D0845782

Dollars, Diplomacy, and Dependency

Dollars, Diplomacy, and Dependency

Dilemmas of U.S. Economic Aid

An Institute for the Study of Diplomacy Book

Robert F. Zimmerman

Lynne Rienner Publishers ■ Boulder & London

Published in the United States of America in 1993 by
Lynne Rienner Publishers, Inc.
1800 30th Street, Boulder, Colorado 80301

and in the United Kingdom by
Lynne Rienner Publishers, Inc.
3 Henrietta Street, Covent Garden, London WC2E 8LU

Library of Congress Cataloging-in-Publication Data

Zimmerman, Robert F., 1939–
Dollars, diplomacy, and dependency : dilemmas of U.S. economic aid / by Robert F. Zimmerman.
p. cm.
Includes bibliographical references and index.
ISBN 1-55587-362-6 (alk. paper)
ISBN 1-55587-399-5 (pbk.) (alk. paper)
1. Economic assistance, American—Developing countries.
2. Economic assistance, American—Government policy—Developing countries. I. Title
HC60.Z48 1993
338.9'173—dc20 92-43597
CIP

British Cataloguing in Publication Data

A Cataloguing in Publication record for this book is available from the British Library.

Printed and bound in the United States of America

The paper used in this publication meets the requirements of the American National Standard for Permanence of Paper for Printed Library Materials Z39.48-1984.

This book is dedicated to my parents,
Joan Orner and Robert E. Zimmerman.

They taught me that above all we must accept primary responsibility for our personal well-being and for achieving our goals in life. They taught me to respect the integrity of every human being, always to pursue the truth, and never to turn away from an opportunity to serve our country and the ideals to which it was originally committed.

Contents

Foreword

Hans Binnendijk

Director, Institute for the Study of Diplomacy

This publication is one of a continuing series issued by the Institute for the Study of Diplomacy that deals with U.S. foreign relations, often through open discussion of controversial subjects. Building upon an Institute symposium on the compatibility of short-term U.S. diplomatic pursuits with long-term development interests, Robert Zimmerman's analysis and reflections make a very timely contribution to the continuing debate on the future role of U.S. aid programs in the post–Cold War era.

Drawing freely upon his own insider's knowledge and experience, Zimmerman analyzes points of conflict among such diverse goals as those dealing with democracy, human rights, conflict resolution, strategic and military concerns, and economic, humanitarian, and commercial interests. He weighs the long-term costs of short-term successes. He examines both theory and practice and illustrates his points with cases from countries in Asia, Africa, and Latin America.

Zimmerman's analysis focuses principally on the use of Economic Support Funds, created in the late 1970s as a flexible foreign policy instrument. In an extensive case study of U.S. programs in Egypt, he explores how aid resources are used to buttress differing U.S. objectives, especially the heavy use of budget support funds in pursuit of political and strategic interests, as opposed to aid for development. He also examines how the overall foreign aid program can be skewed by such pursuits, thereby potentially shortchanging longer-term objectives.

Because Zimmerman believes so strongly that genuine development is inseparable from the growth of democracy and peace in the world, he does not hesitate to express conclusions sometimes highly critical of the U.S. government's approaches to economic assistance. His issue-oriented characterizations of the uses, and abuses, of the aid program may delight some readers and dismay or offend others; they have been welcomed by many in the development community who share his persistent hopes for effective long-term development efforts.

Bob Zimmerman has been described by some in the aid community as "something of a maverick" and "refreshingly iconoclastic." In this book, he bases his analysis on his research and personal experiences covering two decades as a foreign service officer in the Agency for International Development and the State Department, during which he was frequently called upon to evaluate aid programs and projects. He draws inspiration from expressions of far-reaching U.S. goals, especially those of John F. Kennedy and Franklin D. Roosevelt. And he bolsters his own conclusions with those of concerned contemporary observers like Congressman Lee Hamilton and Senators Patrick Leahy and Robert Dole (as well as numerous studies by the Congress, A.I.D., and others), who address the recurrent questions of how and why U.S. resources go to the support of other nations.

With the end of the Cold War and the beginning of a new administration, the time is right for a fundamental reevaluation of the aid agency and its programs. This candid reexamination of the political, economic, and moral dilemmas of U.S. foreign aid addresses just such fundamental questions. Policymakers and academics alike will want to consider its recommendations. While we do not necessarily endorse all of its conclusions, we believe this book will stimulate an important debate.

PREFACE

In late November 1989, Georgetown University's Institute for the Study of Diplomacy convened a symposium to examine the relationship between foreign economic assistance (primarily, but not exclusively, U.S. assistance) and the achievement of diplomatic or political objectives. The symposium questioned whether the use of economic assistance resources to achieve a political objective is compatible with the effective use of such assistance for development purposes. Participating in the symposium were active and retired State Department and Agency for International Development (A.I.D.) officers, including ambassadors and mission directors, and several members of the academic community. These participants represented nearly 500 years of combined experience in the development and implementation of U.S. foreign policy and foreign economic assistance programs. As appropriate and whenever relevant, this study includes insights from this symposium.

This study also draws on over thirty-five interviews with current and former foreign service officers in A.I.D. and the State Department. These officials included ambassadors, A.I.D. mission directors, and other personnel who have served in program planning and evaluation or political reporting positions. I also conducted an extensive study of foreign assistance documents, legislation, and other relevant data from the broad base of literature on foreign assistance, from articles in newspapers and periodicals, and from a personal journal that I maintained throughout a twenty-one-year foreign service career.

This study is informed by the experience of practitioners in coping with complex and uncomfortable realities while developing and implementing U.S. foreign aid policies and programs. In this regard, I must identify my own biases. This effort is based on my experience of twenty-seven years with economic aid and U.S. foreign policy—beginning with the Peace Corps from 1961 to 1963, four years of graduate study in comparative government and international relations, and a doctoral dissertation on the Peace Corps as an instrument of U.S. foreign policy, followed by twenty-one years as a U.S. foreign service officer in A.I.D. and the State Department, seeking effective ways to help others "learn how to fish for themselves."

This study also reflects my personal experience of the United States' effort to advance political-diplomatic objectives with economic aid, and of the compatibility of this effort with the economic and social development objectives of that aid. Like many others, my career began in response to President John F. Kennedy's inaugural address wherein he challenged, "Ask not what your country can do for you; ask what you can do for your country." In that address, he tried to establish the underlying political and moral basis for U.S. assistance policy:

> To those people in the huts and villages of half the globe struggling to break the bonds of mass misery, we pledge our best efforts to help them to help themselves, for whatever period is required—not because the Communists may be doing it, not because we seek their votes, but because it is right. If a free society cannot help the many who are poor, it cannot save the few who are rich.[1]

By the end of 1961, I was a Peace Corps volunteer on my way to the Philippine island of Samar. I returned two years later determined to prepare for a career in international affairs.

In this study, both description and analysis are issue oriented. The work is addressed to the needs of scholars who teach international relations, foreign aid, and development courses; to the U.S. public, which must provide informed support for any viable U.S. foreign aid program; and to U.S. government foreign policymakers and practitioners who are trying to develop new approaches to foreign assistance in the post–Cold War world.

This study, I believe, begins the candid reexamination of U.S. foreign aid that Senator Patrick Leahy (D-Vermont), chairman of the Foreign Operations subcommittee of the Senate Committee on Appropriations, called for in his letter of August 2, 1992, to President George Bush. Expressing his deep concern, Senator Leahy wrote that

> our international assistance program is exhausted intellectually, conceptually, and politically. It has no widely understood and agreed set of goals, it lacks coherence and vision, and there is a very real question whether parts of it actually serve broadly accepted United States national interests any longer. . . . As a whole it is failing to address adequately fundamental American interests in the global population explosion, international environmental degradation on a massive scale, and seemingly ineradicable poverty and hopelessness in the developing world.

Leahy called for "a total reexamination of foreign aid" that would candidly explore "the most basic questions," including the following:

- In the absence of a global military threat to our national security, why should the United States continue to have a foreign aid program? In the post–Cold War era, what specific interests should it serve?
- What goals are we trying to achieve through foreign aid and are we really making any progress toward those goals? How should our foreign aid program be rebuilt to attain those goals?

- If we are to continue to give foreign aid, how should we do so? What is the best, most cost-effective mechanism for providing our aid?
- How do we explain and justify to the American people continued foreign aid?

Virtually all these questions are addressed in this study, either directly or by illustrating why so many past foreign aid efforts have failed to address fundamental development concerns, and by suggesting how these lessons can be applied in the future.

*

Terrence F. Liercke, an Agency for International Development career foreign service officer, provided sustained encouragement and invaluable insight without which this study would have been impossible. He frequently helped retain perspective on the constant tension between ideals and unavoidable compromises in planning and implementing U.S. foreign aid. Terry's knowledge and experience are reflected especially in the discussions of U.S. policy in Latin America, Egypt, and foreign aid personnel.

Ambassador David E. Newsom gave me the opportunity to begin this study at Georgetown University's Institute for the Study of Diplomacy (ISD). Our careers crossed several times and I was privileged to learn from him as he practiced and later taught U.S. diplomacy. Ambassador Newsom became for me the ideal against which all U.S. ambassadors should be measured. ISD and its Martin F. Herz Memorial Fund subsequently provided support for the symposium in November 1989 that provided initial guidance for this study.

David I. Steinberg, a retired A.I.D. foreign service officer currently teaching at Georgetown, also provided invaluable, sustained encouragement and insight, including opportunities to lecture to and obtain feedback from students in his course on U.S. foreign economic assistance.

Margery Boichel Thompson, director of publications at ISD, was a reliable sounding board throughout this study and provided vital editing support. The findings and conclusions of the book, however, are mine alone and do not necessarily reflect the views of the Institute for the Study of Diplomacy.

Finally, I am deeply indebted to my brother, Colonel John E. Zimmerman (USAF Ret.), my sisters, Jan Purcell and Betsy Zimmerman, my daughters, Jennifer and Kathleen, and my best friend, Celia Joy Garney, who provided constructive criticism, encouragement, and, most especially, love, whenever I began to grow weary in this endeavor.

NOTE

1. Roger C. Riddell, *Foreign Aid Reconsidered* (Baltimore: Johns Hopkins University Press, 1987), p. 6.

1

Economic Support Funds: Diplomatic Gains, Development Losses?

The central thesis of this book is that U.S. foreign economic assistance—most notably Economic Supporting Assistance using Economic Support Funds (ESF)—has largely failed to achieve its clearly stated economic and social development goals, primarily because this assistance has been first and foremost a diplomatic tool to promote U.S. political and security objectives. The ESF program's political and development goals, though often carefully and logically linked in policy and program planning documents, become lopsidedly competitive in practice. Using such economic aid to attain high-priority, short-term national security and political (including domestic political) objectives requires extensive compromises in essential development-oriented criteria for planning and performance. These compromises make attaining the development goals of ESF resources impossible and, in some cases, can even affect the development opportunities and impact of Development Assistance (DA) resources.

Such compromises also make it more difficult and expensive to attain and sustain the indirect, unstated but ultimate U.S. foreign policy objective: peace within and between states and thus the security of the United States. The major foreign policy objectives of ESF resources are, after all, those of preventing the outbreak of hostilities or helping to end existing conflicts in ways that will favor U.S. national security. Foreign aid that does not address the causes of violent conflict within or between states cannot create the conditions for peace—no matter how successful that aid may be at buying the tenuous stability of the status quo. Nowhere is this truth more evident than in the Middle East, where, ironically, much U.S. economic aid has actually helped sustain conditions in the region—from Iraq to the West Bank—that are more conducive to violent conflict than to peace.

Finally, in too many cases, diplomacy that relies on ESF assistance primarily as a tool for achieving foreign policy objectives actually creates reciprocal dependencies between the United States and recipient governments. The aid's primary purpose often becomes promoting the stability of the relationship between the United States and the political leadership of the recipient government so that U.S. political objectives can be achieved with some assurance that they will be sustained over at least a medium time frame. The United States depends on these relationships. The recipient government's political leadership also comes to depend on U.S. assistance to secure its primacy vis-à-vis other political elements within the country and to enhance its legitimacy in the eyes of the general population. This study describes such dependency relationships and their often perverse consequences.

U.S. foreign economic aid provided through the Agency for International Development (A.I.D.) fits into three main categories: Economic Support Funds, Development Assistance, and Food for Peace. Additional resources go to multilateral institutions and the Peace Corps. This study focuses primarily on the ESF account because these are the resources most directly aimed at advancing U.S. political and security objectives. Moreover, ESF resources account for more than half of all U.S. bilateral economic assistance. In 1989, for example, ESF resources totaled $3.4 billion and DA $2.7 billion, while multilateral institutions received approximately $1.3 billion.[1] ESF resources constitute all or most of the economic aid provided to all of the countries discussed in Chapters 5, 6, and 7.

In this book I describe how the United States has used the ESF foreign economic aid program, and sometimes other aid, to advance U.S. political objectives; demonstrate how these processes undermine the stated development objectives of that assistance; and attempt to show how failure to achieve these programs' development objectives ultimately undermines the original short-term political and security objectives while making attainment of longer-term political, economic, and security objectives all the more difficult. Finally, the failure to apply effective development-oriented criteria also undercuts A.I.D.'s own reputation and influence as a development agency.

Reflecting on the compatibility of, or conflict between, the diplomatic-political purposes of foreign assistance and its other, economic development objectives has special relevance today because U.S. policymakers, development practitioners, and the general public are raising serious questions about the future role of U.S. aid programs in the post–Cold War world. These questions reflect many new realities: the end of superpower competition for political and strategic advantage in the Third World; unprecedented opportunities to use aid resources in Eastern Europe, where there are greater expectations that the aid can effectively advance U.S. political and—one hopes—developmental objectives; a corresponding lack of enthusiasm and resources for foreign aid to the Third World, which often appears insufficiently committed to addressing impediments to the effective use of development aid; greater potential than ever before for violent ethnic and other low-intensity conflict[2] in many countries throughout the Third World and in Eastern Europe and the former Soviet Union; difficulty in resolving the contradictions that arise when the efforts to stimulate economic growth create gaps in equity; an overwhelming debt crisis throughout the Third World; and an increasingly serious threat to sustainable development from continuing environmental degradation.

In such circumstances, the United States can ill afford a confusion of motives or processes for allocating resources to the Third World, Eastern Europe, or even the states of the former Soviet Union. Neither the United States nor other donors can afford to miss the opportunities created by the rapidly changing international environment. Identifying new approaches and criteria for implementing aid programs that can advance both development and diplomatic objectives requires a candid review of the record of U.S. economic aid throughout the Cold War.

Over the past half century the United States has spent $233 billion on foreign economic assistance.[3] It has used at least half of this assistance, particularly the ESF account, to advance short-term country-specific political objectives related to global strategic, political, and security goals and to respond to global economic requirements. When viewed from the political perspective, the record includes several significant short-term successes. One of the most obvious has been that of encouraging a sustained Egyptian-Israeli dialogue toward an expanded peace process in the Middle East—averting further war-related setbacks to Egyptian development—and enabling Egypt to endure the break in its relations with other Arab states—especially the cutoff of their aid—until these states, realizing that the original break was not in their interest, resumed relations with Egypt.

A second major success was that of obtaining Pakistan's cooperation with U.S. efforts to provide support to Afghan rebels resisting the Soviet occupation of Afghanistan. Ironically, the United States earlier had cut its aid program to Pakistan in reaction to Pakistan's refusal to end its secret effort to develop nuclear weapons. Resisting the Soviet invasion of Afghanistan became a higher political objective forcing the U.S. government, including Congress, to resume a massive ESF program. Pakistan's cooperation was essential in creating the military stalemate that led to Soviet withdrawal from Afghanistan.[4] An unexpected additional result was the increased impetus this outcome gave to internal political reform in the Soviet Union itself and to Soviet withdrawal from Eastern Europe.

U.S. economic aid also supported the generally successful containment of Soviet efforts to extend communist influence throughout the so-called Third World, including Soviet support for Cuban and Nicaraguan subversion efforts in Central America. Finally, this aid helped obtain and sustain U.S. military bases and intelligence facilities in all regions of the world.

Nevertheless, today there is widespread evidence that foreign aid, some project-level successes with DA funds notwithstanding, has not helped produce the broad-based economic and social development results expected. A.I.D., in a major 1989 review of the purposes and impact of foreign assistance, asked whether today's U.S. assistance has been fostering "development towards independent prosperity or simply postponing the day of reckoning for governments unwilling or unable to take the politically painful steps needed for their own development." The study tentatively concluded that "all too often, dependency seems to have won out over development. . . . Only a handful of countries that started receiving U.S. assistance in the 1950s and 1960s has ever graduated from dependent status."[5]

Why is this so? Were expectations too high? Were they raised unnecessarily by the development-oriented rhetoric used to sell programs to the Congress and the U.S. public? Was there no clear consensus on the development objectives of foreign assistance, in particular Economic Supporting Assistance? Was there a lack of understanding of the obstacles both to U.S. interests and to development? Were the processes of planning, decisionmaking, and implementation too complicated?

For most of these questions, much of the answer begins with the adverse impact on the allocation and implementation of *all* U.S. foreign economic aid resources of allocating so much to the ESF account, and its predecessors, to promote U.S. political and short-term special interest objectives. This has generally been true from at least the late 1950s, even though agency documents and most public pronouncements always stressed more lofty, moralistic aid objectives. The U.S. public may have been willing to support aid programs that taught people how to fish; they have rejected simply buying the fish for other countries, except in disaster situations. But, using aid as a political tool results precisely in buying fish for "key allies" rather than helping them stand on their own. Nevertheless, the unavoidable political realities of the Cold War, coupled with a limited constituency in support of foreign assistance among a generally uninformed U.S. public, may have precluded alternative approaches.

The types of U.S. assistance over the past four decades and the shifting regional focus of that assistance reflect the high priority of political over development objectives. Regional priorities for U.S. aid began with our European recovery effort after World War II. South Asia and Southeast Asia became priority areas during the Vietnam War in the 1960s. From 1977 to 1989, Israel and Egypt received 47 percent of total economic aid. During the 1980s, aid to Central America rose sharply to $1.3 billion in 1989, surpassing Asia. Aid to Africa stabilized at about $500 million until the early 1990s, when it increased to $800 million.[6]

Military aid increased from 25 percent of total aid in 1978 to 37 percent in 1988. Over the same period, development assistance decreased from 33 percent in 1978 to 26 percent in 1988. ESF remained at or near 50 percent of all economic aid throughout the period. Food aid fell from highs of $5 billion per year in the 1950s and 1960s—20 percent of the program—to $1.6 billion in 1990, or 10 percent of the program.[7] It is worth noting here that both military and economic aid are included in the annual aid package sent to Congress. This practice tends to give the U.S. public and the press a distorted image of both types of aid.

During 1990 the focus shifted again—ironically—back to Europe, where it had originally begun as a response to the rising threat of Soviet communism. Today, however, the aid program is responding to the collapse of

Soviet communism and the perceived need to consolidate the political gains in Eastern Europe and the emerging successor states of the former Soviet Union. The United States, the West European donors, and Japan are redirecting significant portions of their assistance resources to support emerging free market and democratic reforms in the region. As this process continues, reflection on our past use of economic assistance to advance diplomatic and political objectives can provide useful lessons.

The purposes of this study are

- To examine the relationship between U.S. foreign policy objectives and the implementation of U.S. foreign economic aid, particularly through the ESF account;
- To address the compatibility of shorter-term U.S. political and security objectives with the furtherance of longer-term economic development in less developed countries (LDCs) through U.S. foreign economic aid; and
- To draw conclusions from the examination of these two questions regarding the future course and purposes of U.S. foreign economic assistance.

Finally, a few words about the organization of the book. Chapter 2 provides a brief history of the U.S. foreign economic aid program, the evolution of aid rationales from the late 1940s through the early 1980s, and the purposes of U.S. foreign policy. It describes the primary aid instruments and sets forth my reasons for focusing on the Economic Support Fund.

Almost all supporting documents for U.S. foreign assistance stress the linkages between development and political objectives. Development, however, means many things, often depending on one's objectives. Chapter 3 establishes operating definitions of *modernization* and *development*, with particular attention to the differences between these two often interchanged concepts. Given the intensity of the debate on these concepts, Chapter 3 does not attempt to reconcile the differences, but only to clarify the concept of development against which this study assesses U.S. foreign economic assistance.

My own definition of development began with my Peace Corps experience. It was further informed by Gunnar Myrdal's *Asian Drama* and other works, P. T. Bauer's *Dissent on Development*, and Norman Jacobs's *Modernization Without Development: Thailand as an Asian Case Study*; by my experience with A.I.D. from 1968 to 1989; and by observations about the differences between development and modernization I gleaned from U.S. aid policies in the Middle East, the 1990–1991 Gulf crisis, and the collapse of Soviet communism in 1989–1990.

Chapter 4 describes the differences between words and deeds in the aid planning and implementation processes and draws upon such key documents as the Country Development Strategy Statement and the Congressional Presentation. Chapter 5 looks at the U.S. assistance relationship with Egypt. It describes foreign policy and assistance processes in Egypt, including their relationship to other programs in the Middle East, and assesses their impact on the achievement of political and development objectives. Chapter 6 expands on this example by looking at attainment of political and development objectives in several other country-specific cases, and Chapter 7 focuses on key lessons learned.

Chapter 8 addresses attainment of global U.S. foreign policy objectives concerned with peace, human rights, and political, social, and economic development. This chapter includes brief discussions on the roles played by the PL 480 program and the Peace Corps in U.S. foreign policy. Chapter 9 suggests a possible new approach for U.S. foreign assistance that might better serve both political and development objectives.

NOTES

1. A.I.D., *U.S. Overseas Loans and Grants: Obligations and Authorizations* (July 1, 1945–September 30, 1990), Office of Planning and Budgeting/Bureau for Program and Policy Coordination, p. 4. Chapter 3 provides more information on each of these aid instruments, and Appendix II.1 presents the U.S. International Affairs Budget in a pie chart.

2. Senator David L. Boren, "Preface," in *Low-Intensity Conflict: Old Threats in a New World*, ed. Edwin G. Corr and Stephen Sloan (Boulder: Westview Press, 1992).

3. A.I.D., *U.S. Loans and Grants*, p. 4.

4. For a detailed analysis by a senior Pakistani diplomat, see Riaz M. Khan, *Untying the Afghan Knot: Negotiating Soviet Withdrawal*, an Institute for the Study of Diplomacy Book (Durham, N.C.: Duke University Press, 1991).

5. A.I.D., *Development and the National Interest* (Washington, D.C.: A.I.D., February 1989), pp. 111–112.

6. Lee Hamilton, "Foreign Assistance: Which Direction Now?" *Foreign Service Journal* (February 1989), p. 28.

7. Ibid.

2

The Origins, Purposes, and Instruments of U.S. Aid Diplomacy

One undeniable lesson of World War II and interstate relations since then is that national security cannot be secured unilaterally. Political and economic security demand increasingly complex interaction and cooperation with countries in all regions of the world. Even the internal economic and political conditions among the least developed countries will affect U.S. economic, political, security, or moral interests.

THE HISTORICAL CONTEXT OF SECURITY AND DEVELOPMENT AID

Robert E. Osgood believes the disillusionment created by World War II stimulated a climate of opinion in the United States "conducive to a recognition of the primacy of national interest and the necessity for an objective calculation of national power." He suggested that this recognition created a widespread consciousness that U.S. security "depended on the course of events beyond the Western Hemisphere" and became "the necessary basis for the growth of political realism, the vital balance wheel needed to restrain and give direction to the nation's egoistic and idealistic impulses."[1]

U.S. foreign policy leaders have rarely addressed foreign affairs and the country's role without reference to perceived moral ideals and responsibilities. Robert Bellah suggested that World War II gave U.S. citizens such faith in U.S. political institutions that they attempted to transfer them wholesale to other countries through the foreign aid program.[2]

The original architects of U.S. policies toward the less developed regions of the world were determined to avoid a recurrence of the hard times of the Depression and the four years of world war. These statesmen sought a "liberal international order" that would provide both bread and freedom. They wanted, as Nicholas Eberstadt suggests, "to capture the most beneficial economic workings of the trade and finance arrangements associated with the Age of Imperialism and at the same time to protect the weaker peoples of the world against imperial subjugation and anti-democratic oppression."[3]

From the end of World War II through the formative 1950s and 1960s, governments felt a "moral obligation to provide aid."[4] But the moral arguments were also always linked to the national interest. Franklin D. Roosevelt dedicated the United States to the policy of the good neighbor, but in another statement that highlighted the importance of the national interest, he also declared, "Our foreign policy is . . . to defend the honor, the freedom, the rights, the interests, and the well-being of the American people."[5] In his last address to Congress, Roosevelt warned that a peaceful world required an economically healthy world. The main job was reconstruction—not relief—and it had to be done largely by local people and their governments. "They will provide the labor, the local money, and most of the materials. The same is true for all of the many plans for the improvement of transportation, industry, agriculture, and housing that are essential to the development of the economically backward areas of the world."[6]

The Economic Cooperation Administration (Marshall Plan), established in 1948 in response to the alarming advance of Soviet communism throughout Eastern Europe, was the first massive government-sponsored approach to foreign assistance. The plan supported the postwar reconstruction of Europe. It was immensely successful in Western Europe. The Soviet Union did not permit those parts of Europe under its occupation forces to participate in the reconstruction program. The Marshall Plan experience became a benchmark for foreign assistance, though there were obvious differences between the reconstruction of the advanced states of Europe and the former colonies in Africa, Asia, and Latin America.

Following passage of the Mutual Security Act of 1951, Congress terminated the Marshall Plan (in 1952) and transferred its functions to the new Mutual Security Administration (MSA). This act provided for military aid, defense support, and economic and food aid assistance. It united in one agency the activities previously executed under both the Economic Cooperation Act and the Mutual Defense Assistance Act.

Throughout most of the 1950s, U.S. foreign aid policies followed comparatively clear principles and operational rules. Morality-based appeals remained strong factors in favor of development aid. In a sense, these were simpler times. Development was still equated with economic growth and modernization of infrastructure and institutions. U.S. aid planners, in particular, had not yet had to face the complex and confusing realities—often with country-specific variations—inherent in a development process that went beyond attempts to stimulate economic growth. Economists were the elite members of the aid fraternity.[7] They could build economic models and provide blizzards of supporting statistics. Other factors, communist-inspired subversion and guerrilla war, were only beginning to add to the difficulty of defining the relationships between security and social-political development that would challenge foreign assistance efforts.

Ambassador George C. McGhee defined the moral and national self-interest dimensions of the challenge for foreign aid in a 1962 speech entitled "The American Ambassador Today." He emphasized that U.S. policy sought to hasten the progress of the less developed nations. The stability and cohesion of the free world depended on these nations' continued progress toward their goals through peaceful and orderly methods. Otherwise, they might succumb to extremist appeals from leaders whose purposes and programs were opposed to those of the free world community:

> Our response to the challenge of development has become, in our time, a great crusade in the light of which most historical movements fail. . . . *The interests of neither the United States nor the host country will be promoted by aid programs which do not face up to this challenge*. . . . [It is] a question of making sure that our aid, in responding to the economic and political needs of the moment, *does so in ways which contribute to the long-term development goals that we and the host country share*.[8] (Emphasis added)

President Kennedy's message to Congress on March 1, 1961, established the Peace Corps' original vision and purposes. The rhetoric directly linked political and development objectives, and the moral tone was evident. Kennedy believed that the freedom of the United States and freedom's future around the world depended "on the ability to build growing and independent nations where men can live in dignity, liberated from the bonds of hunger, ignorance, and poverty." He proposed the Peace Corps to "recruit and train American volunteers, sending them abroad to work with the people of other nations."[9]

Eighteen years later, Dame Judith Hart, then British minister of overseas development, echoing Kennedy, continued the argument that moral imperatives and political interests can overlap.[10] Moreover, she pointed out that even as aid donors helped the people in poor countries to meet their basic human needs, they also needed to recognize and address basic human rights. When these needs—rights—were met, then "for the first time, [these people] will have the opportunity for full participation within their own societies. They will have the opportunity to determine for themselves how best to create a legal and political structure which protects and advances their rights."[11]

Thirty years have passed since Ambassador McGhee and President Kennedy raised these moral challenges and defined the United States' role in assisting other nations toward sustainable economic and social development. The priorities for development assistance that would help promote the economic and social well-being of the people in the less developed countries have varied over time in different countries and regions. Nevertheless, the option vigorously to pursue development objectives was always possible, if not overridden by higher priority political objectives. What has happened in the intervening years to the original vision and inspiring commitments?

The first compromises began well before President Kennedy's stirring vision and challenge. During the Eisenhower years, military and development assistance were separated. While political aid and military grants to friendly countries accounted for only one-sixth of U.S. foreign aid between 1949 and 1953, between 1953 and 1961 they made up over half of this aid.[12] Perceived—and sometimes real—communist threats and advances in Asia and other parts of the decolonizing world drove these changes. The United States designed its security assistance, primarily in the form of assistance to police forces and other paramilitary forces engaged in counterinsurgency efforts, to help struggling governments maintain political stability while they undertook other economic and social development programs.[13]

President Kennedy refined the security and development linkage by arguing that development aid was security assistance. He believed this linkage would encourage the people and Congress to support economic aid. "I urge those who want to do something for the United States . . . to channel their energies behind the new foreign-aid program to help prevent the social injustice and economic chaos upon which subversion and revolt feeds."[14]

In essence, Roosevelt, McGhee, and Kennedy shared the premise that preserving the security of the United States and advancing other U.S. interests demanded long-term U.S. involvement in developing and maintaining world order.[15] U.S. military and economic aid became major instruments for this involvement. In the Foreign Assistance Act of 1961, Congress established Kennedy's "new foreign-aid program," creating the Agency for International Development to administer the economic aid that would advance U.S. foreign policy objectives.

WHAT HAS THE U.S. PUBLIC EXPECTED?

At first glance, the people of the United States appear to have assumed that U.S. national interests included resolution of development problems in the LDCs. The Chicago Council on Foreign Relations found remarkable constancy in the U.S. public's willingness to provide assistance to the desperately poor. In a 1982 survey, nearly 60 percent of the respondents polled by the council said "combating world hunger" was a "very important" objective. This survey reflected previous findings that combating world hunger ranked far ahead of "protecting American business abroad," and even ahead of "defending our allies' security" or "matching Soviet military strength," as an international concern.[16]

Curiously, the U.S. public limited its support for combating world hunger to humanitarian aid and disaster relief. This might indicate that many either do not understand the long-term nature of the development process or that they do not believe that government can effectively deliver development aid. They appear to prefer that aid be chaneled through private voluntary organizations (PVOs) or other nongovernmental organizations (NGOs). The U.S. Presidential Commission on World Hunger showed that 77 percent of the U.S. public favored "aid to combat hunger"; however, when put in terms of economic assistance, only 49 percent were in favor.[17] Explaining this contradiction, Eberstadt suggested that the U.S. public believed that foreign aid programs for the world's poor might be defective or "positively injurious." He added, "The stronger the public's commitment to the world's poor, the more forcefully it would reject programs that seem untrue to that commitment."[18]

Eugene Wittkopf and James McCormick, on the question "Do you think it would be best for the future of the country if we take an active part in world affairs or if we stay out of world affairs?" found that from the 1950s through the 1980s roughly two-thirds of the U.S. public have consistently supported an active role for the United States.[19]

However, since the 1950s, the people of the United States have changed their views considerably on what purposes economic aid should serve. Wittkopf and McCormick reviewed a series of polls between 1955 and 1957 on whether economic aid should be used to support countries willing "to stand by us" in opposing communist aggression. The average level of support was 81 percent. In nine other surveys between 1949 and 1955 on the use of economic aid as an instrument of economic development, the level in favor averaged 71 percent.

But support for foreign aid declined significantly in the following decades. In each of its surveys, the Chicago Council on Foreign Relations asked: "On the whole, do you favor or oppose our giving economic aid to other nations for purposes of economic development and technical assistance?" The council found on average that only 50 percent of the respondents favored aid for these purposes. While people accepted containing communism as an important goal of U.S. foreign policy, they were changing their minds. By the end of the 1980s they were dissatisfied with foreign aid of any kind.[20] They also vastly overestimate the share of the U.S. budget that goes to foreign aid. They seem not to understand that well over 70 percent of all U.S. aid dollars are spent in the United States for goods and services. These misperceptions affect their conclusions about foreign aid.

The 1988 Bipartisan Task Force on Foreign Assistance of the House Committee on Foreign Affairs found that many of those who make and implement foreign aid programs doubted that foreign assistance was achieving its purposes. This doubt is reflected in the restrictions, earmarks, and conditions amended to foreign aid legislation in order to make the aid more responsive to every interest, from the newborn child to the rain forest.[21] After the collapse of the Soviet Union in 1991 and the end of the Cold War, support for foreign aid shrank to the point where members of Congress were willing for the first time to question openly the sacred cow of all aid programs, assistance to Israel.

There is evidence, including my own experience, to suggest that the U.S. public would prefer that assistance help people to stand on their own—

that it teach them how to fish, rather than provide the fish to them. The implication of the Chicago Council's findings may be—as Eberstadt, Wittkopf, and McCormick appear to suggest—that the U.S. public's declining support for foreign assistance reflects a feeling that economic aid has failed to fulfill this objective. This feeling is understandable, given the gap between the stirring appeals in the original foreign assistance documents and the way much of the aid has actually been allocated, as well as its limited impact on development. Roosevelt believed that foreign aid should meet exacting standards with clear and morally legitimate purposes and programs that prosecuted their objectives directly and effectively. Perhaps, had U.S. policymakers, the U.S. Congress, and the practitioners of foreign aid followed these criteria, the developmental impact of foreign aid would have been far closer to the expectations set forth in the early rhetoric.

Steven Sinding, director of the Population Division at the World Bank, reconfirmed this perspective when he suggested that in the future "we might be well advised to simply return to our earlier goals and actually apply the sound development-oriented criteria and implementation processes that have long been set forth in all our handbooks and policy papers, but rarely ever adhered to for the time necessary to have sustainable impact."[22]

U.S. FOREIGN POLICY OBJECTIVES AND INTERESTS

It is easy to discern what were the primary global U.S. foreign policy objectives during the Cold War. The first priority was, and remains, the physical security of the United States. This objective required containing threats to national security from direct attacks on the United States or through attacks on a country that provided strategic military facilities deemed essential for the military protection of the United States.

Thus, the second objective was to ensure the political security of and cooperation with strategically important states. This objective required efforts to counter alien influences that threatened the political values and processes of the United States. Such efforts might include promoting democracy, protecting basic human rights, maintaining historic relationships, creating a supportive international environment, addressing ethnic issues and interests, and accommodating leadership relationships—all with countries where establishing political processes counter to these interests could affect the political security of the United States.

Promoting economic security and growth was the third objective. This objective entailed active opposition to acts by foreign countries that harmed the U.S. economy. It required promoting free trade, providing investment opportunities, ensuring access to technology and raw materials, attracting foreign investment, and promoting the principles of the market economy.

The fourth major objective, promoting humanitarianism, derived from the belief that humanitarianism is an essential part of the American soul. This required being able and willing to respond to man-made conditions of impoverishment and sudden natural disasters anywhere in the world.

At the country and even regional level, pursuit of strategic political objectives required developing and advancing more specific intermediate objectives. Moreover, the priorities among these shorter-term, political objectives frequently varied because the relationship between those objectives and the larger national interests were indirect and subject to differing interpretations and conditions on a country-by-country basis.

U.S. foreign economic aid could advance at least two of these foreign policy objectives: promotion of political security and economic growth. Country assistance program documents that justified assistance requests ranked "sustainable development" high in the hierarchy of objectives. Nevertheless, the specific diplomatic and political objectives at the country and regional level almost invariably fell into the following hierarchy:

- Support for political stability
- Containment of the political-economic influence of another power
- Obtaining of rights for military facilities
- Maintenance of diplomatic access necessary for achieving selected political-security objectives
- Achievement of support for issues of importance to the United States, for example, in the United Nations
- Provision of humanitarian assistance to the poor
- Advantages for commercial enterprises
- Enhancement of human rights and democracy
- Enhancement of the United States' image

In practice, ESF-based aid diplomacy focused on maintaining stable relationships with, and providing stability for, governments that support short-term U.S. political and security interests. Programs to promote democratic principles and protect basic human rights had far lower priority.

ADVANCING POLITICAL OBJECTIVES WITH ECONOMIC ASSISTANCE: THE FOREIGN AID INSTRUMENTS

Diplomacy is both an art and a science that translates foreign policy objectives into results. Smith Simpson, a retired diplomat, public servant, and professor, has defined diplomacy as

> the means by which governments seek to achieve their objectives and gain support for their principles. It is the political process by which a

> government's foreign policies are first nurtured and then guided to their destination of influencing the policies and conduct of other governments. It thus can be defined as the process by which policies are converted from rhetoric to realities, from strategic generalities to the desired actions or inactions of other governments.[23]

Two other terms—*diplomatic* and *politic*—might also be kept in mind. According to the *American College Dictionary*, *diplomatic* "suggests a smoothness and skill in handling others, usually in such a way as to attain one's own ends and yet avoid any unpleasantness or opposition." *Politic*, a synonym, "emphasizes expediency or prudence in looking out for one's own interests."[24]

Clearly, U.S. foreign economic assistance, most notably ESF, has been a major instrument for advancing U.S. political objectives—often with emphasis on "avoiding opposition," "expediency," and "prudence." Other U.S. foreign assistance instruments include agricultural credits, trade policies, commercial investment, cultural exchange programs, military assistance, and sometimes even something as specific as sending a surgeon to operate on a foreign leader. This study focuses on Economic Support Funds because these resources directly promote U.S. political objectives, though, on occasion, Development Assistance, PL 480 food aid, and the Peace Corps also serve political objectives.

Foreign policy administrators tend to look for the easiest of these instruments to apply. Bradshaw Langmaid, a thirty-year A.I.D. career officer, contends that spending money is far easier than orchestrating other instruments. The diplomat without an aid program has to work much harder to advance U.S. objectives. "It is easier to walk into a ministry and have a substantive discussion on your agenda when that ministry has a financial interest in the outcome or perceives that it does."[25] In this sense, an economic or military aid program can clearly be an expedient tool to help reduce opposition and unpleasantness in U.S. relationships with a country whose cooperation is required to attain a U.S. objective.

Economic aid also serves other purposes. Some may be intended, while others are unintended and possibly negative in the long run, particularly when they are incompatible with attainment of sustainable economic development objectives. Ancillary objectives include symbolism, political legitimacy, and sometimes even emergency humanitarian interests.

Virtually all of the ambassadors interviewed for this study stressed that U.S. political objectives are not necessarily opposed to development objectives. Ambassador Edward E. Masters believed that "development is a diplomatic [political] objective, if only because it is so essential to long-term political and social stability, without which the advancement of U.S. diplomatic objectives becomes very difficult, limited and sometimes impossible."[26] As noted earlier, President Franklin D. Roosevelt clearly recognized the linkages between peace and development. His last address to Congress warned, "We cannot succeed in building a peaceful world unless we build an economically healthy world." Roosevelt and his advisers believed that foreign aid had to have exacting standards. It required "clear and morally legitimate purposes" and its programs should "prosecute their objectives directly and effectively."[27] Despite the inherent wisdom in these statements, U.S. foreign aid policy and practice since the early 1960s have more often supported short-term expediency than long-term morality.

Foreign economic aid provided through the Agency for International Development fits into three main categories: Economic Support Funds, Development Assistance, and Food for Peace.[28] Additional resources go to multilateral institutions and the Peace Corps. Though this study and its conclusions relate primarily to ESF aid, a brief description of the nature of the other major economic aid instruments will help retain perspective.

Economic Support Funds

Traditionally, the United States has provided considerable economic assistance on a grant or loan basis to countries of special political importance. Beginning in the 1950s, this aid was called Security Supporting Assistance (SSA) and was used primarily to help relieve recipient countries' balance of payments pressures. Throughout the 1960s, major SSA recipients were Vietnam, Thailand, and the Philippines. As the Vietnam war came to an end, the 1973 Foreign Assistance Act changed the title to the Economic Support Fund. ESF resources serve several U.S. political and security objectives, including enhancing prospects for peace in the Middle East, enhancing political stability, promoting economic reforms important to long-term development, promoting economic stabilization through budget and balance of payments support, and assisting countries that allow the United States to maintain military bases on their soil.[29]

ESF resources became increasingly important in the 1980s when the Reagan administration changed the focus of U.S. foreign aid from trying to promote basic human needs—which relied on DA resources—to preserving political stability while promoting macroeconomic reform. The basic human needs (BHN) approach, given its welfare orientation toward basic health, mother and child survival, and nutrition services, and given the restrictions against using DA for balance of payments support, had not directly stimulated broader-based, sustainable economic growth. This approach did not address developing countries' policies for allocating, mobilizing, and distributing the resources that most affect economic growth.

A.I.D. conditioned its ESF balance of payments and budget support assistance on host governments' implementation of economic policy reforms. In Central America, for example, A.I.D. believed the governments should undertake economic stabilization and structural adjustment reforms to achieve self-sustaining economic growth, the return of private capital that had been sent abroad, and strengthened civilian, democratic governments.[30] In practice, however, these types of conditions were seldom enforced.

Conflicting development and political objectives are evident in the allocation and use of ESF resources. The number and variety of countries receiving ESF raise complicated questions regarding the criteria used to select them.[31] Moreover, many countries receive both ESF and DA resources, and sometimes even ESF resources are used for humanitarian and developmental projects. The weight given to the broad range of political contexts that may affect U.S. security interests is important because of the impact political-security concerns can have on planning and implementing DA or ESF assistance programs.

Because ESF resources are a diplomatic tool, they can be used in the broadest spectrum of circumstances, so long as important U.S. political interests are involved. The U.S. government, through A.I.D., considers the following factors when deciding how best to deliver ESF resources: (1) what foreign policy objectives the United States is trying to achieve, (2) what economic and development needs are most pressing for each country, (3) how much assistance A.I.D. is providing and how quickly the funds need to be disbursed, (4) what program objectives A.I.D. is advancing, and (5) whether any unique funding-control concerns are present.[32]

Congress directs A.I.D. and the State Department to implement ESF to the maximum extent possible on the basis of development criteria, but it provides no such criteria. The State Department plays the primary role in budgeting ESF resources. Congress provides that ESF will have the flexibility to include cash transfers, yet some ESF countries get cash transfer treatment on more flexible terms than others. Israel, for example, receives all of its annual ESF grant of $1.2 billion as a cash transfer, while Egypt through the second half of the 1980s was allowed to obtain only $115 million in cash transfer out of its total annual $815 million in ESF. Moreover, A.I.D. and the State Department, under pressure from Congress, have tried to apply increasingly tough economic reform performance conditions on cash transfers to Egypt. Pakistan, during the Afghan War from 1980 through 1990, became the third largest recipient of ESF aid, while the administration and Congress set aside their previous concern about Pakistan's nuclear weapons program. Such disparities can be found for all ESF recipients where U.S. security objectives have been the determining variable.

ESF is supposed to alleviate the causes of economic and political disruption that threaten the domestic political stability and independence of strategically important countries. Originally, ESF provided balance of payments support and financed commodity import programs for those countries needing foreign exchange to undertake difficult, long-term economic policy adjustments. In countries where economic and political stability was at stake and there was some concern about how effectively the recipient government would use the funds for special development needs, A.I.D. missions have used ESF to finance capital infrastructure projects, trade and private enterprise promotion, and projects of direct benefit to the poor.[33] These are also the types of projects usually funded through the regular DA account.

When A.I.D. provides ESF resources through projects (as opposed to cash transfers or commodity import support programs), it administers these resources according to the same planning and implementation processes used for DA funds. The A.I.D. field mission will identify project opportunities in cooperation with the recipient government and then complete the planning process with support from A.I.D./Washington as necessary. The A.I.D. administrator implements the ESF program in cooperation with, and under the overall policy direction of, the secretary of state. The secretary of state, in turn, holds responsibility for ESF under Section 531(b) of the Foreign Assistance Act.

ESF has averaged over $3.2 billion for fiscal years 1989 through 1991, and Congress retained this level in the FY 1992 Continuing Resolution.[34] This level is down from $3.9 billion in 1987. Between 1979 and 1987, the ESF program grew faster than the other major economic assistance programs. In 1979, A.I.D. provided $1.9 billion in ESF support to twelve countries and two regional programs. The level grew in 1987 to $3.9 billion to forty-eight countries and four regional programs and represented 52 percent of the total U.S. bilateral economic assistance program.[35]

Development Assistance

Development Assistance is the second major assistance category. It provides grants to support social and economic development programs. DA totaled approximately $2.3 billion in FY 1989 but had dropped to $1.3 billion for FY 1992.[36] Except for sub-Saharan Africa, Congress generally allocates these resources to functional accounts such as health, population, education, agriculture, and rural development. A special type of DA is the Development Fund for Africa ($500 million in FY 1989, $800 million in FY 1992), for which Congress appropriates without earmarks to such functional accounts. The DFA, like ESF, can be used for balance of payments support.

The project planning and implementation processes for DA and ESF are essentially the same. Generally speaking, foreign service officers responsible for economic aid prefer working with DA funds precisely because economic development and basic human needs–oriented criteria receive higher priority in the planning and implementation of DA projects. However, many countries in Africa, Latin America, and Asia receive both ESF and DA. In these instances, some distortion of the aid processes occurs simply because of the difficulty of applying two different sets of criteria within the same country.

All DA funds are provided through projects. These projects are personnel-intensive (as are those portions of ESF provided through projects).

In all A.I.D. field missions, a project officer is responsible for the initial project identification, much of the planning, and all subsequent monitoring of the implementation process. The recipient government[37] will usually assign a counterpart project officer to coordinate implementation activities with the A.I.D. officer. Performance conditions, especially regarding the actual disbursement of funds, can be applied to both the recipient government and private contractors who implement the projects. DA programs tend to experience less pressure to compromise such criteria or to release funds simply to facilitate larger political interests. A.I.D. also provides U.S. resources through the DA account to Housing Guarantee programs, Foreign Disaster Relief Assistance, the Private Sector Investment Program, and American Schools and Hospitals Abroad.

Food Aid (PL 480)

Food aid is the third major component of U.S. economic aid. Food aid is provided through the Food for Peace program in close cooperation with the Department of Agriculture. The United States has provided food as a major component of its foreign aid programs since 1947, following establishment of the Organization for European Economic Cooperation and subsequent passage of the Marshall Plan, which was enacted into law as the Economic Cooperation Act, a part of the Foreign Assistance Act of 1948.[38]

Food assistance remained under the Mutual Security Act and its predecessor legislation until the passage of the Agricultural Trade Development and Assistance Act of 1954 (Public Law 480, or PL 480). The Mutual Security Act had stressed the use of money and materials, including food commodities, for security assistance. The passage of PL 480, however, required greater use of food as a tool for economic development.

In Section 2 of PL 480, Congress promoted international trade between the United States and foreign nations, and the use of foreign currencies generated from food sales to encourage economic development, purchase strategic materials, pay U.S. obligations abroad, promote collective strength, and in other ways foster the foreign policy of the United States. In addition, the PL 480 program tries to make the most efficient use of U.S. surplus agricultural commodities, thereby reducing surpluses and promoting the economic stabilty of U.S. agriculture.[39]

The PL 480 legislation establishes four basic objectives: to expand exports of U.S. agricultural commodities, to combat hunger and malnutrition, to encourage economic development in developing countries, and to promote the foreign policy interests of the United States.[40] In many countries, the United States uses PL 480 resources as balance of payments assistance to help ensure the internal political stability of strategically important recipient countries. The Department of Agriculture implements this food aid under Title I concessional loans that recipient governments use to relieve pressure on their national budgets as they try to meet food import needs for their people.

Implementation of the PL 480 program requires coordination among several government agencies. To facilitate coordination, the secretary of agriculture established the Interagency Staff Committee (ISC). Chaired by the Foreign Agricultural Service (FAS), the ISC in effect makes program decisions on the secretary's behalf. Membership includes the Office of Management and Budget (OMB), A.I.D., the Departments of Agriculture (USDA), State, Treasury, Defense, and Commerce, and other agencies with an interest in local currencies generated from the sale of food commodities under Title I.

Through the 1980s, until new legislation turned management of Title II over to USDA, an ISC subcommittee coordinated the Title II and Title III grant programs, which were used to meet emergency food needs or to support development projects usually managed by private voluntary organizations (PVOs). The subcommittee membership included OMB, USDA, State, and A.I.D. Of these agencies, A.I.D. was the only member with the necessary expertise and with sufficient operational staff overseas to do the job in most of the recipient countries. A.I.D.'s Food for Peace Division chaired the committee. Within the Food for Peace Division, program officers supported projects designed in the field for each type of PL 480 program, commodity specialists provided information on technical details such as packaging and storage requirements, and a support staff provided statistical and narrative information.[41]

In addition to enabling recipients to feed their people, the food assistance program, through resale of agricultural commodities, also generates funds for the partner government. These resources then help finance other development projects. On the negative side, depending on the recipient government's policies, food aid can cause economic distortions. For example, free provision of food for sale at low prices can become a disincentive for local production by dampening demand for local products and undercutting prices farmers receive for their crops.

To address the disincentive problem, the Congress, in Public Law 95-88, added the Bellmon "determination" in 1977 to the PL 480 legislation. A few minor changes were added in subsequent legislation in 1979 and 1990; but as of 1992, the Bellmon determination prohibited shipments of any U.S. agricultural commodity "unless it is determined that . . . the distribution of the commodity in the recipient country will not result in a substantial disincentive to or interference with domestic production or marketing in that country."[42] Nevertheless, in countries where the PL 480 program is used to keep the overall aid levels high for U.S. political purposes (as we shall see in the Egypt case), these certifications sometimes followed the guidelines only loosely. For example, there might be different determinations depending on how the word "substantial" is defined.

Grants and loans under the Food for Peace program from its inception through 1990 totaled $40 billion. Food assistance in 1990 totaled $1.6 billion.[43]

The United States Peace Corps

The Peace Corps has been a significant U.S. foreign policy instrument. President John F. Kennedy's message to Congress on March 1, 1961, established the Peace Corps' vision and purposes and clearly suggested a direct link between U.S. political-security and development objectives in those areas of the world where people were struggling for economic and social progress. "Our own freedom, and the future of freedom around the world, depend, in a very real sense, on the ability to build growing and independent nations where men can live in dignity, liberated from the bonds of hunger, ignorance, and poverty."[44]

On September 22, 1961, Congress passed Public Law 87-293, the Peace Corps Act. In this document, Congress declared that the Peace Corps would send qualified men and women from the United States to help meet the needs of developing countries "for trained manpower, and to promote a better understanding of the American people on the part of the peoples served and a better understanding of the other peoples on the part of the American people."[45]

Clearly, learning about other peoples and enabling them to learn about the American people and values relates directly to all diplomatic objectives. Effective diplomacy requires understanding of other cultures and languages. Dialogue between U.S. diplomats and host country officials who have some understanding of the values and attitudes that affect U.S. perceptions and behavior facilitates all U.S. diplomacy. The first goal relates more directly to development objectives, the achievement of which is more long term in nature. This is the goal that is receiving more attention, as recipient countries request volunteers with more advanced skills or experience than are usually available from generalists with liberal arts degrees. Peace Corps volunteers (PCVs) are also now part of the United States' response to the rising prospects for democratic change in Eastern Europe and the former Soviet Union.

Between 1961 and 1990, the Peace Corps sent 130,000 volunteers to ninety-eight countries in Asia, Latin America, and Africa. By the end of FY 1990, the Peace Corps had approximately 6,700 volunteers in seventy-five different countries. The Peace Corps' budget in FY 1962 totaled $30 million. By FY 1966 it had quadrupled to $114 million and remained over $100 million for the rest of the decade. A retrenchment in Peace Corps activities and an attempt at organizational change during the 1970s resulted in a reduction in the organization's visibility and funding, which dropped from $98 million in FY 1970 to $86 million in FY 1978, but fluctuated at higher levels during the 1980s, reaching $153 million in FY 1989.[46]

Active Peace Corps volunteers are not directly involved in diplomatic activities. In the early years, the first Peace Corps director, Sargent Shriver, and his successors intentionally distanced volunteers and their development activities from the development and diplomatic efforts of A.I.D. and embassy officials. This separation was necessary to preserve the Peace Corps' apolitical image and to avoid suspicion that volunteers were CIA agents or otherwise engaged in subversive political activities.

Any political impact from the Peace Corps in the short run would likely result from the perception of the volunteers' presence as an expression of U.S. goodwill. Coupled with their participation in development activities, PCVs can indirectly create general goodwill toward the United States, which may later affect the diplomatic dialogue carried on in government ministries. The Peace Corps has become a major source of foreign experts and knowledge at all levels in the public and private sectors. Today, volunteers are often active participants in the planning and implementation of A.I.D.-funded development projects and provide insights useful in the Country Development Strategy Statement (see Chapter 4).

Multilateral Institutions

Multilateral institutions have functioned as important conduits for indirectly advancing U.S. political objectives. Since the mid-1970s, the United States has relegated the funding of large-scale infrastructure projects like roads, power plants, and irrigation schemes from bilateral DA resources to multilateral institutions. In the 1990s, the United States is also turning more of the balance of payments role over to multilateral institutions, particularly for aid to Eastern Europe and the former Soviet Union. The United States provides funds to the International Monetary Fund (IMF), the World Bank, the Asian Development Fund, and the African Development Fund. U.S. contributions to these four institutions totaled nearly $1.5 billion in FY 1990. This represents about 13 percent of all U.S. economic aid for that year.[47]

An advantage of multilateral institutions is their capacity to provide aid with conditionality that is based on economic criteria rather than on narrower U.S. political interests. Multilateral involvement helps to remove the United States from taking sole responsibility for the reforms suggested by these institutions in their assistance packages. Other donor countries have also welcomed the "shield" the IMF and the World Bank offer, particularly in those countries where they too have only marginal political interests.

Enforcement by the IMF and the World Bank of tough development-oriented conditions can help the bilateral donors to protect themselves from political pressure—whether exerted by the recipient country or other special interests—to provide aid for purposes other than those that directly promote conditions for sound economic growth. Multilateral institutions can also provide cover for donors seeking to avoid the political entanglements that go with bilateral aid provision. As A.I.D. has cut staff positions, it has also let the World Bank conduct most economic analyses on developing countries. Nevertheless, U.S. political interests increasingly have influenced decisions on whether or not a given country could obtain aid from multilateral institutions and on the nature of the conditionality exacted. This has been especially true in countries receiving high levels of ESF assistance, such as Egypt.

Another difficulty faced by the United States, unlike other major donors, is its process for replenishing international development aid provided through multilateral institutions. Foreign aid is always a controversial issue in the U.S. Congress. Many members in both parties tend to oppose allocations for the multilateral institutions because they believe that these institutions too readily make funds available to countries who actively oppose the United States, or who have socialist, state-controlled economic systems. Alternatively, some members think that the conditions are too lenient. The intensity of opposition varies from year to year, depending on the nature of difficulties the United States has experienced with certain Third World nations.

In any event, opposition may delay or even cut appropriations for multilateral institutions. The unpredictability of U.S. support, along with the politicized nature of U.S. opposition to certain countries, interferes with the development planning and implementation processes of these institutions. When this happens, it can irritate friends of the U.S. or other donors.

This brief description of the origins, purposes, and major economic instruments of U.S. aid diplomacy sets the stage for the remainder of this study. As indicated at the outset, the focus is on the use of ESF resources to advance U.S. political objectives and on the impact of this process on the promotion of economic, social, and political development objectives. Such objectives, as outlined in aid legislation and country programs, often appear to be fully consistent with the high-minded goals set forth by Roosevelt, Kennedy, McGhee, and others during the formative years of U.S. foreign aid. Chapter 4 begins the analysis with a discussion of the differences between myths and reality in the way ESF aid purposes are established, and the processes and interests that actually govern the way the aid is implemented. But first, Chapter 3 will discuss the differences between modernization and development.

NOTES

1. Robert Endicott Osgood, *Ideals and Self-Interest in America's Foreign Relations* (Chicago: Phoenix Books, imprint of The University of Chicago Press, 1953), p. 19.

2. Robert Neelly Bellah et al., *The Good Society* (New York: Random House, Knopf, 1991).

3. Nicholas Eberstadt, *Foreign Aid and American Purpose* (Washington D.C.: American Enterprise Institute, 1988), pp. 19–20.

4. Riddell, *Foreign Aid Reconsidered*, p. 3.

5. As quoted in A.I.D., *Development and the National Interest*, p. 13.

6. Eberstadt, *Foreign Aid*, p. 22.

7. The World Bank–sponsored Workshop on Participatory Development, February 26–27, 1992, recognized that the major bilateral and multicultural donors had relied too much on development approaches driven by measures of economic performance and "the elite" who controlled the relevant statistics: the economists. The World Bank intended to eliminate the bias for economists and obtain a better balance between political-social scientists and economists on its staff and their promotion criteria. This finding is a telling admission that this fundamental weakness has plagued all bilateral and multilateral foreign aid programs and approaches from their inception.

8. George C. McGhee, "The American Ambassador Today" (Address delivered at the Fourth Graduation Exercises of the Senior Seminar in Foreign Policy, Foreign Service Institute, Washington, D.C., June 8, 1962).

9. John F. Kennedy, "The Peace Corps," Message to Congress, March 1, 1961, *Vital Speeches* 27, no. 11 (March 15, 1961), pp. 325–326.

10. Riddell, *Foreign Aid Reconsidered*, p. 8.

11. Ibid.

12. Eberstadt, *Foreign Aid*, p. 31.

13. A.I.D. provided aid (both equipment and technical advisers) to police forces, particularly in Latin America and Southeast Asia, throughout the 1960s and early 1970s until Congress, reacting to the Vietnam War, prohibited such programs. During the 1980s, some aid to police forces in Central America was resumed but focused on increased professionalism and reduction of human rights abuses.

14. Eberstadt, *Foreign Aid*, p. 31.

15. James A. Nathan and James K. Oliver, *Foreign Policy Making and the American Political System*, 2d ed. (Boston: Little Brown, 1987), p. 1.

16. John E. Reilly, ed., *American Public Opinion and U.S. Foreign Policy* (Chicago: Chicago Council on Foreign Relations, 1983). As quoted in Eberstadt, *Foreign Aid*, p. 18.

17. Graham Hancock, *Lords of Poverty* (New York: The Atlantic Monthly Press, 1989), p. 4.

18. Eberstadt, *Foreign Aid*, pp. 17–18.

19. Eugene R. Wittkopf and James M. McCormick, "Was There Ever a Foreign Policy Commitment?" (Paper prepared for the Annual Meeting of the American Political Science Association, Washington, D.C., September 1–4, 1988), p. 9.

20. Ibid., pp. 16, 31.

21. Hamilton, "Foreign Assistance," p. 27.

22. Steve Sinding, interview with author, Washington, D.C., March 6, 1991.

23. Smith Simpson, *Perspectives on the Study of Diplomacy*, Occasional Paper (Washington, D.C.: Institute for the Study of Diplomacy, Georgetown University, 1986), p. 3.

24. *The American College Dictionary* (New York: Random House, 1970), p. 341.

25. Bradshaw Langmaid, deputy assistant administrator, Bureau for Science and Technology, A.I.D., interview with author, Washington, D.C., May 31, 1989.

26. Ambassador Edward E. Masters (Ret.), interview with author, Washington, D.C., August 1989.

27. Eberstadt, *Foreign Aid*, p. 22. Eberstadt provides an excellent and concise review of the concepts and purposes that lay behind early U.S. foreign assistance efforts.

28. See Appendix Figures II.1 and II.2 for the balances among these programs.

29. GAO, *Foreign Aid: Improving the Impact and Control of Economic Support Funds* (Report to the Chairman, Subcommittee on Europe and the Middle East, Committee on Foreign Affairs, House of Representatives, GAO/NSIAD-88-182 Economic Support Fund, June 1988), p. 8.

30. GAO, *Central America: Impact of U.S. Assistance in the 1980s* (Report to the Chairman, Committee on Foreign Relations, U.S. Senate, GAO/NSIAD-89-170, July 1989), p. 38.

31. See Appendix Figure V.

32. GAO, *Improving the Impact*, p. 15.

33. A.I.D., *FY 1990 CP,* main volume (February 1989), p. 45.

34. Marianne O'Sullivan, "Foreign Aid Funds Enacted," (*Front Lines*, A.I.D. newsletter (May 1992), p. 2.

35. Ibid., p. 9.

36. Ibid.

37. A.I.D., under its new Mission Statement (September 1990), now prefers to use the term *partner government.*

38. Richard F. Calhoun et al., "Food for Peace: Analysis of Organization and Administration" (A.I.D. Management Report, March 4, 1966), p. 26.

39. Ibid., p. 28.

40. Beatrice L. Rogers and Michael B. Wallerstein, *PL 480 Title I: A Discussion of Impact Evaluation Results and Recommendations* (A.I.D. Program Evaluation Report No. 13, February 1985), p. 2.

41. Ibid., pp. 29–30.

42. U.S. Congress, "The Agricultural Trade and Development Act of 1954" (known as PL 480) as amended, Section 403(a)(2).

43. A.I.D., *U.S. Overseas Loans and Grants*, p. 4.

44. Kennedy, "The Peace Corps," pp. 325–326.

45. U.S. Congress, "The Peace Corps Act," *United States Statutes at Large*, 87th Cong., 1st sess., 1961, vol. 75.

46. GAO, Peace Corps: *Meeting the Challenges of the 1990s* (May 1990), pp. 9–12.

47. A.I.D., *U.S. Overseas Loans and Grants*, p. 4.

3

MODERNIZATION AND DEVELOPMENT

The very complexities of development have made it difficult to determine the proper purposes of development assistance and how they relate to larger U.S. political and security objectives. This condition continues to some extent today, despite considerable rhetoric about the need to make foreign aid more effective.

THE PROBLEM OF DEFINING DEVELOPMENT

The Cold War context limited the time, resources, and talent available within government agencies to study the development process in depth. Although project and program evaluations sometimes provided insights about development, few policymakers were prepared or able to apply these insights, especially if the lessons challenged conventional wisdom, or threatened country program objectives related more to preserving "stability" in government-to-government relations than to supporting changes in power relationships throughout a developing society.

Many practitioners and development theorists also reflect confusion when they argue that it is chauvinistic or even "imperialist" to attach development performance conditions to aid, asserting that such efforts constitute pressure to force our perceptions about development and change on different cultures. While such a position appears "open-minded," it ignores the fact that the very economic and social goals that the recipient nations claim they want all but dictate substantial, timely, and difficult change in traditional social and political processes. Applying such nonintervention theory would mean that U.S. aid cannot be used to help empower recipients to someday stand on their own. Instead, aid programs would become largely welfare oriented and only serve to relieve recipient governments of their responsibility to ensure their peoples' welfare. Indeed, this is the net effect of much current politically driven aid.

Finally, within the Agency for International Development, "economic development" from the early 1960s to at least 1988 was defined primarily in standard economic terms that focused on rates of growth, balance of payments, employment statistics, and other such quantifiable criteria. A.I.D.

officers who tried to argue that controlling and restrictive political systems could be a major cause of underdevelopment *and* a major obstacle to generating social and economic development were generally ignored, or reminded that political issues were the State Department's responsibility. A.I.D. could not address political issues, they were further told, because projects that empowered people could destabilize a friendly government and undermine other aid efforts. In the Cold War context these were compelling arguments.

Nor, over the past twenty-five years, has Congress ever undertaken a serious study of the development process and its implications for the aid program. Few members of Congress have cared to spend much time on foreign aid issues. Foreign aid has had low priority because it has little impact on relations with constituents. Moreover, in the politically charged debate over the proper stance of the United States in world affairs, a vote the "wrong way" on a particular assistance program—in Central America during the 1980s for instance—could adversely affect one's reelection prospects.[1] In 1983, an internal A.I.D. review of congressional action on foreign aid objectives from 1961 to 1982 found that "only when a program is perceived as extremely important to peace (aid to Israel) or as serving the interests of a large segment of American society (Food for Peace) or as demonstrating purely humanitarian concerns in an emergency (disaster aid) is there little difficulty passing authorization and appropriations bills." Less well-understood objectives, such as development of a remote country or security aid to an ally whose domestic policies are distasteful, create serious problems. "Not only is there a lack of broad grass-roots support, there is substantial grass-roots opposition, resulting in reluctance by many members of Congress to support so unpopular a program."[2]

Thus, Congress has remained unable to delineate a coherent set of development objectives and priorities for foreign assistance. Moreover, executive agencies, including A.I.D. and the State Department, have not tried to develop and defend a coherent vision for foreign aid. The 1989 A.I.D. study on foreign assistance also found that priorities for U.S. aid had become less focused. Some champion humanitarian aid for its own sake, others hold political and national security considerations paramount, and others seek commercial advantages. Special interest groups advocate aid for particular countries or programs.[3]

Professor Golar Butcher of Howard University, a former A.I.D. assistant administrator for Africa, compared the lack of a consistent definition of development to fashion's "long-skirt, short-skirt problem." The focus has shifted from basic human needs to infrastructure to the marketplace. Professor Butcher advocates conceptualizing development strategy from a larger framework. "Do we really want to focus on moving people away from their underdevelopment? Do we want to get them not just narrowly self-sustaining but into the industrial world?"[4]

Unfortunately, as the former colonial powers began to look for ways to help newly independent states in the Third World, the successful precedent of the United States' first major attempt at foreign economic aid, the Marshall Plan, impeded understanding about the role foreign aid could play in the development process. The Marshall Plan approach led donors and recipients alike to believe that external aid could be a major determinant in development, when in fact it could only be a helpful but insufficient tool. In brief, the Marshall Plan was successful because it provided resources to governments and people in previously successful industrial states who needed to rebuild their factories, but not to change social, economic, and political structures or to create totally new ones with new values and attitudes.

Failure to recognize or act on this reality led to the kind of problem described by Butcher. As thinking on development evolved, foreign aid proponents and practitioners shifted among a succession of factors they saw as the "missing link" in the development process. First was the need for capital, then physical infrastructure, followed by agriculture. Then came the need for strong public institutions, followed in the 1980s by establishment of the free market as the best way to stimulate the economic growth that would create jobs and expand participation in the economy.[5]

By the early 1990s, the focus had shifted to "good governance." Though this concept touches on the issue of political processes, its initial formulation by the World Bank and the United Nations Development Program (UNDP) seems to focus on reducing corruption and improving administration rather than empowering people as individuals to control their own destinies. To A.I.D.'s and the U.S. government's credit, however, most of the new Democratic Initiatives projects pioneered in several Latin American countries and beginning in appropriately small-scale projects in many of the former East bloc states do focus on empowerment of people.

Gunnar Myrdal, Sweden's Nobel Prize–winning economist, was a major architect of development theory in the 1950s and 1960s. In *Development and Underdevelopment*, Myrdal argued that a government's central planners should control the divisive forces within developing societies by centrally managing the necessary social and economic revolution. He believed that economic development was a task for governments—as in Sweden's own socialist-oriented approach—and that their plans should contain a system of intentionally applied controls and impulses to get development started and keep it going. For Myrdal, failure to adopt the central planning approach would mean "continued acquiescence in economic and cultural stagnation or regression which is politically impossible in the world of today."[6]

P. T. Bauer, noted British development theorist, disagreed with Myrdal. In his controversial treatise *Dissent on Development*, Bauer argued that extensive state control over economic and social life placed a premium on the exercise of political power. This situation created considerable stress and anxiety among the active elements of the society as they intensified their struggle for political power. Bauer observed that extensive state control over economic life often meant the public would "blame the government for all economic grievances, whether genuine or spurious, including adverse effects of economic change." Since practically all change affects some groups adversely, political tension would increase. Bauer concluded that such all-important political action diverted the energies and resources of able and ambitious men from economic activity to political life. "And the direction in which the activities of able, energetic and ambitious people are employed is clearly a major influence on the level and progress of economic attainment of a society."[7]

In retrospect, with the failure of Soviet communism and even the increasing evidence of the failure of socialist-oriented nations such as Sweden to fulfill people's need to believe they can control their own destinies, it is hard to believe that Bauer was discounted for so long by so many development specialists. Many U.S. foreign aid economists and practitioners considered Bauer's views on individual liberty, work ethic, self-responsibility, the free market, and the dangers of central planning out of place in the Third World context.

Norman Jacobs extended the development debate by defining basic differences between modernization and development. Jacobs uses *modernization* to denote the maximization of a society's potential within the limits set by a society's goals and structure. In this sense, modernization improves techniques for coping with change *within* the existing, traditional environment. In contrast, development seeks maximization of a society's potential *regardless of any limits* currently set by a society's goals or basic structure. Jacobs saw *development* as an open-ended commitment to *productive change*, "no matter what the consequences might be on existing goals or existing ways of doing things." Development depended on a commitment to objectivity, where "innovation is accepted or rejected on the objective grounds of whether or not it contributes to maximizing the society's potential."[8]

This definition of development recognizes that commitment to change and empowerment, with all their inherent risks, is *essential* in any development process. However, the consequences of certain changes on the political process, particularly the configuration of power, cannot always be foreseen and may create even more difficult problems. These possibly destabilizing consequences strike fear in those who currently wield power in developing countries, as well as among many aid donors, development experts, and diplomats who rely on stability and predictability in government-to-government relations. Such instability can also be threatening to the small farmer who wants nothing more than to grow and sell his crops in peace.

U.S.-Thai relations in 1973 provide an example of the weakness of U.S. commitment to understanding and promoting the development process, even for a close ally in the Vietnam War. During 1972–1973, the A.I.D. mission's Program Research Office in Bangkok, Thailand, carried out a series of seminars to introduce the Myrdal, Bauer, and Jacobs perspectives, among many others. The seminars included A.I.D. personnel, Thai academics and government officials, other U.S. embassy officials, and the donor community. The seminars (eleven in all) examined the Thai political process and administrative behavior to determine their impact on the implementation of the aid program. Though the series was successful in terms of participation and the quality of the discussions, many participants discounted Bauer's perspectives and considered Jacobs's views "insensitive" to traditional cultures. Moreover, the United States had committed itself to steep reductions in the aid effort prior to the 1973 Thai student uprising, and did not appreciate the new opportunities for development aid created by the emerging democratic political process. This decision "created the impression that the United States did not care for the new, democratic government, which was partly true."[9]

Indeed, on October 25, 1973, Robert Nooter, then assistant administrator of A.I.D.'s Bureau for Supporting Assistance, told A.I.D. mission staff that although Thailand had "high priority for its key geopolitical position in terms of our overall Southeast Asian political-military strategic requirements," because of its large foreign exchange reserves, "in the eyes of the U.S. Congress, Thailand does not really qualify for long-term economic aid [and] has a low priority from a development aid perspective."[10] An internal memo to the deputy chief of mission and the A.I.D. director, responding to this perspective, argued the case for supporting the emerging Thai democracy and not cutting the program. It concluded, "We had resources when we needed bases and Thai support for our effort in Vietnam. We had resources for the police and army generals. . . . Now, when we have a government of Thailand 'of the people, by the people, and for the people'—or at least better prospects for this than ever before, we may have no way to help and thereby make up for our very serious lack of understanding in the past."[11]

The only aspect of Thai political and social development issues that appeared relevant was the confusion the changes created for those U.S. diplomatic and development aid officers more concerned about avoiding U.S. entanglement. In the end, perceived aid management interests prevailed. The United States reduced its aid to Thailand to modest levels and never established any significant programs in direct support of the democratization process.

By 1980, Myrdal himself began to confirm some of Bauer's earlier fears regarding the dangers of governmental control over development processes. At a trade union–sponsored seminar, "Capital and Economic Development," held in Stockholm on September 10, 1980, Myrdal startled the audience when he criticized many of the elite in developing countries for mismanagement and lack of concern. He charged that international development assistance was almost entirely ineffective and instead was contributing to the perpetuation of social and economic evils in the recipient countries. His extemporaneous comments were later reiterated in an interview with TT, the Swedish news agency.[12]

Myrdal admitted he had changed his mind about "the traditional model of assistance to the developing countries." He called instead for international charity that would go only to those countries whose people faced death by starvation. Myrdal criticized the "scandalous political situation" in many of the developing countries, noting that the peoples of underdeveloped countries were represented at international aid conferences by elites who lacked the will to solve the problems of the vast majority. He argued that without broad social reform in developing countries, the assistance would be of little use to the people in real need. He suggested that the only thing donors and recipients really accomplish at international conferences on how to improve the economies of the developing countries was "being polite to one another."[13]

Myrdal appeared to echo Bauer's view that foreign aid can become a crutch for crippled political leaders who lack the will to promote the policies, attitudes, and behavior patterns conducive to self-sustaining political and economic development. R. M. Sundrum also suggested that development economics needed to "understand the nature of the process which has transformed the developed countries in the past, why it has not occurred in the lesser developed countries, and what may be done to promote it in the future."[14]

Interestingly, though Myrdal and others moved toward recognition of the role of the political process in 1980, A.I.D., the World Bank, and the UNDP did not begin to address this issue for another eight to ten years. In part, this was due to the Cold War context in which political development was almost a taboo subject. If aid donors, especially the United States, tried to stress political development, they might seem to be trying to unseat the very government they were supposed to be supporting. The focus remained on economic development efforts, although some aid programs tried to address political issues through grassroots community development projects. The collapse of the Soviet empire shook much of the conventional wisdom about the role of central planning in development economics and encouraged aid donors to put political reform conditions on aid to Central and Eastern Europe, the Soviet successor states, and much of the developing world.

This wide spectrum of perspectives on development has impeded consensus on a limited set of measurable objectives for foreign aid that might serve both political and development purposes. As a consequence, foreign aid has become a collection of programs to serve the diverse interests and views of development represented by the many participants in the U.S. policy process: Congress, special interest groups, and many agencies in the executive branch.

The Hamilton Task Force on Foreign Assistance found that the Foreign Assistance Act's thirty-three different objectives were "so numerous that they cannot provide meaningful direction or be effectively implemented."

Although military aid had fewer objectives, the task force found those objectives "overly politicized, leading us to expect too much in foreign policy terms from what is being provided or sold," and concluded that "mixing security, military, development, and humanitarian objectives makes evaluation and congressional oversight difficult."[15]

REDEFINING DEVELOPMENT AND ITS IMPLICATIONS FOR U.S. FOREIGN AID OBJECTIVES

Throughout 1988, 1989, and 1990, A.I.D. and the U.S. Congress considered new approaches to foreign aid. The IMF, the World Bank, the UNDP, and other major donors also sought more effective ways to provide additional aid to LDCs, whose combined debt in 1990 exceeded $1 trillion.

During the March 1988 appearance of A.I.D. Administrator Alan Woods before the Senate Foreign Relations Committee, Senator Jesse Helms asked whether the United States could really aid the development of a country without addressing the root causes of its underdevelopment. Ambassador Woods, expressing doubt that it could, identified the root causes as inappropriate economic policies. These impeded the broad economic growth needed to create the resources to pay for water, health, education, and other services. At the same time, Congress had directed A.I.D. to intervene directly to help improve the health, education, and general welfare of the people of developing nations. "The longevity of such programs," he concluded, "depends on the capacity of the recipient countries to sustain them, and that brings us full circle—back to the absolute need to get the economies of developing countries pointed in the right direction and growing."[16]

Woods's response reflected the traditional stress on economic planning issues while ignoring the probability that the political process could also impede development or that the political process is relevant in different ways to both modernization and development. Nor did Woods address the implications of these issues for U.S. foreign assistance programs.

Modernization, Development, and Democratization

Because political factors are fairly obvious, yet difficult to influence, aid donors have taken them as givens, undertaking little further effort to analyze them or to understand how they affect the use of foreign aid as a development tool. Herein is a major reason for the limited impact of aid on the causes of underdevelopment. For too long, even among Western scholars, conventional wisdom in modernization theory has argued that democracy depends on first achieving strong economic development. The collapse of communism in the Soviet Union and Eastern Europe provides compelling evidence that the reverse may be true: Development efforts that include stimulation of democracy actually improve the prospects for sustainable economic growth, because it ensures the broadest possible participation by empowered people.

At what point does the development process begin to require a change toward greater democracy? How, in turn, does democracy reinforce the sustainability of socioeconomic development? History provides clear evidence that authoritarian political systems and highly centralized bureaucracies can initiate basic modernization of institutions and infrastructure. They can modernize basic education through provision of school buildings and teachers of reading, writing, and math skills. Authoritarian systems can provide basic health care, including potable water systems. They can build power plants, roads, bridges, and irrigation systems, and they can even establish agricultural research stations. All of this modernizing infrastructure can greatly facilitate further social and economic development, but it is not sufficient.

To go beyond modernization and develop self-sustaining political, social, and economic institutions requires active participation *from* and *with* an increasingly empowered, innovative and knowledgeable population. Such a human resource base depends on, among other things, libraries in schools and universities committed to expanding access to information and exchange of ideas, research, and experience. Today's information and communication research technologies demand an inspired, imaginative work force, free to seek and create knowledge in all economic, scientific, and social endeavors. As David Steinberg suggests, "A.I.D. in the past concentrated on 'modernization'—but now with 'governance' an issue (along with human rights and democracy), it needs to consider how to move toward 'development' as defined in Jacobs's terms."[17]

Jacobs emphasizes *change* as the vital element in the development process. Empowerment, which he also seems to have intended, is part of this change process. Throughout the remainder of this study, the word *development* should be understood to include the concept of empowerment of people as individuals and groups seeking to control their own destinies.

Governmental institutions have a vital role in the human resource development process, but that role—in a democracy—primarily involves creating opportunities for individuals, organizations, and institutions to imagine, plan, and manage their own development. Governments can help, but to be effective they should do so on terms established by such individuals and their organizations. By determining what material, informational, and financial resources are available, who has access to them, and what taxes are to be derived from new wealth, the political process sets the parameters for development of human resources, as well as the opportunities for participation in the social and economic growth of the nation.

Self-sustainable development invariably creates new power, both in individuals and organizations. Are the governing elite committed to development of, rather than on behalf of, the people? What is the elite's attitude toward power and its growth in different sectors of the society? Do they accept or oppose the probability that this new power will somehow affect their capacity to control challenges to their positions? Do they view new sources of power as a net gain or loss for the political process? Do they accept or reject change in the sources of political power as a desirable maximization of the society's potential?

Answers to these questions determine the existence or not of a favorable environment for the development of political democracy. Thus, political processes that encourage new power for individuals, organizations, and institutions can be evolving toward democracy even if the system itself still lacks many of the institutions often included in traditional Western definitions of democracy—elections, for example, have often been centrally programmed referenda with predetermined outcomes. Perhaps the most vital element in the process is the emergence of independent power sources—pluralistic institutions—outside the established government that can compel the government to respond to the people's desires for change.

In summary, and recognizing that the wealth of a nation resides more in its people than in any other resource, this study finds that, ideally, the highest levels of sustainable economic development are most likely to occur where at least the following four conditions exist or are clearly developing.

- The *education process* provides good basic knowledge, free inquiry, and research. Such education begins in elementary school and culminates in universities that are unfettered by police, military, or religious intervention. The media are free, and libraries exist that have uncensored texts and the means to expand their holdings continuously.
- *Business enterprise* (capital and labor) can encourage change in policies through the political process when such change is necessary to create continual productive, innovative investment and growth by individuals and business organizations. Support and pressure for change should be possible through political parties, interest groups, labor organizations, and direct lobbying of the formal government structures.
- The *legal system* can effectivly define and enforce respect for rights, the fair production of wealth, and possession of property independent from government control. The laws and courts create and enforce rules fair to all economic enterprises and individuals. Corruption is addressed through effective sanctions that ensure free, fair political and economic competition and growth. All people have access and opportunity to use this legal system.
- *Individuals* can identify their personal needs and objectives and improve and expand their knowledge and skills without coercion by any organization, whether governmental, religious, educational, or economic. Instead, through provision of libraries, training programs, and guarantees for a free press, the government creates opportunities for innovative individuals to profit from their efforts for productive self-growth.

The political process determines the role of these four elements in the development—read empowerment—of people. To the degree that governmental and other political leadership encourage progress toward the realization of these elements, the political process can evolve toward full political democracy.

This perspective should dispel the misperception that modernization of infrastructure or welfare programs constitutes development. It is essential that we understand the difference between development aid that will help empower people—the essence of development—and assistance that only supports the modernization of infrastructure or social welfare services.

The Compatibility Problem

The conflict between developmental and political objectives in the implementation of foreign aid programs further illustrates the differences between modernization and development. Richard M. Cashin, a former A.I.D. mission director, suggests that the central compatibility issue is "the extent to which development assistance can and should be sheltered from the ebb and flow of shorter-term political and strategic considerations."[18] The traditional perspective holds that since development assistance programs (both the ESF and DA varieties) are diplomatic tools, the real question is how they should be deployed and presented in furthering U.S. national interests. Holders of this view tend not to be concerned about preserving long-term development goals. Cashin points out that differences in view derive from the subjective nature of the concept of the national interest, including the lack of intellectual rigor in its application.

Further complicating the issue is the pronounced difference in time horizon between development practitioners and politically driven diplomats, who "try to keep things calm on their watch in the particular country concerned."[19] These differences could further damage development objectives if, as some studies have suggested, A.I.D. were reconstituted within the State Department.

Cashin recalled his experience as director of A.I.D.'s Office of Central African Affairs in the mid-1960s, when he quarreled with an opposite number in the State Department. President Kwame Nkrumah of Ghana had requested over $100 million in PL 480 assistance. The State Department wanted a favorable reponse even if not the full amount. Rejection would "rock the boat" politically, something that would not be in our "national interest"; in other words, the United States depended on Nkrumah's support for U.S. objectives in Africa. Cashin argued that Ghana's economic mismanagement should not be rewarded. Many Ghanaian friends of the United States pleaded that the United States should not prop up Nkrumah economically and thereby only prolong his increasingly oppressive regime. "It came down to a question of who was the proper custodian of the national interest, and it was made very clear to me that the State Department had that mandate. In this case, the issue went to the administrator of A.I.D. and we eventually prevailed, but not without a struggle."[20]

W. Haven North, a retired A.I.D. officer, recalls the stress he experienced in trying to cope with the conflict between development and political objectives. He once tried to transfer a million dollars from the large Kenyan program to another country program for an important development activity. The U.S. ambassador to Kenya opposed the transfer, and the State Department said, "You can't do that; it will send the wrong signal; we'll endanger our base rights." For North this type of argument typifies the "lack of clarification of the relationship of development interests to political objectives; of 'now' objectives as opposed to political objectives that are long-term."[21]

These examples raise important questions: Can failure to achieve development objectives undermine the sustainability of the political achievements originally obtained with the aid levels? Is achievement of political and social development objectives in the recipient country relevant to U.S. national and diplomatic interests? The Congressional Presentation documentation, to be reviewed in the next chapter, certainly makes such linkages. If a recipient country's leadership or other politically important elements believe that the aid relationship is not achieving actual development—or even their own political objectives—what are the consequences for U.S. political objectives? Will even more aid be required to make the relationship palatable?

To the extent that the local leadership may not care about achieving development objectives, negative findings may not affect the short-term relationship. Nevertheless, others in the elite or politically aware population may recognize that the assistance relationship does not provide developmental benefits and might use this failure to discredit that relationship. In such cases, ironically, failure of U.S. assistance to stimulate development could contribute to delegitimization of a government in the eyes of its people.

John Sullivan, former A.I.D. assistant administrator for Asia, suggests that such confusion over economic aid purposes and approaches was symptomatic of a more serious ailment: schizophrenic assistance relationships.[22] Schizophrenia in this case refers to the process by which political assistance, whether it is called security assistance or ESF, is originally given for a political purpose and then given a development twist, with all the latter's attendant planning and implementation requirements.

The U.S.-Egypt aid relationship demonstrates this difficulty. Although U.S. aid to Egypt essentially supports U.S. political objectives, the program is laden with development objectives that are not attainable in the existing political-security context. Sullivan and others have suggested recognizing that political money is a legitimate diplomatic tool for advancing U.S. national interests. It is not something bad. These resources should be managed separately by the State Department and a separate A.I.D. would manage the development funds.[23]

The General Accounting Office (GAO) tried to determine the feasibility of such an approach in the Egyptian case. It found, however, that neither the Congress, the Reagan administration, nor many Egyptians were comfortable with an unconditional transfer of resources based on a quid pro quo security relationship.[24] The GAO concluded in Egypt's case that the best approach was to accept the political purposes of ESF but, reflecting congressional interest, continue trying to have developmental impact. The problem is that the expectations for achieving development impact with money given for political quid pro quos have been raised to the point where they exceed the possible.[25]

Cashin's response to the compatibility dilemma is a plea "for the space and time to work toward genuine development, rewarding virtue where we find it, biding our time where we do not, accepting the fact that we will sometimes seem to be acting at cross purposes with shorter-term U.S. political goals." Perhaps the real issue from a domestic political standpoint, Cashin observes, is whether it is feasible to isolate political considerations and "whether the United States is prepared to support an aid program not tightly linked to current international relations."[26]

IMPLICATIONS FOR FOREIGN AID AND THE PROMOTION OF PEACE

The 1990–1991 Gulf crisis illustrates the consequences of politically driven aid policies that may have helped modernization but not the empowerment of people, and which have done more to sustain the causes of conflict than to promote the conditions of peace.[27] This experience and other U.S. foreign aid policies in the Middle East and other regions suggest that using economic aid to preserve a political status quo or to prevent hostilities does not deter war in cases where political leaders feel compelled to use war as a means to turn their people's attention from domestic political and economic failure, to gain political and military control over another state's territory, or to advance some messianic purpose.

Economic aid that does not address the economic, social, and political causes of conflict cannot create sustainable conditions for peace—within or between states. Experience demonstrates that foreign aid can be a modernizing tool, yet fail to stimulate development defined in terms of increasingly empowered people. As already noted, modernization does not necessarily result in new processes and organizations that ensure the participation of people in determining their own development objectives.

When economic and/or military aid is provided primarily to advance a diplomatic objective, such as persuading a state to opt for peace over war or to cooperate against a threat to peace, the funding levels usually range in the hundreds of millions of dollars. Often, the United States provides direct cash grants or, as was the case with Iraq, large agricultural credits. When transferred through projects, such aid tends to support highly visible projects that will absorb high levels of aid, such as power plants, other large infrastructure projects, and commodity imports. The most important considerations are the aid levels and their rapid transfer to the recipient government. While such assistance may help modernize infrastructure or transfer some technology, its primary purpose is to demonstrate a quick "payoff" for cooperation with the United States toward a given security objective, "in the cause of peace" or any such related political objective.

Generally, such aid does not contribute to the development of social, economic, and political power in people, as individuals or groups, *throughout* a society that might help restrain the call to war. In the case of Iraq, not unlike Argentina when it initiated the Falklands War, it is this lack of such societywide political strength that impels leaders like Saddam Hussein to use war to obtain additional resources or divert public attention when popular dissatisfaction threatens political stability.

By comparison, aid that focuses on enhancing people's capacities—human resource development rather than simply improving basic living conditions—does not require such large projects or enormous sums of money. It does require time, patience, and committed cooperation between donor, recipient governments, and people who want to empower themselves. Economic aid can become a major factor in a peace process when a recipient country's leaders want to expand political, economic, and social pluralism in their societies. Such development expands the nature and sources of power in a society and creates special interests that would be damaged by war. It also stimulates the growth of different types of organizational power throughout a society that will tend to resist war as a viable policy option.

Iraq is a striking example of a modernizing state capable of waging war but not empowering its people to live well in peace. A key lesson would appear to be that economic assistance can most effectively advance the cause of peace when it is allocated and applied toward the empowerment of people.

NOTES

1. Larry Q. Nowels, Library of Congress Research Service, interview with author, August 1989.

2. A.I.D., "Historical Look at Objectives of Foreign Aid: Congressional Action and Legislative Changes 1961-1982" (August 22, 1983), p. 36.

3. A.I.D., *Development and the National Interest*, p. 19.

4. Professor Golar Butcher of Howard University, at a symposium on foreign aid and diplomacy, sponsored by Georgetown University's Institute for the Study of Diplomacy (ISD), Washington, D.C., November 30, 1989.

5. Hamilton, "Foreign Assistance," p. 29.

6. Gunnar Myrdal, *Development and Underdevelopment* (Cairo: National Bank of Egypt, 1956), pp. 63–65.

7. P. T. Bauer, *Dissent on Development* (Cambridge: Harvard University Press, 1972), p. 87.

8. Norman Jacobs, *Modernization Without Development: Thailand as an Asian Case Study* (New York: Praeger, 1971), p. 9.

9. David I. Steinberg, interview with author, August 25, 1992.

10. Robert F. Zimmerman, "Thailand's Position on the Map of U.S. Priorities" (Memo to Edward E. Masters, deputy chief of mission, U.S. Embassy, and Roger Ernst, director, U.S. Operations Mission [A.I.D.], October 26, 1973). This memo, written with the support of many A.I.D./Thailand mission personnel, argued against cutting the economic aid program to Thailand.

11. Ibid., p. 4.

12. Swedish News Agency article quoting Myrdal, provided to the U.S. Mission to the United Nations in a cable from the U.S. embassy in Stockholm on September 17, 1980 (UNCLASS STOCKHOLM 4068).

13. Ibid.

14. R. N. Sundrum, *Development Economics: A Framework for Analysis* (London: Wiley, 1983), p. 78.

15. *Report of the Task Force on Foreign Assistance to the Committeee on Foreign Affairs, U.S. House of Representatives*, 101st Cong., 1st sess., Document 101–32, February 1989, p. 27.

16. Robert F. Zimmerman, "A Root Cause of Underdevelopment: The Political Context and Its Implications for the Future of Foreign Assistance" (Paper delivered at the American Political Science Association Annual Meeting, Washington D.C., September 1989), p. 2.

17. Steinberg, interview.

18. Richard M. Cashin (retired A.I.D. career foreign service officer and participant in the ISD symposium), letter to author, January 2, 1990.

19. Ibid.

20. Ibid.

21. W. Haven North (former career A.I.D. officer), ISD symposium.

22. Dr. John Sullivan, ISD symposium.

23. Ibid.

24. Carol Shuster (evaluator, U.S. General Accounting Office), ISD symposium.

25. Ibid.

26. Cashin, letter.

27. This example is discussed in Chapter 8.

4

Processes and Purposes: Myth or Reality?

Establishing and implementing a coherent set of development assistance purposes within the hierarchy of U.S. foreign policy objectives has remained a difficult and largely unsuccessful undertaking throughout the history of U.S. foreign economic aid. A March 1992 GAO study concluded that because A.I.D. has to address so many objectives, "the agency has no clear priorities or meaningful direction."[1] The study noted that A.I.D. had begun to take steps to improve its strategic management but found that it still lacked "a clearly articulated strategic direction that was shared by key internal and external groups." The GAO continued:

> Throughout much of its history, A.I.D. has had to address the sometimes competing concerns of a wide range of groups that are concerned with its mission or have a stake in A.I.D.'s services and resources. The Congress plays a major role in shaping A.I.D.'s programs through legislated requirements and various directives. The State Department carries out U.S. foreign policy and has significant input in determining the types of programs A.I.D. provides and the countries in which A.I.D. delivers assistance. The Office of Management and Budget exercises great influence over A.I.D.'s operating expense budget and staff levels.
>
> Within A.I.D., development professionals differ on the direction of A.I.D.'s program. Recipient countries and organizations that implement A.I.D. projects are concerned with the levels of funding they receive, the types of projects and programs funded by A.I.D., and the administrative requirements that govern participation in A.I.D. activities. Attempting to respond to a number of groups, A.I.D.'s program has grown too large and unfocused for its operating expense and staff levels.[2]

One of A.I.D.'s major handicaps is that it does not control its own destiny. A.I.D.'s other handicaps include significant weaknesses in its leadership and personnel management, excessive bureaucracy, a lack of vision for itself, and the courage to challenge those other groups and agencies that have so badly confused foreign aid purposes. This chapter describes the effect on the implementation of the economic aid program of the different bureaucratic interests within the executive branch (including A.I.D.), Congress, and various government agencies; of domestic special interests; and of the interests of recipient countries.

THE POLICY, PROGRAM, AND PROJECT DESIGN PROCESS

The two most important aid planning documents are the Country Development Strategy Statement and the Congressional Presentation. These documents set forth the purposes and rationales that link the aid program to the larger U.S. political objectives. There is, however, considerable difference between the U.S. economic aid planning guidance and documentation presented to Congress and actual implementation as dictated by the real world of U.S. political objectives, bureaucratic processes, and special interests.

The Country Development Strategy Statement (CDSS)

The CDSS has provided the analytical basis for a proposed assistance strategy in each recipient country. The CDSS guidance recognizes that "insightful analysis of the host country's development prospects and problems . . . is the key to a successful strategy." In the CDSS, the A.I.D. mission can "think through its assessment of the basic development problems and opportunities faced by the host country and the role that A.I.D. can play."[3]

The CDSS describes the U.S. political, security, and economic interests and objectives in each recipient country. It analyzes economic conditions, including how these may affect political and social stability in the country. State Department guidance for the CDSS states that "successful economic development is essential to the achievement of U.S. foreign policy goals in less developed countries." While accepting that responsibility for development lies with the countries themselves, the guidance states that, "the international community, both public and private, can clearly play an important supporting role. A key to effective U.S. participation in that process is a well thought out development assistance strategy. . . . The strategy must be grounded in the development needs of the country, our opportunities for making effective interventions, and the resources available to achieve our foreign policy objectives."[4]

The CDSS establishes the U.S. aid strategy by describing the nature and scope of economic and social development problems and the approaches the A.I.D. mission intends to follow in each relevant sector, for example, agriculture, education, health and family planning, energy, water/wastewater, transportation, environment, irrigation, and public administration. It defines the linkages between economic and social development, the long-run political stability of the country or region, and the focus of the intended aid activities. Whenever relevant, the CDSS describes how U.S. aid complements other donors' activities.

Unless a dramatic political change in the recipient country or in the strategic environment necessitates a shorter-term revision, the A.I.D. field mission and appropriate U.S. embassy staff prepare the CDSS once every five years. The A.I.D. mission director supervises the process—which can take several months—but the mission Program Office, with inputs from all mission divisions, coordinates the actual drafting. If the political environment, including U.S. political objectives and the host country's political condition, proves relevant, the embassy usually leads the analysis process. The ambassador personally approves the final document and may sometimes participate in discussions on key issues and projects. In most cases, missions use A.I.D./Washington personnel via temporary duty (TDY) assignments to help draft the CDSS. They also rely heavily on personal service contracts to bring in consultants who can provide expertise in agriculture, public administration, education, cultural, and to some extent political analysis. Consultants also help prepare sections in the CDSS (and project documents) that address special interest concerns such as the environment, women in development, children, and human rights.

The CDSS guidance recommends that, to the extent possible, key host country analysts and decisionmakers participate in the CDSS development process. This generally occurs in countries that receive Development Assistance rather than Economic Support Funds and where any necessary political analysis of U.S. political-strategic interests does not require classification. Upon completion, the embassy will send the CDSS to Washington for final review and approval after any necessary further discussion on particular issues or proposed program approaches.

The A.I.D. FY 1991 CDSS Guidance required the CDSS to address both "the basic issue of whether an economic assistance program continues to be important to the U.S. interest in a particular country and identify the highest priority investments which the U.S. can undertake in pursuit of our development and foreign policy goals."[5] Despite this instruction, the analyses for U.S. economic assistance country programs generally either (1) fail to describe how achievement of development-oriented project and program objectives can affect advancement of overarching U.S. political objectives or, given all the other competing special interests, (2) have little impact on the actual design and implementation of the aid programs. This weakness reflects the ambiguity concerning what the proper purposes and implementation approaches for U.S. economic assistance are or should be. The CDSS during the 1970s began asking "Who is poor? Why? What are we doing about it?" During the 1980s, as A.I.D. again began to address macroeconomic issues, the CDSS had to move away from the standard BHN analyses to other issues and the analysis process required more political economy–oriented expertise, which A.I.D. did not have. More on this and other weaknesses later.

The Congressional Presentation (CP)

The CP is the administration's formal request to Congress for funding. In effect, it tries to "sell" the administration's foreign aid program to Congress. The CP is prepared annually by the embassy and its A.I.D. mission in each recipient country, as well as by the A.I.D. and State Department regional bureaus and country desks in Washington. Recipient country officials have no direct role in preparing the CP, but they may be involved in planning the projects presented in the CP.

The CP reflects the broad political and economic analyses set forth in the CDSS. It describes the ongoing and proposed project activities and puts these in the context of the overall mission strategy outlined in the CDSS. Like the CDSS, the CP appears to place "sustainable development" high in the hierarchy of political objectives. These requests almost uniformly argue that assistance resources are required to support economic and social development in the recipient country. The CP reiterates CDSS contentions that cooperation and stability in U.S. relations with the recipient country are necessary to pursue U.S. national interests in particular countries or regions.

Since the primary objective of the CP is to sell the administration's foreign assistance program to Congress, the tone will be positive. At this point in the process, the more positive arguments will focus on the economic development objectives, including their intended beneficiaries. The documentation and testimony by State Department and A.I.D. officials will try to emphasize successes—or, perhaps more often, progress toward successful project completion. They will try to avoid initiating discussion on adverse project, program, or policy-dialogue experience and the complications and contradictions inherent in the development process.

Though perhaps understandable, this practice can have negative consequences for both diplomatic and development objectives, if only because it contributes to the often adversarial tone during congressional hearings and to the impression that the administration is hiding or covering up its failures. The hearings also provide congressional and public advocates or opponents of foreign assistance, usually through special interest groups, an opportunity to review the record set forth in the CP and to propose their own programs with the aid approaches they believe appropriate.

Sometimes, members of Congress or special interests use these hearings to send messages of praise or criticism to specific countries that may be receiving assistance. During the 1980s, several countries in Central America bore the brunt of such criticism, usually on human rights issues. While the testimony of the administration's representatives will defend the record of recipient countries or try to explain shortfalls on human rights issues or in project activities and economic reform efforts, often the administration will welcome some criticism if it reinforces behind-the-scenes negotiations that the Department of State and A.I.D. might be engaged in with recipient governments on the same problem areas. For example, congressional statements were helpful in the case of the long pipeline of unexpended funds in the Philippines during the 1980s. A.I.D. was able to use these expressed concerns to get the attention of the government toward resolution of such problems.[6]

In these cases, the U.S. Congress uses the CP process to become an important and helpful actor in U.S. diplomacy. The process does not end until Congress accepts the CPs, with additional modification, after completion of congressional hearings by all Senate and House foreign relations committees.

The following excerpts from the FY 1990 CPs reflect perceived relationships between development and U.S. political objectives in these regions.

> *Africa*
>
> For FY 1990, A.I.D. is requesting . . . $83.3 million in Economic Support Funds . . . to support strategic interests justified on political and security grounds. To the extent practicable, the ESF resources will be utilized so as to maximize their development impact and to complement and support [Development Fund for Africa] and PL 480 initiatives. The Administration also requests $171.5 million in PL 480 resources which we intend to use to the greatest extent possible in support of our programmatic objectives.

The CP asserts that the Development Fund for Africa (DFA) supports "sustainable, broad-based, and market-oriented economic growth in Africa" through four strategic objectives: improving public management of African economies by redefining and reducing the role of the public sector and increasing its efficiency; strengthening competitive markets so as to provide a healthy environment for private sector–led growth; developing the potential for long-term increases in productivity in all sectors; and improving food security.[7]

> *Latin America and the Caribbean (LAC)*
>
> Our primary goal in the region is broad-based economic growth in order to sustain an environment conducive to stable, democratic governments and to protecting our major security interests. These interests include access to petroleum and other industrial raw materials, and to unimpeded use of the sea lanes adjacent to North America and the Panama Canal. Thus we have strong reasons for seeking to prevent the seizure of power by anti-democratic forces anywhere in the region, and for actively supporting civilian, democratically elected governments which are now in office in most countries. . . . Our interests and those of the LAC countries will be secure only if these countries can achieve faster, sustainable growth and their people enjoy broad participation in that growth.[8]

> *Asia and the Near East*
>
> In Asia and the Near East, A.I.D.'s programs directly serve many of the most important national security objectives of the United States. As a result of these programs and of the overall success of U.S. foreign policy, pressing national security issues are now being transformed into promising opportunities for political and economic progress. . . .
>
> In the Middle East, a fragile peace based on the Camp David Accords between Israel and Egypt continues to provide time for all parties to seek a durable solution to persistent violence and political conflict. Moderate Arab nations such as Jordan, Tunisia, Morocco and Oman will

> continue to receive U.S. aid. Assistance to improve the quality of life of Palestinians living on the West Bank and in Gaza is also proposed.
>
> [And finally,] developmental and humanitarian objectives in the Asia and Near East region remain major U.S. foreign policy concerns. Great progress has been made in the region, particularly in generating improved economic growth and in substantially increasing food production. It is equally true, however, that most of the world's poor live in the densely populated countries of this region. If the United States is to have a significant impact on world poverty, then Asia and the Near East must be the focus of our efforts.[9]

These CP statements clearly relate development to the achievement of U.S. political objectives. They confirm that long-term development is in the U.S. national interest. They even imply a shared consensus on the concept of development. As we shall see, however, the reality is sometimes very different.

Project Planning

Under the direction of the secretary of state, the Agency for International Development implements the policies and programs established through the CDSS and CP processes. The United States spends the bulk of all assistance resources through A.I.D.-managed project activities that address specific problem areas in education, health and family planning, rural and urban infrastructure, water, and other such sectors. In FY 1992 A.I.D. was responsible for administering assistance funds totaling approximately $7.5 billion and managing more than 2,000 ongoing programs and projects in over seventy countries.[10]

The design process begins with a project identification document (PID). The PID describes the development problem and the approach the A.I.D. field mission intends to follow in addressing the problem. PIDs are generally approved in A.I.D./Washington, though this practice varies by regional bureaus and depends on the cost of the project and the nature of any special issues such as environmental impact, the role of women, or political sensitivity.

The project design process involves discussions with recipient country officials and their participation in drafting the project documentation. The documentation outlines purposes to be served; financial, personnel, and other project inputs; and the project outputs in terms of personnel trained, health clinics built, family planning services provided, irrigation canals built, and so on. The plan describes administrative requirements, recipient country legislative actions, and other reforms, and underlying assumptions about the economic, social, bureaucratic, and (sometimes) political environment that can affect project implementation and goal achievement.

Project documents include "social soundness" analyses of the social, cultural, and administrative environment. Project documents also contain financial and economic rate of return analyses and sections on how the project takes into account special interests like women in development or environmental concerns. Field missions usually obtain short-term outside consultants to undertake the studies necessary to prepare this documentation. The A.I.D. officers primarily concern themselves with managing the process: contracting with consultants, setting up meetings with host country officials, arranging travel itineraries, and preparing the necessary project documents. In exceptional cases, project officers or other mission personnel may participate in the analysis process. Unfortunately, these analyses generally include little political analysis. Moreover, there is rarely coordination in a single project document, that is, the social scientist does the social soundness analysis but is not asked for his or her views on the economic analysis or vice versa.

Most field missions now have full authority to plan and approve all project activities up to $10 million at country level. They involve A.I.D. central staff in the project drafting process. Project planning is time consuming and can take two or more years to complete, depending on the different views that recipient country ministry and U.S. economic assistance officials have over definition of purposes, inputs, administrative responsibilities, and funding levels.

THE DIFFERENCES BETWEEN WORDS AND DEEDS

The CP descriptions of the relationships between development objectives and U.S. foreign policy objectives draw on the in-depth analysis provided in each country's CDSS. Unfortunately, development assistance professionals in A.I.D. and the Department of State who developed these documents—and Congress, which provides the resources—are often unable to implement these aid resources in programs consistent with the developmental and political objectives outlined in the CPs. Planning and analysis weaknesses, bureacratic processes, and U.S. policy objectives often work against the economic development-related objectives set forth in the CDSS, CP, and project documentation.

Relating Political and Development Objectives in the CP and Project Planning Process

Many critics in Congress believe that A.I.D. spends too much time planning and justifying its programs and not enough time implementing them. Representative Lee Hamilton (D-Indiana), noting that the annual CP weighs more than most members of Congress can lift, candidly admits that few, if any, read it. In addition, A.I.D. and State annually send to Congress some 700 required notifications of project changes or descriptions of new projects not included in the CP. These notifications generate additional correspondence between Congress and A.I.D., adding to the reporting burden. The country strategy statements, regional strategies, policy papers, and reports to Congress "threaten to engulf us."[11]

Ironically, while there is more information than anyone can use effectively, much of this information remains incomplete or is intentionally designed not to tell the whole story. While information on implementation disputes between A.I.D. or recipient governments and contractors, or other differences over project purposes or budgetary contributions is available, it is rarely freely offered. To do so would risk having Congress or other competing bureaus or agencies suggest reductions in funding and reallocation to other less troublesome projects. Dealing honestly with difficulties in delivering aid also could be used to undercut support for the aid program among U.S. citizens who already believe the aid is simply wasted.

It is important to remember that Congress is a major player in this process, along with all the special interests who want to ensure funding for their agendas. Sometimes even Congress does not want the candid perceptions of foreign service officers on the public record, especially if these perceptions contain information that would upset the premises of either a current policy or a particular project activity favored by Congress or a special interest group. Thus, negative assessments, however accurate, often will simply be ignored, disregarded by all concerned, or even classified when their publication would be politically damaging.

A telling example in light of the U.S. conflict with Israel over the use of Housing Guarantee Loans in the West Bank in 1991–1992 is a late 1970s A.I.D. evaluation of the U.S. Housing Investment Guarantee Program (HIG) in Israel (often referred to as simply the Housing Guarantee Program). The evaluation illustrated how foreign policy considerations create tensions between the different political and development objectives served by ESF aid. During this evaluation, Robert Berg, then an A.I.D. associate assistant administrator whose responsibilities included the agency's evaluation process, found that no one in the U.S. embassy in Tel Aviv had thought about the connection between the program and its political objectives. There was no program logical framework (logframe)[12] drawing the tight connections between what the A.I.D. programs were expected to accomplish in developmental terms and what the United States was trying to accomplish politically.[13]

Up to the mid-1980s, before Congress became concerned about ensuring that U.S. business interests were not losing export opportunities, tracing the use of resources in Israel had always been difficult because the assistance was provided as cash transfers, which went into the overall pot of resources. The HIG program was different, however, because these resources are traceable to the household door. The HIG program could be used only within Israel, not in the West Bank and Gaza. Moreover, the housing had to go to the poorest 50 percent of the Israeli population. At that time, the Israeli population included over 450,000 Arabs, most of whom were in the poorest 50 percent of the population. Yet, Arab mortgage holders under the HIG program had received less than 1 percent of the loans rather than the 25 percent one would have expected, given their percentage of the poor population. The Israeli government explained that many of the Arabs had changed their names, presumably making it harder to tell who was Arab and who was Jew.

Nevertheless, the evaluation concluded that there was blanket discrimination against the Arab population. It cited efforts to keep Arabs off balance with numerous regulations, such as requiring advance approval of construction plans. Without the approved plans, Arabs could not get approval for construction. Without approval to begin construction, they could not obtain loans. This treatment of Israeli Arabs was difficult to understand, especially given the closeness of these Arabs' ties with other Arabs in the region. More important, this treatment contravened the original purpose of the aid program to Israel: to foster peace, stability, and reconciliation in the area.

The United States wanted Israel to demonstrate its goodwill to the rest of the Arab world by providing decent housing to its own Arab poor. Thus, the HIG program would help build confidence and help the peace process. Instead, the program subsidized discrimination and undermined the peace process. The evaluation, however, never saw the light of day. By classifying and terminating further action in light of its findings, *both* the HIG program's developmental purpose and the U.S. diplomatic objective of fostering a better perception of Israel in the Arab world were subordinated to other political objectives, including domestic special interests that drive the U.S.-Israeli relationship.[14] While other hard-hitting evaluations have been published, they did not threaten a relationship as this one did.

Bureaucratic interests also come into play during the CP process. While aid officials may be motivated by their beliefs in the diplomatic and development objectives of the program, they may also try hard to protect their turf and resources. Unfortunately, some do this by avoiding candid discussions of the complexities of development, some of which even A.I.D. professionals do not understand. Their lack of vision and courage to confront real issues, coupled with simply presenting positive images to Congress and the U.S. public, have hindered understanding of the nature of development.

Economic and social development is neither neat nor short-term. It is more like trying to work one's way through a swamp with all sorts of submerged obstacles. The complexities are hard to explain in briefing papers limited to one or two paragraphs. They are even harder to understand in the few minutes that members of Congress and other ranking officials usually allow themselves to read the background material.

Addressing all of the different development and political objectives in a single document is also difficult. This, in turn, makes determining the success or failure of economic assistance in advancing development or political goals even more difficult. Senate Majority Leader George J. Mitchell (D-Maine) drew attention to this problem in 1990 when he refused to support President Bush's request for $800 million in immediate economic aid to Nicaragua and Panama until the president produced a long-term foreign aid plan. He criticized the administration for approaching foreign aid on a country-by-country basis, in one-shot increments, with no long-term view of how all the country programs should fit together. "The administration does not have a five-year plan or a three-year or a two-year plan for foreign aid; indeed they offer no plan at all."[15]

Senator Mitchell's observation, however, was describing a weakness in the process in which all previous administrations and congressional sessions have participated since the inception of foreign aid. His criticism of the lack of a long-term plan was disingenuous, because Congress itself has long opposed funding commitments for longer than two years, primarily because this would commit the next Congress. Moreover, Congress appropriates funds only on a yearly basis.

Another major factor that affects the CP process is the conflict between two different cultures—Congress and diplomacy. Roger L. Hart, a former foreign service officer, suggests that many foreign service officers consider Congress an alien culture that they "despair of understanding. Conversely, from the Hill the State Department often appears complacent and untrustworthy."[16] He believes such misunderstanding at the working level is a major cause of the friction over foreign policy issues. This friction derives from the separation of powers built into the U.S. Constitution. Inaccurate stereotypes compound the problem. Hill staffers see foreign service officers as "elitist, too cautious, evasive, and inclined to take the foreigner's point of view," while from the State Department, Hill staffers appear "hostile, superficial, prone to leak, and ignorant of the purposes of diplomacy."[17]

Hart sees less such friction between A.I.D. officers and Hill staffers because A.I.D. generally has to maintain continuous, informal communication at the working level on aid project and program issues. Nevertheless, during the CP process, State and A.I.D. coordinate preparation of all documents. Sometimes this coordination creates friction because A.I.D. gets caught between State and Hill staffers when the latter—because of their A.I.D. contacts—may know more about problems with the aid process than the State Department may want in the public record.

Another source of friction derives from the conflicting requirements of diplomacy and democracy. As Hart observes, while diplomacy requires continuity, experience, secrecy, or discretion, "American democracy . . . resists the idea that experts are any better than the rest of us, likes to throw the rascals and their policies out, and demands full public information. Congress is the most democratic branch of the government, as the framers intended, but the Foreign Service is the closest to an elite among American career public employees." The cultural gap between democracy and diplomacy is reinforced by the divide in Washington "between those who seem to advance through methodical bureaucratic skills and those who appear to rise by political connections or personal magnetism."[18]

Writing is a major problem in both the CP and in project planning. The passive voice appears frequently in planning and analysis documentation because it helps obscure responsibility. The A.I.D. program office in Indonesia once returned a draft project paper to the project officer because he had written several paragraphs entirely in the passive voice. The project officer responded that he and his Indonesian counterpart had been unable to agree on who was going to be responsible for certain project inputs, policy and regulation changes, and other implementation procedures. Coordination with the different ministries and offices involved in the project was incomplete. However, the project paper had to be signed before the end of the fiscal year. There was not enough time to obtain agreement among all parties on who would be responsible for what. The passive voice became the mechanism for obtaining consensus, holding a project-signing ceremony, and obligating funds.

Sometimes the written word even engenders fear. Judith Tendler attributes the A.I.D. project officer's fear to the repercussions candid discussions of problems might evoke from superiors or outsiders. An A.I.D. technician who writes a candid description of a problem or a balanced evaluation of a project might be asked, "What would Congress or the GAO say if they got hold of that!?" Thus, the technician might write cautiously for fear of "betraying" his or her organization and colleagues. "Words were toned down, thoughts were twisted, and arguments were left out, all in order to alleviate the uncomfortable feeling of responsibility for possible betrayal. The writing was finished with a sense of frustration at not having articulated an argument as lucidly, honestly, and convincingly as possible."[19]

Tendler concluded correctly that this type of situation resulted in a certain atrophy of communication through the written word. Her focus was the individual A.I.D. technician, but this problem exists in the State Department and throughout the government bureaucracy. The consequences are more serious, however, when atrophy in communication about assistance programs, including the environment in which they are implemented, causes project failures. Such failures can undercut achievement of development *and* political objectives when they reinforce the perception that the assistance relationship's only purpose is to promote short-term U.S. political objectives.

Weakness in Analysis: The Problem in Addressing Recipient Government Agendas

Another major factor affecting planning and implementation of foreign aid is the political objectives of recipient governments when they seek and accept foreign aid. For example, just as U.S. officials gain contacts through providing aid, so do recipient government officials and other elements in their society obtain access to U.S. leaders and special interests for their own purposes, including internal political balances. A recipient government, for example, may believe that accepting U.S. aid will enhance its prospects for obtaining better trade terms with the United States.

Sometimes, the most important objective of a recipient government is establishing and enhancing its legitimacy in the eyes of its own people. Receiving foreign assistance from a major power such as the United States can be portrayed as a clear vote of confidence for the leadership of the recipient country. Even within a government, those ministries that receive resources gain leverage vis-à-vis other ministries and agencies.

Some types of aid seem to enhance legitimacy more than others. For example, many recipient governments prefer ESF resources over regular DA. They know ESF resources are driven by important U.S. strategic objectives and are available only to countries and governments of great political importance to the United States. Thus, receipt of ESF sometimes enhances the government's prestige and "legitimacy" with its own population, other internal political forces, and sometimes even other aid donors, thereby helping to stabilize a regime. By the same token, once that special relationship ends, the close identification with the United States can become a disadvantage, particularly if critics of the assistance relationship can demonstrate that the aid did not result in tangible, sustainable economic benefits. This clearly has been the case with Liberia, Zaire, and the Philippines.[20]

Clearly, the political objectives of both the United States and the recipient government can be overwhelmingly complex. Moreover, the dominance of the political agenda creates an atmosphere in which establishing an economic and social development agenda may be impossible. Rarely do *both* parties enter the dialogue committed to development as their mutual primary objective. Each participant recognizes this reality; each tries to determine what political or other special interest may be driving the real agenda. Thus, the stated intention of establishing a development agenda lacks credibility.

Berg calls this situation the problem of "parallel duplicity," which makes it very difficult to be explicit. "It's like a marriage when one's real reasons like, 'I wanted economic security or whatever' are better left unsaid."[21] Thus, aid diplomacy requires complex manipulation and signaling in which the recipient often has the upper hand. As Scott Ticknor has observed, "Their power is not fungible; the weakness of a Haiti or Bangladesh in the world system masks their considerable influence in the politics of aid."[22]

Ticknor notes that recipient officials often can control goods, services, and markets to which donors want access. For example, the U.S. PL 480 Food for Peace Program serves the interests of U.S. farmers by providing food to Bangladesh, Egypt, and many other countries. A recipient government official who helps develop a PL 480 package is also opening his or her country's markets for U.S. agricultural exports. When Egyptian officials agree to the annual $200 million U.S.-funded Commodity Import Program, their decisions on whether a communications project will be included or not can help AT&T gain access to the Egyptian market and ensure a competitive edge over the French and German companies trying to capture that market.

Recipient government officials can also command the gates to legitimacy and support for donor countries and the private voluntary agencies that are so often involved in carrying out assistance projects. In these instances, as Just Faaland contends, "paradoxically, the very poverty of Third World countries can be viewed as a resource. Much of the feverish [aid] activity is not necessarily due to keenness to initiate sound projects but rather to international actors' concern to legitimize themselves as humanitarian organizations dedicated to raising the standard of the world's poor."[23] Ticknor adds that political alliances and favors (UN votes, support in the General Agreement on Tariffs and Trade, good press coverage, and the like) are also important resources for legitimization of donor country and voluntary agencies' activities.[24]

Analysis of such linkages and agendas has been largely nonexistent, even in classified documentation, in part because neither A.I.D. nor the State Department has analysts available with the necessary expertise to address these issues. During the Cold War, there seemed to be little bureaucratic interest in such analyses because short-term U.S. political objectives would likely have overridden most options that might have emerged. Moreover, foreign service diplomatic personnel have also been disinclined to become involved with a major policy dialogue on recipient country development issues, because their primary interests are the promotion of U.S. national interests with the country at hand. This lack of interest in development, in turn, often inhibits the use of other experts from academia or contractors who could provide the analysis if requested.[25]

Using long-term economic tools to accomplish short-term political objectives causes other analysis problems when the political situation and need change substantially by the time ground is broken on an assistance project or the overall aid program is initiated. When political objectives are overriding but cannot be explicitly addressed, the result is faulty or incomplete economic and financial analysis in the project design process. Since bad economics rarely makes good politics, when a long-term project is poorly designed, it can generate a political issue—and become part of the problem.[26]

As noted earlier, A.I.D.'s logframe could sort out the different political factors that affect the implementation of foreign aid programs for either diplomatic or development objectives. If preparation of the logframe is not truly collaborative, with recipient country participation, including government officials and other nongovernment experts, the process can be artificial and contorted. Such collaboration on each section of the matrix requires time and candid recognition of the political and bureaucratic contexts of each his also assumes that all the officials involved on both sides have in one another.

Steinberg has suggested that the planning process also would be more realistic if it applied *two* logical frameworks for presenting the overlapping assumptions of A.I.D. and the recipient government. Projects and programs are normally defined in economic terms, but the real decisions are political. The forces at work in these two logical frameworks are centrifugal; they pull apart because the unstated political objectives in the assumptions column are normally more powerful than the economic objectives. There is a major need to address A.I.D. activities in terms of the power of the political objectives of the donors vis-à-vis the recipient's political agenda. Could they pull the project apart once started?

A.I.D. technicians tend to believe that the U.S. embassy's political section should address these issues and the tensions they raise. The difficulty is that the political section is often more concerned about some current destabilizing event and has no time to spend thinking through the real implications for the future of what the aid program is doing. Steinberg asks, "When have you ever sat down with a political officer who said to you, 'Look, you are building this infrastructure in Cairo and this is good, but what about all the people from rural areas who are also going to be attracted by the infrastructure? What impact can these people without jobs have for political stability?'"[27]

Even when considered, these issues do not appear in the assumptions column. Moreover, they do not determine whether A.I.D. will do a project. This is unfortunate because such planning might ensure that when A.I.D. begins a project, it would build in collateral activities that might alleviate adverse political consequences of the project. In reality, the logframe is usually prepared last and used to summarize the other project documentation. It has remained a static way of viewing foreign assistance, whether talking about budget support or project aid.

A stark example of the importance of the recipient country's political interests involved mid-1980s plans to provide Peace Corps volunteers to Botswana, which had requested additional PCVs beyond the 250 already present. Botswana's leadership did not seem interested in using more of their own unemployed educated people. During conversations with government leaders, Robert Berg found that they considered the Peace Corps volunteers insurance against the activities of the South Africans pursuing the African National Congress (ANC). Clearly, there was a major disconnect here between what the United States hoped Peace Corps volunteers might accomplish with the poor people in remote areas and what Botswana's government wanted. For Berg, "resolution of this type of problem would depend on whether the State Department political officers are insightful and are basing what they are thinking on who they had lunch with last week or on a profound understanding of the forces at work in a given country."[28]

Weaknesses in Analysis of the Recipient Country's Political Context

A.I.D.'s program planning guidelines for the FY 1991 CDSS considerably expanded the requirement to address host country politics and development strategy, including how the political environment might affect later project or program implementation.[29] Unfortunately, most A.I.D. missions still lack the necessary analytical skills and the time to apply them. Missions usually rely on outside consultants for political analysis. However, unless those who later manage the implementation of aid projects can internalize the consultants' political insights, they will remain vulnerable to sabotage—intended or otherwise—when the project begins to threaten special interests within the recipient's political process.

Resolving this analysis gap remains difficult for A.I.D. because the agency has limited opportunity for inclusion of the discipline of political science into its planning process. Economic growth remains the overwhelming focus of the CDSS. At least until the late 1980s, A.I.D. and other assistance agencies, including multilateral institutions, viewed development primarily as an economic process. These agencies have given little attention to the development of in-house skills in cross-cultural social and political analysis. William Fuller, former deputy assistant administrator in the Asia–Near East Bureau of A.I.D. observed, "It's a pity we are not better informed about the social-political forces that affect policy formulation and support or impede economic reform; in a sense we need to work on understanding the politics of policy reform in the countries in which we work. There is growing sensitivity to that. We are getting better at it but we have a ways to go."[30] As noted earlier, the World Bank, in its February 1992 workshop on participation, also admitted this weakness and specifically called for changes in its staffing mix.

Ambassador David D. Newsom once noted that "it is the nature of the diplomat's job often to bring bad news. But the nation would not be served if diplomats first tested the political waters at home and then tailored their assessment to fit that test."[31] The ambassador was discussing the problem of the regular foreign service officer who is analyzing and reporting on issues that may affect a particular political problem within a given country or between it and the United States. His conclusion applies equally to an A.I.D. foreign service officer who might analyze the political, economic, or social environment within which a given assistance project or program aims to advance U.S. diplomatic objectives—as well as any possible development objectives.

This problem arose during preparation of Indonesia's 1976–1977 CDSS. The initial CDSS draft included an analysis of the Indonesian political-bureaucratic environment and how it might affect implementation of projects intended to decentralize bureaucratic authority to the provinces. Once completed, however, senior mission officials decided to omit most of the analysis from the final CDSS. The analysis discussed Indonesia's closed and carefully controlled political-bureaucratic process, inconsistencies in the Suharto government's commitment to political decentralization, and the extent of corruption throughout the political-administrative structure. Senior mission officials feared that this analysis, even if included only in a classified version, threatened the existing aid program. They feared that some members of Congress might use such "negative" analysis to challenge the mission's rural decentralization projects and recommend cutting the project or the aid program in general. Leaving the political analysis out was easier than responding to congressional inquiries or adjusting the current program's purposes and the processes for attaining them.[32]

Thus, many CDSSs tended to be dishonest even about unclassified problems such as Berber power in Morocco or the Chinese in the private sector in Indonesia.[33] This type of programming conflict can arise in almost any aid relationship. Moreover, classified analyses have limited value if they cannot be discussed with recipient governments in the interest of improving project implementation and achieving objectives. Recipient governments have been frequently unwilling to accept explicit political-social analysis because they view it as "intervention" by "outsiders."

If government officials express such concerns, U.S. officials generally back off when specific U.S. political objectives, including shorter-term U.S. special interests in the business, agriculture, university, and PVO communities, are the highest priority. Planning and implementation issues tend to become important for the recipient country's political leadership and for the U.S. ambassador only when these adversely affect the diplomatic process or its objectives.

Inadequate Dialogue on the Development Agenda

Given the above analytical weaknesses, it is not surprising that the planning process has often lacked a serious dialogue on development issues and priorities between A.I.D. and recipient countries prior to creating an ESF aid program. Any dialogue is often limited to discussions on project ideas initiated by U.S. officials or on U.S. plans for disbursing the funding as quickly as possible. Generally, proposed projects will be limited to the current congressional mandate or the administration's perception of "what will fly" in the CP.

Such planning flaws affect later implementation. When planning negotiations do not include the recipient country's inputs, recipient countries tend to accept the project as A.I.D.'s project, not theirs. Unfortunately, one aid official's approach may well not be another's. Some mission directors try either to create aid programs that reflect their personal visions, which they pursue even when reality suggests a different approach, or to act as quasi-ambassadors and keep the recipient government happy. The programs of such directors often become a grabbag of small projects to satisfy different ministers, in emulation of those ambassadors who approach the A.I.D. program as a slush fund to facilitate their access to government officials. Sometimes, the limited size of the aid program in comparison to those of other donors argues for such an approach. A program of only $20 million in a country that is getting $1–2 billion in other donor assistance offers little opportunity for significant development impact attributable to the United States. Thus, it seems to make more sense to use the aid in ways that will smooth the ambassador's access to government officials so that he or she can advance other U.S. short-term political objectives.

DETERMINING THE TYPE AND LEVEL OF ECONOMIC ASSISTANCE: THE MESSAGES IN THE METHOD

The primary purpose of U.S. economic assistance is to support the diplomatic processes that promote overall U.S. foreign policy objectives. Establishment of an ESF assistance level and the subsequent transfer of these resources are the two most important acts supporting the diplomatic effort.

Establishing the Assistance Level

U.S. foreign policy objectives and domestic political considerations weigh most heavily at the level-setting stage. Determination of aid levels involves lengthy dialogue between U.S. and recipient government officials. Often, this process begins when a head of state visits the White House or when the U.S. president is visiting a key foreign country. During discussions between the two leaders, the subject of economic and military assistance will almost inevitably arise. Usually, State Department and other officials concerned with assistance will have briefed the U.S. president on the possibility of a discussion on aid. If the concerned agencies have already reached agreement on a suggested level, they may suggest that the president make the offer during a state visit, thus ensuring the highest possible visibility and consequent political effect. Alternatively, they may advise the president to avoid making any commitments or even mentioning aid levels.

There are occasions, however, when such planning does not occur and an aid level will come up during the discussions between the two leaders. Sometimes, the president initiates an aid proposal during an official visit; presidents do not like to feel that visitors are going away unsatisfied. When a level is discussed, however tentatively, it often becomes a baseline against which the recipient country will judge the significance of the level actually delivered after completion of the congressional presentation and approval process.

The political objectives of both countries, and even of special interests who lobby for or against certain proposed levels and earmarks, play important roles throughout the process. Often, however, the political objectives are not clearly stated or mutually agreed upon by the parties concerned. If the original level received public attention in a press release (which is often issued for the political purposes of both governments) or in A.I.D.'s annual CP, any lower level will become the subject of often intense, and perhaps misleading, interpretations, depending on the objectives of those analyzing the assistance relationship.

Often, a congressional committee or an individual member of Congress will propose a cut or an increase to make a statement of either displeasure or approval to a recipient government—or even to please a domestic constituent. Moreover, any public debate in the U.S. Congress or through media coverage about the assistance level and U.S. objectives toward the recipient country will also affect how that country will interpret the political or development purposes of the assistance. These perceptions can affect implementation of the assistance program, particularly when the debate has highlighted the political quid pro quo purposes of the assistance. Recipient government officials often resist the efforts of U.S. aid officials to apply development, economic reform, and accountability criteria during transfer of the assistance via cash transfers or development projects.

The 1990 congressional debate over the levels and purposes of assistance to the emerging democracies in Eastern Europe and of programs in Nicaragua and Panama demonstrates how public discussion on aid levels may send different messages about the purposes of assistance. The debate began when Republican Senate Minority Leader Robert Dole (R-Kansas) proposed 5 percent cuts in aid levels to several key allies, including Israel and Egypt, in order to allocate more resources to Eastern Europe and Panama. Dole's proposal would have yielded approximately $330 million for use in Europe and Panama. Critics argued that $330 million spread around Eastern Europe would have little impact, but would seriously affect countries that would lose the money. In some countries, such cuts could mean riots and revolution.

Charles Krauthammer, writing in the *Washington Post*, asked, "What kind of message does it send to American allies and adversaries around the world when those countries that most identify with the United States and its interests are precisely the ones whose aid is cut?"[34] Krauthammer suggested that since the changes in Eastern Europe contribute directly to reductions in the military threat from that quarter, a 5 percent cut in the defense budget's allocation for Western Europe would be more appropriate and also yield $7.5 billion—twenty-three times the amount in Dole's proposal. Other observers suggested that Dole also may have been serving a diplomatic objective by opening the possibility of revisions in Israel's long-standing aid level if Israel did not get more serious about its own peace plan.[35]

It is significant that in this debate neither the proposed cuts to current recipients nor the levels for Eastern Europe were based on analyses concerning economic development–oriented needs, the absorptive capacity of the proposed recipient governments' bureaucracies, past performance, or even current or future economic development purposes. Supporters and opponents alike talked about the political messages in the proposed aid *levels*.

All too often assistance levels, particularly for ESF, are not based on the recipient government's capacity to use the assistance effectively for economic and social development purposes. Does this mean that the CDSS and the CP are irrelevant or fictitious? Not necessarily, but the answer in specific cases depends on the political objectives involved. How relevant the purposes and linkages in these documents are depends on whether aid officials can apply development-oriented criteria when they transfer the resources through the projects developed after determination of the aid level.

Nowhere are political considerations more overriding—and absorptive capacity and development considerations of so little meaning—than in U.S. assistance allocations to the Middle East. U.S. bilateral economic assistance over the past fifteen years has averaged $5–6.5 billion annually, with the Middle East receiving over half of these resources.[36] Israel and Egypt together have averaged about $2.6 billion in ESF aid per year, justfied on the need to protect Israel and extend the regional peace process. Capacity to effectively absorb the aid has not been a determinant in the aid level. Indeed, as the Egypt case demonstrates, Congress and the administration ignored the conclusion of a GAO report explicitly stating that Egypt could not absorb the aid level proposed for FY 1977.[37]

Levels and Leverage

The U.S. government and the recipient interpret aid levels differently. The U.S. leaders often believe that designating a significant level helps provide leverage to get recipient governments to support U.S. positions on political issues in international forums; to facilitate strategic cooperation, including use of military bases and other facilities; to assist special interests; or to undertake economic and administrative reforms that U.S. officials believe will help enhance the development potential of the assistance.

However, when the United States presets aid levels to signal political support for, or to achieve a strategic political objective with, the government in question, it creates a quid pro quo relationship that later undermines the leverage value of the aid—whether for development or sometimes even political purposes. The target government recognizes that the level has been determined by high-priority political objectives and believes that its political support is justification for obtaining these resources.

This has been particularly true with the politically driven ESF account. U.S. relations with Israel provide another example of U.S. inability to deny assistance to an ally even when that ally acts in ways that undercut U.S. political objectives. In March 1991, the United States and Israel agreed to a $650 million compromise aid package that would help Israel cover increased military and civil defense expenses incurred during the 1991 Gulf War. This assistance, despite severe budgetary constraints in Washington, developed from pressures in Congress and the administration to reward Israel for not ıng for Iraqi Scud missile attacks during the war.[38] The Israelis had ılly asked for $1 billion. The compromise level finally reached was, ılly, contingent on Israel not seeking any additional aid or housing loans in FY 1991.

This agreement proved short-lived. In August 1991, in addition to the war-related aid, Israel also asked for $10 billion more in housing loan guarantees to help settle 300,000 Soviet Jews.[39] This request for HIG loans put the Bush administration in an embarrassing situation and threatened the peace process because it raised charges of double standards—not only in the United States but also from members of the Gulf Coalition who saw Israel's settlement policies as a major obstacle to a permanent peace between Israel and its Arab neighbors.

This time, President Bush appealed for the support of the U.S. public as he told them and Congress that he would veto any such aid until after significant progress was made in the Middle East peace process and until other terms and conditions were worked out. Some of these conditions related to economic reforms that Israel would have to implement to improve economic performance. President Bush ultimately prevailed in his challenge to the powerful Israeli lobby on the housing loan issue. Over 70 percent of the U.S. public also opposed the loans, though a primary reason may have been belief that such guarantees should be offered first to hard-pressed Americans.[40]

In reality, however, any U.S. legislative prohibitions against use of HIG resources for West Bank housing are meaningless without an actual cut in the available funds—be they HIG or the annual $1.2 billion ESF grant—since U.S. assistance in any form releases other Israeli funds for the housing projects. Words send one message; continued delivery of billions of dollars in cash grants send another. Moreover, the delivery of cash grants—grants that exceed the annual U.S. economic assistance to all of sub-Saharan Africa—continued even while the Israeli government acted in ways, such as expanding settlement construction, that impeded administration efforts to accelerate the peace process. Such assistance, including aid to Egypt in this linkage, arguably does more to sustain the sources of conflict in the Middle East and even within Israel than to create the conditions for stable peace based on reconciliation.[41]

U.S.–Korean relations during the 1960s and early 1970s also illustrate how a security relationship influenced economic assistance roles in disputed cases. Trade-offs between security and economic needs were common. The Koreans used the security requirements to mitigate what they regarded as antagonistic U.S. demands for policy changes on trade issues and suggestions for political liberalization. The Koreans often used statements by U.S. military officers concerning cooperation with the Korean government to imply support for Korean political or economic objectives.[42]

U.S. threats to withhold aid resources in order to encourage the Korean government to honor previous agreements regarding resource mobilization or economic stability were usually ineffective. But the United States faced a difficult dilemma (as described in an A.I.D. evaluation report): "Since our [U.S.] political objectives could not permit real damage to the Korean economy, and since our funds were never unlimited, we had to use available funds for dual purposes," withholding them for punishment and making them available again. Because failure to meet goals did not result in deobligation of funds, temporarily withholding them did not result in new policies. Conditionality had limited meaning because funds were usually released even when the recipient had not reached previously agreed goals.[43]

Earmarks

When there is an overriding U.S. political objective or even a domestic special interest, the need to deliver a set level of assistance regardless of the content often results in legislation with earmarks that set levels or direct how the funds are to be used in different sectors, such as education, health, BHN, population, or the environment. Some earmarks are needed to maintain certain types of aid, but others have become major obstacles to effective use of economic assistance for either political or development objectives. Most of these earmarks are country-specific allocations in the legislation. The report of the House of Representatives' Task Force on Foreign Assistance found earmarks in FY 1989 for 92 percent of military aid, 98 percent of ESF, and 49 percent of DA. The use of earmarks to protect high-priority recipients has considerably diminished executive branch agencies' discretionary authority over foreign aid allocations. The task force expected this problem to get worse as budget pressures tightened.[44]

Earmarks result from a process in which Congress annually insists on choosing which countries will get aid and at what levels. The administration submits its foreign aid request to Congress in January. Several Senate and House foreign affairs committees and subcommittees hold hearings during which various government agencies (State, Treasury, Commerce, Defense) and innumerable business, university, and PVO interests lobby for their share of the pie and for their view of what U.S. priorities should be. These hearings become a "season of horsetrading . . . among the Administration, Congress and various lobbies, 'earmarking' exactly who will get what."[45]

Inevitably, earmarks from this process leave the administration with little leeway to respond to changing situations and new opportunities to use the assistance resources either for political or development purposes. A 1992 GAO study found that congressional appropriation of funds in functional (for example, education, agriculture, BHN, environment) accounts had reduced A.I.D.'s flexibility to plan coherent programs at the country level. "In effect, strategic planning for development assistance at the country program level has been replaced by a variety of projects undertaken to meet congressional spending directives."[46]

Examples that illustrate negative consequences of special interest activity do not, however, mean that the A.I.D. bureaucracy is incapable of dealing with earmarks created to serve special interests. Many externally imposed priorities help the agency overcome the inertia that can get in the way of new initiatives. The external push for basic human needs efforts or for increased attention to women's roles in development helps energize the agency. These priorities help push forward goals and programs that might not otherwise evolve out of the established programming process.

Organizations, including A.I.D., are more comfortable with existing programs and priorities. Funding shifts entail "interruptions" in what is often seen as important, demanding work and can entail reducing or abandoning efforts related to current priorities. Joseph Stepanik, at this writing A.I.D. mission director in Tanzania, believes that having many objectives creates opportunities for flexibility and imagination in programming aid resources and enhances A.I.D.'s capacity to work with those that are feasible in each recipient's political, economic, and social context. "Our responsibility is to explain our choices to A.I.D./Washington and members of Congress in terms of what can be accomplished toward some objectives and why others have to be set aside, at least temporarily."[47]

Generally, A.I.D. staff have willingly endorsed new emphases, whether internally generated or mandated by Congress, such as those involving the private sector and the environment. The majority of A.I.D. staff tend to play by the rules, and if the rules say support PVOs, they will try to provide that support, mindful of the other priority programs competing for resources. Indeed, observes Barry Sidman, a former career A.I.D. foreign service officer, "It is often the case that in their programmatic application, priorities are not imposed uniformly on all A.I.D. missions and offices; a 'rule of reason' may apply in discrete situations where a general priority or policy objective cannot or should not be pursued."[48]

A 1988 GAO report on the impact of ESF confirmed that linking U.S. political objectives with ESF assistance can affect policy reform efforts. "Generally, the more sensitive the foreign policy interests, the more difficult it is to strongly pursue economic reform and strictly condition the assistance. . . . The State Department said that [much] earmarking is detrimental, in that earmarked countries are normally less willing to agree to reforms that might entail short-run political costs because they know they will receive ESF anyway."[49] Earmarking also limited opportunities to reward countries that did undertake reforms, including democratic political reforms.

Even without congressional action or pressure from the State Department, de facto earmarks emerge through A.I.D.'s programming processes. In these cases, the driving forces are the need to ensure continuity and to avoid sending the wrong signal. Thus, even where a political purpose was not the original impetus behind a given assistance program, the process of giving the aid develops its own political purpose. The original level, however it is set, becomes an earmark that, if cut for whatever reason from A.I.D.'s perspective, lends itself to different interpretations by the host government or its internal or external opponents.

This problem has occurred even in small DA programs in Africa. An important question is often whether the cost of running very small programs is really worth the marginal development impact that the small funding levels for aid projects would create. While the answer is usually no, these projects may be necessary to facilitate the U.S. ambassador's access to government officials so that he or she can pursue other U.S. political objectives.[50] In such situations, something as simple as a ribbon-cutting ceremony for a health center can be an opportunity for dialogue on a new item in the U.S. political agenda.

Unfortunately, the problem becomes more than preserving assistance as an access tool. As noted above, the assistance level becomes a symbol of U.S. engagement and interest in a country. The aid becomes a country's quid pro quo and a measure of commitment that it uses as a bargaining chip. Sometimes even A.I.D. supports the "entitlement," arguing in the CP process that aid level cuts, even if good program decisions, "would send the wrong message."

The President's Commission on the Management of A.I.D. Programs in March 1992 noted that when A.I.D. sets an aid level in the CP, it raises recipient country expectations and reduces A.I.D.'s negotiation leverage. When Congress repeats these levels in the appropriation legislation, it establishes country earmarks. "*This combination of publicized country levels and 1-year funding forces A.I.D. managers to obligate funds prematurely and ineffectively.*"[51] The commission recommended that A.I.D. no longer specify proposed levels for individual countries.

These examples clearly demonstrate how assistance levels are set or retained for political reasons and not on the basis of how well the recipient uses the aid for development objectives. The primary issue is whose immediate political priority comes first.

OPERATIONAL OBJECTIVE #1: SPEND THE MONEY

The administration proposes assistance programs and Congress appropriates funds and authorizes their expenditure for each fiscal year. Until FY 1988, A.I.D. had to obligate all resources—ESF and DA—for specific project activities by the end of the fiscal year in which they were appropriated.[52] Since 1988, ESF programs have had two fiscal years to obligate the funds allocated to them; DA programs remained limited to one year. Even with this relaxation, the pressure to obligate funds within one year remains high. Failure to obligate one year's authorized resources could lead to a cut in the amount authorized for the next year because the earlier resources are still available.

Cuts in aid levels can have serious political implications simply because the aid level has often been the primary means for obtaining a political objective. As a result, the GAO found, A.I.D. "emphasized project design and obligation of funds more than program effectiveness and results, due partly to a budget cycle in which most funds are returned to the Treasury if not obligated in the year appropriated."[53]

Another type of deadline relates to an important symbolic event, such as a signing ceremony with the president of a given country or during a visit by a U.S. dignitary. Sometimes the ceremony occurs during a foreign leader's visit to the United States. When this happens, there is little time to discuss implementation procedures, each party's contributions of personnel and funds, and differences over project purposes—or even to fully examine underlying assumptions of the project. Instead, the important event is signing the agreement with as much publicity as possible. Hidden from view, for months or even years thereafter, lower-ranking operational staff in A.I.D. and the recipient country's ministries will confront the unresolved issues. The delays create frustration and mutual recriminations over who is responsible for project difficulties. The cost of this often confused planning process, including the drawn-out exchanges of project implementation letters and meetings over different understandings, is hidden from public scrutiny until an evaluation determines that a given project is slowly going nowhere.

In the 1960s, the Commodity Import Program (CIP) was the preferred approach for providing balance of payments support. The CIP program enabled the United States to allocate high aid levels in the form of dollar credits or loans, which were then used to purchase U.S. goods, including tobacco products, corn, wheat, steel rods, locomotives, buses, and many other such commodities. It was thought the CIP program would avoid the long implementation delays associated with aid projects. In fact, however, the processes for responding to bids, including challenges by disgruntled suppliers, also led to long delays in delivering the goods. Moreover, the CIP goods had little development impact for the poor and tended to encourage excessive consumption spending by recipient governments. Finally, in the 1970s, the CIP programs were discouraged in favor of smaller projects that would directly address the basic human needs of the poor.

During the 1980s, though the CIP approach remained available at lower levels, direct cash transfer grants became the preferred way to overcome project programming delays and other accountability issues, while quickly moving high levels of aid. With cash transfers, the A.I.D. mission director or the ambassador hands over a U.S. Treasury check to the recipient government. Throughout the 1970s, A.I.D. and Congress opposed unrestricted cash transfers because of the fungibility factor: either the cash transfer dollars or the freed-up foreign exchange could be spent on champagne glasses or—worse—arms purchases. Accounting for fund usage was difficult if not impossible. In the late 1980s, significant change in the policies regarding cash transfers reflected new perspectives on how cash transfers can affect diplomatic or development objectives.

The GAO has found that cash transfers serve four major purposes: (1) U.S. political commitments to Egypt and Israel; (2) security-related commitments to base-rights countries; (3) economic stabilization in countries facing serious balance of payments difficulties; and (4) promotion of economic policy reform.[54] By the end of the 1980s, the cash transfer had become commonplace. Congress loosened conditions on cash transfers as an aid tool, though it has attached conditions requiring that the dollars not used to repay debts to the United States must be spent on U.S. goods, shipped on U.S. vessels. In 1987, the United States provided 60 percent of ESF aid in cash ($2.3 billion), 31 percent in project aid ($1.2 billion), and 9 percent in the Commodity Import Program ($359 million). Moreover, while in 1979 only Israel, Turkey, Jordan, and Nicaragua received cash transfers, by 1987 twenty-six countries were receiving them.[55]

Increased use of cash transfers would facilitate reductions in large overseas missions because they require no administrative structure in-country and move more money with fewer people. This became an important consideration, particularly in the 1980s, with increased terrorist threats to U.S. citizens working abroad. The State Department welcomes and urges cash transfers for this reason and because it believes that cash transfers more directly advance political objectives. Cash transfers also can help recipients remain in compliance with IMF stabilization programs, primarily because they enable some recipients to stay current on their U.S. debt payments and, because of the fungibility factor, on their other debt payments. The Foreign Assistance Act requires that U.S. aid be suspended when a country remains in arrears in its debt repayments.[56] Cash transfers also avoid embarrassing pipelines of unspent resources that often develop when project activities slow down.

Finally, another argument in favor of cash transfers is that even successful project completions create demand for continued operations and maintenance (O&M) funding and related O&M-oriented bureaucratic structures. Many recipient countries have major difficulty providing sufficient funds in their national budgets to cover O&M costs. Moreover, sometimes due to their different social cultures, many countries have been unable to develop effective O&M management systems for large and widely dispersed projects. In cases like Egypt, where large-scale power and water infrastructures are involved, the United States faces embarrassing breakdowns of U.S. equipment if it does not commit to continuing involvement in operation and maintenance of these projects.

Whichever reason applies in a particular case, it reflects the priority placed on either moving money quickly or promoting political and developmental objectives the best way possible. The evidence suggests, particularly in ESF countries, that spending the money is more important than ensuring ıe resources stimulate development-oriented change and new institu- capacities in the agriculture, education, social, and political arenas. In uıe case of Liberia, for example, transferring resources to the Doe government was more important than guaranteeing that the funds would not be diverted for the personal gain of government officials.[57]

The GAO has found that cash transfers appear to have little impact in U.S. efforts to encourage economic policy changes that might stimulate more rapid and sustainable development. A.I.D. officials have difficulty linking specific policy changes directly to U.S. cash transfers. Even where cash transfers influence economic policies, they often do not have immediate benefits for general populations; sometimes austerity measures and subsidy cuts have short-term adverse consequences.[58]

The choice between cash transfers and project assistance should depend most on the objectives of the aid program. If specific U.S. political objectives are paramount, cash transfers clearly have more advantages. If, however, we are committed to development defined especially in terms of empowered, increasingly skilled, and democratically oriented people, project assistance is vital. If provided and received with shared development objectives, such aid can be more carefully targeted and less expensive, and can provide more people-to-people interaction, from planning development projects through their implementation. It is this interaction that best facilitates the interchange of ideas, insight, imagination, and the type of *reconciliation* between peoples that becomes the basis for stable peace—the most overriding U.S. political objective.

SPECIAL INTERESTS: PUBLIC AND PRIVATE

Special interests affect the nature of economic assistance programs even when those programs are meant to achieve a specific political objective. Special interests outside of government are most common. However, special bureaucratic and even personal interests exist within government organizations. These interests can and do affect the allocation and implementation of economic assistance resources. Indeed, the 1992 GAO report on A.I.D.'s management clearly stated that different presidential administrations have appointed many senior-level officials to A.I.D.—and to other federal agencies—who then advance the short-term agendas of these administrations. The GAO concluded, "Some career professionals are increasingly concerned that A.I.D. is becoming more focused on advancing the overseas interests of U.S. business than on improving the living standards in developing countries."[59] With the end of the Cold War and the increased importance of economic competition, this practice will become more prevalent.

Nevertheless, those special interests that most actively seek to obtain and direct economic assistance resources include universities, farmers, business and labor organizations, religious groups, PVOs, and lobbyists that advocate causes concerning the environment, women in development, overpopulation, world hunger, children, human rights, and even specific countries like Israel. As of July 31, 1990, 277 U.S. voluntary and other private organizations were registered with A.I.D. and eligible for development aid funding. They received over $1 billion in grants, contracts, U.S. government–owned property, freight subsidies, and food aid. The GAO found that these organizations often conducted their programs independently, with A.I.D.'s financial and technical support, to meet goals in areas such as disaster assistance, microenterprise development, child survival, environmental preservation, and democratic institution building. In FY 1990, A.I.D. financed 475 active contracts, grants, or cooperative agreements with 265 U.S. universities totaling about $805 million in cumulative obligations.[60]

The Departments of Agriculture and Commerce often also try to promote and protect the interests of their "constituencies" among U.S. farmers and business people. When this happens, they are like nongovernmental special interests. Promoting the overseas interests of U.S. business is properly within the charters of the Departments of Commerce and Agriculture. However, when such activity is directed through A.I.D., the essential result is that economic assistance resources become more like subsidies for U.S. businesses rather than direct support for *development* in the recipient country as defined earlier in this study.

Domestic Special Interests and the U.S. Congress

From a developmental standpoint, many special interest groups do promote sound economic and social development objectives. Indeed, the efforts of U.S. universities, PVOs, business investors, and labor groups are absolutely essential for timely development of people and institutions in aid-recipient countries. Nongovernmental organizations can be more creative than government-led efforts—when the special interests are targeted toward development of others.

PVOs, for example, can advance U.S. national and political interests. They deal with sensitive issues and groups or individuals in politically sensitive project activities that do not require direct U.S. government involvement, such as human rights projects, legal aid organizations, and democratic institutions. They can also provide quick, flexible responses for individuals and organizations that they help. PVOs can focus programs more narrowly and have less cumbersome reporting requirements and bureaucracies. Finally, PVOs have an educational role vis-à-vis A.I.D. and State on what is happening in a country.[61] A significant weakness of PVO projects, however, is that they are often costly and less replicable than they appear to be, and may require a great deal of management attention.

These PVO and NGO efforts presuppose that their objectives are useful within an LDC's political and social context. Problems begin to arise when a given special interest's objective may be unwelcome in certain country-specific contexts. For example, energetically promoting women's participation in every development project, particularly when earmarks to spend a set level of funding are attached, can create resistance in Muslim countries. When forced to pursue such project priorities, A.I.D. can find itself creating tensions with the recipient government that can affect other development or even diplomatic efforts. The dilemma for the United States is that it must try to find the right balance, even if only on the margins of its projects, in applying sound development criteria. Such criteria must include greater participation by women simply because an aid recipient that does not seek to broaden the base of people participating in the development process probably cannot effectively use external aid.

Special interests lobby Congress and other federal agencies to obtain earmarks for funding levels on selected project activities in specific countries and on a global scale. They seek special amendments to foreign assistance legislation. They also lobby A.I.D., either through direct contacts or by asking a House member or a senator to call the A.I.D. administrator on their behalf. Such calls often result in "adjustments" in contracts, reprogramming of funds from one project to another, or extension of projects that should end. In such cases, the special interests often seem more interested in their own survival than in the development objectives of the projects in question.

Whatever the source of their interest in the aid program, members of Congress undoubtedly affect implementation of that program at least as much as any other major special interest group. The congressional process results in the various committees, or individual members, looking at different parts of the whole program. They focus on them, work hard on them, and earmark or restrict them. The result is a series of micromanaged special interest allocations and restrictions that undermine the coherence of the total program.

Even the GAO has addressed the impact of Congress on A.I.D. management: "Congress plays a major role in shaping A.I.D.'s programs and operations by appropriating program funds in separate functional accounts and various other earmarks and directives, *often designed to respond to various U.S. constituencies.* It also directly influences A.I.D.'s resources by separately appropriating operating expenses" (emphasis added).[62] M. Peter McPherson, former A.I.D. administrator, observed, "It's not so much the intention of Congress to micro-manage, as it is that the process, with its multiple power centers, doesn't generally focus on the whole. . . . There's no question that the earmarks and restrictions make it more difficult for us to do what the American people expect us to do. We can't use the money well."[63]

When special interest groups try to operate in the complex economic development environment, they tend to undermine interrelated U.S. political and development objectives. This group-based politics frequently guarantees that the least domestic political consideration will outweigh the greatest development consideration. Representative Hamilton believes, however, th earmarks, conditions, restrictions, and reporting requirements reflect the serious doubts of Congress about the manner in which the executive branch administers the program. He sees the "micro-management" issue as a "symptom of the lack of confidence that often comes about because Congress thinks the law has not been appropriately administered by the executive." Congressional monitoring of cash transfers to Egypt, for example, became necessary "because one year the cash was used to pay a military debt, in what some of us at least thought to be a violation of the law."[64]

The American Farm Bureau Federation and the United States Maritime Administration are two particularly effective lobbyists. Often their interests come into direct conflict, as was the case with agricultural assistance to Poland in 1990. The Maritime Adminstration has sustained strong congressional support for the 1953 Cargo Preference Law, which requires A.I.D. to ship 75 percent of U.S. humanitarian aid on U.S. vessels. In the dispute over food aid to Poland, U.S. agricultural groups argued that this law cut their profits because the higher U.S. shipping costs could reduce grain shipments as much as 40 percent. During a House debate in late 1989, Representative Fred Grandy (R-Iowa) noted that while a Polish ship carrying 11,500 tons of grain sorghum charges $26 a ton, a U.S. vessel charges $84.95 a ton for an identical cargo.[65] This conflict between two U.S. domestic interests directly undercuts both the political and humanitarian objectives of U.S. policy in Poland.

Such arguments are not easily resolved, because they involve vital and seemingly legitimate national interests. The shipping law helped subsidize privately owned U.S. ships so that there would be a U.S. cargo fleet available in time of war. It also preserved jobs for U.S. workers. Farmers say the shipping law subsidizes the maritime industry on the backs of U.S. farmers; labor interests charge that agriculture is the most subsidized sector in the U.S. economy.

U.S. food aid to Nigeria provides another example of how the agricultural lobby can drive an aid program in counterproductive directions. A trade dispute arose because Nigeria decided in 1986 to ban wheat and other basic food imports in an effort to boost domestic agricultural production. Nigeria had imported over $250 million of U.S. wheat per year, making it the sixth-largest U.S. wheat importer. U.S. agriculture groups urged U.S. retaliation unless Nigeria reopened its markets to U.S. wheat.

Nigerians resented U.S. pressure to end the ban, and reacted strongly to former U.S. Ambassador Princeton Lyman's charge that the import ban was counterproductive because it encouraged smuggling. In Nigerian eyes: "The Americans miscalculated how important this issue is to us. They don't seem to understand that our primary objective is economic self-sufficiency, and making money for American wheat farmers pales by comparison."[66] Moreover, the ban was applied to all countries that had exported wheat, rice, and other food items to Nigeria. Ironically, Nigeria had imposed the ban as part of a structural adjustment package that had received IMF and World Bank endorsement and that the United States had encouraged both bilaterally and through the international institutions.[67]

Richard Uku, a Nigerian diplomat then studying at Georgetown University, suggested that from the Nigerian viewpoint, the U.S. change in stride, when it became apparent that U.S. wheat farmers would incur substantial losses from a cessation of Nigerian importation, seemed to indicate double standards. "It called into question the sincerity of purpose behind the professed American commitment to African development. At least this was the underlying sentiment behind Nigerian criticism of American pressure to end the ban."[68]

The special interests of U.S. farmers are also behind the Zorinsky amendment, which prohibits U.S. assistance to developing countries if such assistance will increase their capacity to compete with U.S. agricultural products. The amendment reads:

> *Sec. 546.* None of the funds appropriated by this or any other Act to carry out chapter 1 of part I of the Foreign Assistance Act of 1961 shall be available for any testing or breeding feasibility study, variety improvement or introduction, consultancy, publication, conference, or training in connection with the growth or production in a foreign country of an agricultural commodity for export which would compete with a similar commodity grown or produced in the United States; *Provided*, That this section shall not prohibit: (1) activities designed to increase food security in developing countries where such activities will not have a significant impact in the export of agricultural commodities of the United States; or (2) research activities intended primarily to benefit American producers.[69]

One of the major objectives of U.S. assistance efforts over the past five years has been to get developing countries to adopt economic policies that will stimulate their own economies. Among the policy reforms pursued is establishment of more private sector, export-oriented programs. The Zorinsky amendment and protectionist trade barriers against sugar are examples of the kinds of barriers that Congress can erect to undercut the development objectives and cancel out benefits created through otherwise effective assistance efforts. Instead of aid that "teaches people how to fish," this type of legislation helps to ensure that U.S. taxpayers will have to continue indefinitely providing welfare-type assistance to foreign governments while subsidizing a U.S. special interest.

While it is conceivable that food transfers without development-oriented performance conditions can still serve U.S. political objectives, they cannot contribute much to stimulating self-sustaining development. Not least, as the Nigeria case demonstrates, such interests can even create diplomatic headaches. In all of these cases, the determining and limiting factors have been U.S. domestic special interests. Neither legitimate diplomatic objecti nor sound development objectives mattered in the end.

Government Agencies with "Special Interest" Impact

U.S. government agencies sometimes have a "special interest"–type of impact on the objectives, planning, and application of economic assistance resources.[70] The Departments of Treasury, Commerce, and Agriculture, OMB, and even the intelligence community, for example, all play important roles as they serve the interests of certain constituencies among the U.S. public, to wit, farmers, U.S. exporters and domestic producers, and even political parties in the next election.

Appropriate ESF resource use is sometimes an issue between A.I.D. and Treasury. When a country is not complying with IMF debt repayment requirements, Treasury, to protect U.S. balance of payments interests, may recommend that ESF be provided as a cash transfer to help the country meet its debt obligations. A.I.D. may argue that converting project funds to cash will adversely affect project implementation and the aid program's development objectives. Congress may want more aid to go to the Export-Import Bank. Treasury, however, has not intruded deeply into programming areas as has OMB.

Because it is a more direct participant in the political process, OMB is attentive to the pressures of different voter constituencies and how these might affect the president's goals and objectives. OMB sees more of this overall picture than each of the other players and will negotiate the fund request process before it goes to Congress, attempting to best serve the president's overall domestic and foreign policy objectives. This places OMB in opposition to A.I.D. and the State Department on some issues, especially on budgetary allocations for different countries. Sometimes OMB plays the broker or middleman, but it always supports the president's goals.

For example, OMB becomes directly involved in A.I.D.'s operating budget and staff levels, and it claims a role in the implementation process because instances of poor management can cause political problems for the president. Large pipelines of unspent aid funds can inspire domestic pressures to use the resources to fight U.S. poverty, thereby undercutting the president's annual aid requests. These pressures cause expedited planning and expenditure at project levels that can result in less effective performance toward stated project goals. A.I.D. country directors and even the U.S. ambassador can be embarrassed by pipelines of unspent funds, which can lead to OMB or congressional inquiries into their implementation performance.[71]

The Department of Agriculture (USDA) plays a major role in U.S. aid policymaking and implementation, particularly with the PL 480 food program. As noted in the cases of food aid to Poland and wheat exports to Nigeria, USDA promotes the interests of the U.S. farmer by ensuring that aid programs like PL 480 help increase U.S. agricultural exports. Moreover, because this aid often provides balance of payments support to strategically important countries, USDA and the Department of State often support each other when setting food aid levels. The State Department's support of short-term political stability through food aid meshes with USDA's interest in expanding exports.

A.I.D., however, may point out that highly concessional food aid undercuts programs to increase agricultural productivity and economic development in the recipient country. In these cases, the Bellmon amendment will come into play. The amendment requires USDA to certify that U.S. food aid does not discourage local food production. Sometimes, however, as will be shown in the Egypt case, considerable debate occurs between A.I.D., the State Department, and USDA over the nature and extent of any disincentive. Creative language will be found to allow the food aid to continue, thereby keeping the overall aid level high.

PERSONNEL

A.I.D. career foreign service reserve officers cooperate with their colleagues in the Department of State and its embassies overseas to manage foreign assistance resources. Both A.I.D. and State foreign service officers rotate between posts in Washington and overseas. In FY 1989, A.I.D. personnel totaled 4,400, of whom 1,732 were direct-hire foreign service officers. Some 1,200 of these officers worked overseas while the remainder worked in Washington with the 2,700 civil service employees who help provide programming and administrative support for the worldwide $8 billion economic assistance program.[72]

The number of personnel in any given U.S. embassy community depends on the importance of the country to the United States and on the scope of that country's aid programs and reporting requirements. Because U.S. personnel responsible for economic assistance work actively with the recipient government's ministries, in urban and rural areas, with the private sector, and in university-linked projects, they have unique opportunities to develop understanding that is sometimes deeper than is possible for other diplomatic officers. Often, they have provided unique insight and information about a given country's social-political events to diplomatic officers in the embassy community and the State Department. During the 1986–1989 period of crises in the Philippines, for example, the U.S. ambassador frequently relied on the A.I.D. mission director for insight on issues that affected U.S.-Philippine relations.[73]

Nevertheless, these opportunities do not translate into diplomatically relevant information and analysis unless the development officers themselves are aware of their possible relevance and inclined to communicate them. Sadly, many career officers are either unaware of such possibilities or simply do not want to risk "rocking the boat." Moreover, A.I.D. personnel are reluctant to gather political information because they do not want to be seen as spies. Their purpose is managing and implementing the aid program's project portfolio. Thus, their contribution to diplomacy derives from the perceived relationships between assistance activities and specific U.S. political objectives.

The relationships developed between diplomatic officers and all personnel responsible for economic assistance can also affect opportunities to draw on each other's insights. Each country team includes the A.I.D. director, who will generally attend the ambassador's regular morning briefing sessions with the chiefs of all embassy sections. Ideally, all U.S. official personnel should be intimately aware of the different U.S. economic and political objectives in a given country. In reality, this has seldom been the case—although that may be changing—because most development assistance personnel have tended to focus most on their technical specialties on project planning and implementation activities, on reporting requirements for A.I.D./Washington and Congress, or on other time-consuming communications with the host government.

"Turf issues" can come into play. An A.I.D. officer inclined to write and think about political issues would require explicit encouragement from the mission director and, more important, from the ambassador *and* the diplomatic staff. Moreover, diplomatic and economic assistance officers alike have experienced considerable difficulty in accepting the "idea that Foreign Service officers are neutral bureaucrats with no views of their own."[74] This problem is serious because it directly affects the quality of analyses on issues related to advancing both political and development objectives, including recognition of linkages between these objectives in different country contexts.

Weaknesses in current analyses were noted earlier. John J. Maresca, a senior foreign service officer, addressed this problem in 1986 while assigned as a diplomatic research associate at the Institute for the Study of Diplomacy at Georgetown University. Though his comments are based on his State Department experience, they apply as well to A.I.D. foreign service officers. During an earlier assignment in Washington, Maresca was disconcerted to find upon return that his colleagues' attention "was absorbed by the bureaucratic process—who had approved which memo, the exact in-box in which it stood, which bureaucratic fiefdom might have sufficient clout to prevail." He found them uninterested in the substance of the issues, about which they seemed to have no views. Even the most qualified officers were reluctant or unable to debate the substance of policies. Maresca suggested that Foreign Service fear of Congress, the media, opinion groups, and political parties was part of the problem. While foreign service officers responded when called for briefings, testimony, and escort work, they were generally passive toward these institutions and limited to responding when asked. Finally, Maresca observed:

> Our criteria for advancement are based primarily on traditional-mythical personal traits and a rather ponderous type of analytical and writing ability. . . . The officers we identify for promotion tend to be safe, well-rounded ones, who have stayed out of trouble and can write mellifluous reports. . . . What experts need is real in-depth knowledge of a specific subject. What leaders need is passion, a confident belief in their ideas, and the ability to bring these ideas to fruition. But our promotion precepts are carefully tuned to downgrade those who are too specialized, or who are stubborn or who get so caught up in specific ideas that they become involved in confrontations.[75]

Ignorance of local languages and political cultures seriously impedes aid project design and implementation, as well as the use of aid to advance political objectives. However, as Maresca notes, the most telling irony is that language and area specialization often hinder a foreign service officer's career. Management expertise is more highly valued than these skills. Countless State Department and A.I.D. studies have recognized this weakness, as has Congress. Writing in the *Foreign Service Journal*, Senator Paul Simon (D-Illinois) recommended that the State Department "ought to place less emphasis on MBA-like management skills, and more on those qualities that have always made an excellent diplomat: foreign languages, area expertise, sensitivity to other cultures, and a firm grounding in our own traditions, history, and values."[76]

U.S. Ambassador to Nigeria Lannon Walker also noted that there is little room at the top for real experts, because managers and generalists seem to get the promotions into the Senior Foreign Service. He believed that because the personnel system tended to discriminate against experts, "in the process, the Foreign Service is not performing its primary function—to produce the very best language, area, functional, and interfunctional experts to assure that the essential foreign service jobs are performed and performed well. . . . If the Foreign Service fails to maintain its expert cadre throughout the ranks in the race to become managers, it will have failed in its basic mission."[77]

That mission clearly must include understanding the political cultures that can so decisively affect the prospects for either development or political objectives. But the time, commitment, and effort required for learning languages and foreign political cultures leaves one little opportunity to master the State and A.I.D. management culture. Moreover, sometimes area and language expertise enables an officer to understand recipient country political or social realities in ways that cause him or her to question an existing policy or to suggest an alternative approach for advancing a program. Such questioning, challenging the traditional ways of doing things, can become a threat to bureaucratic and policy stability.

These attitudes and concerns about adhering to standard operating practices almost ensure, except for the most disciplined, that most officers will not develop working competence in the recipient country's language or become comfortable in their knowledge of the culture and history of the country. A common practice is to waive language training because the officer with the particular technical expertise is needed in the field immediately. Language training in the field usually suffers because other programming duties invariably take priority. Often, even those with fluency in the language have known little of the history and culture of the country. A related problem is that officers are rarely assigned to a mission for longer than four years and there is frequently no overlap between the departure of an officer and his or her replacement. This practice disrupts continuity and makes it difficult for a successor to establish contact with host government personnel.[78]

Another operational reality is that diplomatic and development assistance officers operate in different worlds. In larger missions, they tend to socialize in different circles. Their different work objectives divide them. Wherever aid stimulates development, it will create some dissatisfied people, even among the embassy's diplomatic and economic development officers. There is no avoiding the conflicts that derive from providing development assistance that must serve different, often conflicting, political and development purposes.

Personnel implementing economic assistance projects may accept and hope that their development efforts will stimulate change. Both development assistance and diplomatic officers accept that programs that work toward pluralism and more open societies are the best way to stimulate sustainable development. Political pluralism, however, creates uncertainty, complicates cultivation of political contacts among governing circles, and makes the reporting effort more complex. The diplomatic officer observes and analyzes the host government and the political-economic issues that affect that government and its relationship to the United States, as these may affect attainment of U.S. political objectives. When political change threatens the stable government-to-government relations that facilitate diplomacy, it adds to the frustration all foreign service officers face.

Masters believes that the A.I.D. foreign service officers and the State Department's regular foreign service officers are unfortunately often in conflict with one another. Such conflict might be resolved through more joint staff meetings at division levels. These meetings would broaden each officer's understanding of the social-economic-political contexts in which they operate and "enable them to better articulate the interrelationships of diplomatic and development objectives."[79]

Finally, the size of A.I.D. missions is often a major cause for concern and sometimes even conflict between A.I.D. and State. In part, the higher personnel level is the inevitable consequence of reporting requirements established by Congress. Nevertheless, these large staffs require extra privileges and support services, including special embassy or military shopping facilities that can lead to friction with the host government and the local population. With their families, embassy staff often create their own community and tend not to communicate with the local people except in defensive ways.

Such tendencies negate the potential value foreign service families could have in promoting U.S. ideas and practices.

ACCOUNTABILITY AND EVALUATION: AUDITORS AND PROJECT DOCUMENTATION

Even though it is well understood that short-term diplomatic or other U.S. domestic political considerations often impede adherence to sound, development-oriented performance criteria, Congress has legislated no less than 288 individual reporting requirements to provide information on both one-time and continuing aid activities. These reporting requirements on A.I.D.'s $7.5 billion program are second only to those for the Department of Defense, whose budget has averaged at least $300 billion. According to the Bipartisan Task Force on Foreign Assistance of the House Committee on Foreign Affairs, A.I.D. provides Congress over 700 notifications of project changes each year. In addition, "the numerous directives, restrictions, conditions, and prohibitions in the foreign aid legislation, and in committee and conference reports . . . result [in] an aid program driven by process rather than by content and substance."[80]

Many of the requirements governing the use of assistance funds address basic accounting procedures to ensure against corruption. Through FY 1989 at least, impact evaluations focusing on performance against original project or program purposes were not included in routine accountability requirements, nor were any of A.I.D.'s other routine project evaluations. In other words, expenditures must be accounted for, but no comparable accounting is required on whether such expenditures changed life in the recipient country. That is more difficult to trace and, some would argue, irrelevant, because the primary purpose so often appears to be to move the money, not to stimulate change.

In large and controversial programs, in addition to routine accounting requirements, there have always been innumerable ad hoc requests from Congress for information on specific project activities. Constituents who lose bids on projects generate congressional inquiries, as do constituents who face bureaucratic delays or penalties of some kind levied by the host country. Individual members of Congress or committees also will ask the GAO to undertake independent evaluations and studies of project-specific or country-wide assistance programs.

The constituent contractor-generated reporting requirements can be particularly troubling. They add to already onerous reporting requirements and take A.I.D. and other embassy officers away from important implementation activities. They create frictions between A.I.D. project officers and the contractors, as well as between A.I.D. officers and their host country counterparts. These frictions impede implementation of development projects. Often they foreclose possibilities for dialogue on larger development issues, which are the heart of the delicate donor-recipient relationship, and on whether the local people will experience the benefits of that relationship.

The counterproductive nature of many congressionally imposed restrictions on foreign aid is not lost on people seriously concerned about the diplomatic and development objectives of that aid—the foreign service officers and contractors who must implement the programs. Some members of Congress also believe that present legislation requires too much accountability. Nevertheless, even with the hundreds of reports every year, effective accountability remains elusive. Moreover, the reporting does not prevent cases such as that of Liberia, where the inherent incompatibility of certain objectives and implementation processes was consciously overlooked or set aside in light of other U.S. political objectives.

Two GAO evaluators, Carol Schuster and Jess Ford, candidly recognize that aid administrators are sometimes reluctant to press accountability issues for fear of jeopardizing other important political and security interests. "They make the case that the quid-pro-quo—foreign aid for peace in the Middle East or foreign aid in return for access to military bases elsewhere—is the issue of primary concern to the United States. They maintain that accountability often takes second billing."[81]

Nor, at least up to late 1989, has the A.I.D. evaluation process addressed such issues through official documentation, which would be the only way to compel corrective action or enforce performance conditions. These weaknesses undermine all objectives—be they those of the the recipients or the providers of the assistance. In the end, as Leonard Rogers, a career A.I.D. civil service officer observed, "Accountability for results has been overwhelmed by bean counting. . . . We can't be accountable if we can't specify our objectives in advance. Confusion over purposes means accountability is impossible."[82]

The GAO sees the net effect of the ongoing tension between the executive branch and Congress as being that A.I.D. "has no clearly articulated strategic mission." Instead, its multiple objectives confuse the process for assessing congressional intent regarding the direction of the foreign assistance program. They impede development of consensus between Congress and the executive branch on program priorities, and they "reduce the possibility of A.I.D. being held accountable for achieving any particular objective."[83]

Representative Lee Hamilton believes that because A.I.D. spends too much time planning and justifying what it is doing, it does not leave enough time to implement projects and determine their impact. Morover, because project papers take two years to produce, another year to get funding, and another year to get the contract team in-country, conditions change and the project has to be redesigned.[84]

These processes help explain why there are so many disconnects between political and development objectives and the assistance programs that are supposed to advance those objectives. The volume of information and analysis overwhelms the decisionmakers. Even useful analysis gets lost in the reams of reports. Those who spend weeks and months trying to understand a problem or political environment often find that no one has time to read or exchange views on their analyses. Thus, staff officers try to prepare two- to three-paragraph briefing papers that are expected to provide the insight for decisions to spend billions of dollars.

Hamilton sees A.I.D. personnel as a unique resource and believes that only the United States has overseas staff capable of staying up-to-date on economic conditions in the recipient country and engaging in dialogue with local experts. "[However,] the present system of accountability saps this unique asset as employees sit at word processors rather than work in the field. The process may keep A.I.D. people busy; it may also make them irrelevant."[85]

The additional consequence of irrelevancy is that many A.I.D. and State Department career professionals will experience a change in personal objectives. A.I.D. development officers face a situation similar to that which so disturbed John Maresca, Lannon Walker, and Senator Simon in their reflections on the diplomatic corps. Since development-oriented expertise counts for so little and can have no impact on the development process, the professional tends to find satisfaction not from the content of work on development issues but from personal progress in the bureaucracy. This success, however, places a premium on going along with the bureaucracy's management processes for spending resources.

The performance criteria that count are those related to obtaining and moving resources. As Hamilton correctly recognizes, concern about the development impact of those resources becomes irrelevant. Or perhaps an officer's concern might even become "career limiting" if it leads him or her to question why additional resources continue to go where they are achieving no measurable impact.

NOTES

1. GAO, *A.I.D. Management: Strategic Management Can Help A.I.D. Face Current and Future Challenges* (Report to the Administrator, Agency for International Development, GAO/NIASD-92-100, March 1992), p. 2.

2. Ibid., p. 3. See Appendix Figure I.3 for a diagram of groups and organizations concerned with A.I.D.'s mission.

3. A.I.D., "FY 1990 CDSS Guidance" (State 340628, October 31, 1987) and U.S. State Department CDSS Guidance Cable (State 340629, Part I, October 31, 1987). It should be noted that in 1992 A.I.D. and the State Department were considering dropping the CDSS.

4. Ibid.

5. A.I.D., "FY 1991 CDSS Guidance" (Final draft cable, cover memo from A-AA/PPC, Cliff Lewis, December 6, 1988), Introduction, p. 2.

6. Leonard Rogers, Program Office, A.I.D. Near East Bureau, interview with author, October 15, 1990.

7. A.I.D., *FY 1990 CP*, Annex I: Africa pp. 28–29.

8. A.I.D., *FY 1990 CP*, Annex III: Latin America and the Caribbean, pp. 21, 25.

9. A.I.D., *FY 1990 CP*, Annex II: Asia and the Near East, pp. 28–29.

10. GAO, *A.I.D. Management*, p. 2.

11. Hamilton, "Foreign Assistance," p. 30.

12. The logical framework (logframe) is a project-planning tool developed by A.I.D. in the 1970s to present the linkages between project inputs, purposes, and goals and the underlying assumptions that would affect project/program success. The linkages appear in a four-column matrix. Unfortunately, A.I.D. program officers have rarely used this tool as it was originally intended. Poor training, lack of analytical skills, and even short-term political considerations prevent effective use of the logframe. The weakest part is the fourth column, which is supposed to delineate relevant underlying assumptions at each phase of the project. See Appendix Figure IV.1 for the logframe matrix.

13. Robert J. Berg, president, International Development Conference, interview with author, Washington D.C., August 8, 1989.

14. Ibid. Berg provided this description. He had conducted the evaluation during his tenure as A.I.D.'s deputy assistant administrator for the Bureau for Planning and Policy Coordination.

15. Helen Dewar, "Mitchell Hits Emergency Aid Request," *Washington Post*, April 3, 1990.

16. Roger L. Hart, "State and Congress: Culture Shock at the Working Level," *Foreign Service Journal* (November 1988), p. 24.

17. Ibid.

18. Ibid.

19. Judith Tendler, *Inside Foreign Aid* (Baltimore and London: Johns Hopkins University Press, 1975), pp. 50–51. Though now dated, this book remains the most comprehensive description of the mechanics of A.I.D. While an updated version would be helpful in teaching the aid process, such an effort at this time (1992) would be impossible, given the wide disarray in the agency's bureaucracy, the current conflict between Congress and the executive branch over foreign aid policy and purposes, and the lack of vision within A.I.D. and the courage to at least raise its own voice in the debate.

20. Chapter 6 provides more detail on these and other countries where the United States has used aid for political purposes.

21. Berg, interview.

22. Scott Ticknor, "The Aid Charade and Recipient Politics" (Paper delivered at the American Political Science Association Annual Conference, Washington D.C., August 29, 1988), p. 9.

23. Ibid., p. 10.

24. Ibid.

25. This issue is also discussed in the section on personnel later in this chapter.

26. Bradshaw Langmaid, acting assistant administrator for Science and Technology, A.I.D., ISD symposium.

27. David I. Steinberg, ISD symposium.

28. Berg, interview.

29. A.I.D., *FY 1991 CDSS Guidance*.

30. William Fuller, deputy assistant administrator, Asia–Near East Bureau, A.I.D., interview with author, Washington D.C., June 13, 1989.

31. David D. Newsom, "Are Diplomats Patriotic?" *Foreign Service Journal* (March 1989), pp. 32–33.

32. This example is based on notes and thoughts on the issues involved that I kept in a personal journal during the period.

33. Steinberg, interview.

34. Charles Krauthammer, "Dole's Nonsense on Foreign Aid," *Washington Post*, January 23, 1990.

35. Thomas L. Friedman, "Senator Dole's Jackpot Question on Foreign Aid Stirs Up Congress," *New York Times*, Week in Review, January 21, 1990, p. 1.

36. *Report of the Task Force*, p. 10 (see note 15, p. 38).

37. The case study on Egypt in Chapter 5 discusses this example.

38. Thomas L. Friedman, "U.S. to Give Israel $650 Million to Offset Its Costs in Gulf War," *New York Times*, March 6, 1991.

39. Ibid.

40. From a segment of the "McNeil-Lehrer Newshour," March 24, 1992, Public Broadcasting System.

41. I will discuss further how such aid sustains the conditions of conflict in Chapter 7.

42. David I. Steinberg, "United States Assistance to Korea: A Policy Dialogue Perspective" in *Korean Challenges and American Policy*, ed. Kim Il-Pyong (New York: Paragon House, 1991), p. 221.

43. Ibid., p. 224.

44. *Report of the Task Force*, p. 27.

45. Friedman, "U.S. to Give Israel $650 Million."

46. GAO, *A.I.D. Management*, p. 11.

47. Dr. Joseph P. Stepanik, mission director, A.I.D./Tanzania, interview with author, Washington D.C., March 20, 1991.

48. Barry Sidman, former A.I.D. career foreign service officer, interview with author, July 1989.

49. GAO, *Foreign Aid: Improving the Impact*, p. 29.

50. Haven North, interview with author, Washington, D.C., May 1989.

51. President's Commission on the Management of A.I.D. Programs, Action Plan, working draft, March 1992, p. 19.

52. The fiscal year runs from October 1 to September 30.

53. GAO, *A.I.D. Management*, p. 2.

54. GAO, *Foreign Aid: Improving the Impact*, p. 15.

55. Ibid., p. 10.

56. Ibid., p. 16.

57. The Liberian example is discussed at length in Chapter 6.

58. GAO, *Foreign Aid: Improving the Impact*.

59. GAO, *A.I.D. Management*, p. 17.

60. Ibid.

61. Fuller, interview.

62. GAO, *A.I.D. Management*, p. 17.

63. M. Peter McPherson, "Advancing U.S. Interests with Foreign Assistance," *Foreign Service Journal* (December 1986), p. 26.

64. Hamilton, "Foreign Assistance," p. 31.

65. "Aid to Poland Sets Off Fight over Shipping," *New York Times*, December 8, 1989.

66. Kenneth B. Noble, "Wheat Rift Splits Nigerians and U.S.," *New York Times*, December 31, 1989.

67. Richard Uku, interview with author, April 18, 1990.

68. Ibid.

69. Foreign Operations, Export Financing, and Related Programs Appropriations Act, 1990, Public Law 101-167 (H.R. 3743), 103 Stat. 1195, approved November 21, 1989.

70. See Appendix Figure I.3.

71. This discussion is based on an interview with Leonard Zuza of the Office of Management and Budget, August 1, 1989.

72. William Haven North, "Development Specialists, Managers and Diplomats," *Foreign Service Journal* (May 1989), p. 39. Also see Appendix Figures I.1, I.2, and III.1.

73. Sidman, interview.

74. John J. Maresca, "Leaders and Experts," *Foreign Service Journal* (March 1986), p. 32.

75. Ibid., pp. 30–31.

76. Paul Simon, "The Tongue-tied Diplomat?" *Foreign Service Journal* (December 1988), p. 31.

77. Lannon Walker, "Language Expertise: Personnel Implications," *Foreign Service Journal* (December 1988), pp. 33–34.

78. Millidge Walker, letter to the author, December 14, 1990. Dr. Walker frequently provided consultant services for project development in overseas missions.

79. Masters, interview.

80. *Report of the Task Force*, p. 27.

81. Carol Schuster and Jess Ford, "Bringing Accountability to Foreign Aid," *GAO Journal*, no. 2 (Summer 1988), p. 33.

82. Leonard Rogers, interview with author, Washington D.C., October 15, 1990.

83. GAO, *A.I.D. Management*, p. 10.

84. Hamilton, "Foreign Assistance," p. 30.

85. Ibid.

5

THE U.S.-EGYPTIAN AID RELATIONSHIP: DEVELOPMENT OR DEPENDENCY?

Perhaps no bilateral assistance relationship is as difficult to describe and understand as that between the United States and Egypt. No other donor-recipient relationship matches the level of funding, the complexity and variety of project activities, and the cash transfer, PL 480, and Commodity Import Program (CIP) modes and conditions. Given the enormous resources committed to advancing U.S. political objectives and the relationship of Egypt's political, economic, and social stability to those objectives, the U.S.-Egyptian aid relationship demands assessment. Egypt alone receives more U.S. economic aid than the rest of Asia and the Near East combined, Israel excepted. Moreover, its mandated level also limits the resources available for all of Africa and Latin America.

Heba Handoussa, an Egyptian economist, notes that any aid relationship is "a mixed motive game rather than a zero sum or purely cooperative game" and that, like trade, dependency on aid "stems from the opportunity cost of forgoing the relationship to either partner."[1] She rejects the notion that the U.S. aid program to Egypt has been simply an annual $1 billion, highly concessional package with no indirect costs or strings. Project conditions, the requirements to buy American, high-priced U.S. consultants, U.S. aid priorities, and—though she does not mention it—the economic policy dialogue requirements all constitute "strings." The result has been an inflated local A.I.D. bureaucracy, which is often referred to as Egypt's "shadow cabinet." This in-country bureaucracy contrasts sharply with Israel's treatment, wherein the United States simply delivers a billion dollars in U.S. cash aid per year, "with no interference from a single U.S. A.I.D. official in-country. It is, therefore, fair to conclude that in Egypt's case the additional strings attached to U.S. aid also assign a greater responsibility to the U.S. for the success or failure of its aid program."[2]

During the February 1989 hearings on the FY 1990 program, Congressman Lee Hamilton wondered whether the Government of Egypt (GOE) would ever carry out the economic reforms deemed so essential to resolving Egypt's precarious economic condition.[3] Although such misgivings have resulted in attempts to place performance conditions on the policy dialogue and to delay cash transfers in order to leverage economic reforms, no one has ever suggested that the aid level be cut because of past poor performance—or unless the Israel assistance package undergoes a similar, proportional cut.

The U.S.-Egyptian assistance relationship demonstrates clearly how using economic aid resources to advance political objectives undermines efforts to use these resources to stimulate self-sustainable economic and social development. Yet, failure of development efforts can also undermine the stability of the Egyptian regime and, as a consequence, limit Egypt's capacity to contribute to the Middle East peace process.

THE PURPOSES OF U.S. FOREIGN POLICY IN EGYPT

Following their defeat in the 1973 war with Israel, increasing disappointment with the Soviet Union and continuing economic deterioration led Egypt's leaders to look for new opportunities in a relationship with the United States. Secretary of State Kissinger's frequent diplomatic trips throughout the Middle East in the early 1970s further encouraged this trend. By decade's end, Paul Jabbar observes, "Cairo was in virtual alliance with the United States, relations with the Soviets were in a deep freeze, and a peace treaty with Israel had returned to Egypt substantially all of its national territory."[4] This same treaty also led to a break with the rest of the Arab world and a cessation of Arab assistance.

The 1979 Camp David Accords created new U.S. foreign policy objectives in the Middle East. With the Camp David doctrine, the United States envisaged a new role for Egypt, believing that peace with Israel would be the first step in a process that would enable Egypt to lead other Arabs to negotiate peace. The hope was "that the Camp David Accords had laid the groundwork for other Arabs, with Egyptian and American help, to follow Egypt's lead."[5] President Sadat sold Camp David to the Egyptian people by stressing the economic benefits of peace and the new relationship with the United States. The United States openly tied its economic assistance program to "sustaining the peace process and maintaining economic conditions favorable to Sadat's survival."[6]

The FY 1981 Congressional Presentation noted that the Egyptian-Israeli peace treaty caused rejectionist Arab states to impose sanctions on Egypt, including withdrawal from participation in development projects in Egypt, and termination of financing for Egypt's defense industry and GOE military procurement. Thus, the U.S. ESF program was "designed to assist President Sadat in his effort to match political achievements with substantial internal economic improvements. . . . U.S. assistance seeks to meet both short and long-term priority development needs."[7] Jabbar observed, "In the minds of Egyptians, their socio-economic crisis is inescapably bound up with the question of peace with Israel and the tight U.S. embrace."[8] Equally clear is the fact that since at least 1979, U.S. regional and global strategic political objectives have determined the levels and priority purposes of the United States' ESF program for Egypt.

U.S. and Egyptian Political Objectives

The United States has four major political objectives in its relationship with Egypt. The fundamental objective is to establish lasting peace between Israel and its neighboring Arab states. The first step toward this goal required peace between Israel and Egypt. In the long term, an essential condition for maintaining peace is that these two states experience the economic benefits associated with peace. The FY 1976 CP characterized Egypt's "determination to move toward peace" as "essential in achieving the progress thus far made," and U.S. economic assistance to Egypt as supporting "the Egyptian Government's policy aimed at seeking a negotiated settlement of a permanent nature which will permit Egypt to turn her energies toward economic development."[9]

The FY 1977 CP noted the successful implementation of agreements to disengage Israeli and Egyptian forces and conclude a second-step military disengagement agreement between Israel and Egypt. The CP concluded that further progress toward permanent peace would depend "specifically on . . . an economic and social atmosphere within Egypt conducive to growth, development, and peace. The objective of U.S. assistance is to foster economic and social development within Egypt and thereby to create the preconditions to a continued and a more permanent peace."[10]

Second, the United States seeks to extend the peace process to include other Arab states, particularly Jordan and Syria. The U.S. expectation is that as these states build their relationship with Egypt and Israel, other Arab states will participate as well.

Third, the United States wants ready access to military facilities and an intelligence relationship with Egypt. The U.S. military aid program helps the United States maintain a close working relationship with the Egyptian military and political leadership. This relationship facilitates unimpeded transit for U.S. naval vessels, particularly those that may have to carry any nuclear weapons, through the Suez Canal. The final U.S. political objective in Egypt is to support political and economic stability, including increased democratization and continued improvement in basic human rights.

For its part, Egypt's fundamental political objectives appear to include reducing tension with Israel (but not at any further expense to Egyptian de facto leadership of the Arab World); resolving the Palestinian problem on terms that will enhance regional stability; retaining a close economic and military assistance relationship with the United States; attaining major powers' and Arab states' acceptance of Egypt's political leadership in the Middle East; containing the growth and appeal of Islamic Fundamentalist ideology and organizations; and stable progress toward democracy, while ensuring that the pace of democratization not exceed the pace of dismantling a socialist-oriented political-economic system that has relied on extensive subsidies to preserve stability.

Economic Objectives

As the cited CPs show, the United States recognizes that Egypt's leadership in the peace process with Israel is unsustainable unless Egyptians experience economic and social benefits. For Egypt, moreover, obtaining political leadership in the Middle East ultimately requires a productive, self-sustaining economy.

Several economic and development objectives affect the impact of the U.S.-Egyptian relationship for both countries. The first priority for most of the 1980s was trying to resolve the debt burden. Prior to the 1990–1991 Gulf War, Egypt's overall debt approached at least $55 billion, about 70 percent of which was owed to public institutions. Of most concern was the Foreign Military Sales (FMS) debt, which exceeded $7 billion by 1990. Egypt faced payment deadlines and the aid cutoff provisions of the Brooke amendment.[11] In the early 1990s, payments on principal would have raised annual FMS payments to over $1 billion. As a reward for Egypt's cooperation against Saddam Hussein's aggression, the administration recommended and Congress approved full forgiveness of the $7.3 billion FMS debt.

Obtaining IMF standby loans with limited reform conditions was another recurring issue. Egypt believed an IMF Standby Agreement would facilitate Paris Club rescheduling of Egypt's debt, enabling Egypt to obtain additional donor assistance and access to private lenders.[12] A third major issue was retaining U.S. aid levels and expanding the cash transfer portion thereof.

THE U.S. ECONOMIC ASSISTANCE PROGRAM FOR EGYPT

The A.I.D. Assistance Structure and Purposes

From 1974 to the mid-1980s, the economic aid program for Egypt supported projects in most sectors and included large-scale PL 480 food assistance. Direct cash transfers became part of the aid portfolio in 1984 and have maintained an annual rate of about $115 million, except for a special additional $500 million appropriation in FYs 1985 and 1986. Entering the 1990s, the program included $115 million minimum in cash transfer, $500 million in project aid, and $200 million in commodity imports, divided equally between the public and private sectors. The United States also provided annual PL 480 food assistance that averaged over $200 million per year into the mid-1980s and then gradually declined to approximately $160 million in 1990.

The Congressional Presentation for FY 1990 stated that the A.I.D.

development strategy and program should support economic stabilization during a period of severe balance of payments pressures; increased economic productivity, particularly in agriculture and industry; development of human resources to provide a skilled work force and to enhance and sustain basic health and family planning services; and improved efficiency of economic infrastructure through investments in water/wastewater and energy, with emphasis on operations and maintenance and cost recovery.[13] U.S. aid officials believe that attaining these objectives in Egypt depends on successful implementation of project-level activities to curb population growth; expand private sector investment to expand employment, develop exports, and facilitate technology transfer; discourage public sector industry; expand land available for housing, agriculture, and the exploding population; dramatically improve Egyptian education and the quality of its graduates at all levels; and develop agro-industry and industrial exports.

Finally, the U.S. Congress has tried to tie the cash transfer element ($115 million annually) in the overall Egyptian portfolio to performance on economic reform issues raised in extensive policy dialogue with the GOE. These issues include interest and exchange rates, subsidies, agricultural prices, and the budget deficit. Since 1984, the policy dialogue has continued with only marginal success, despite linking cash disbursement to major economic reform. Between 1984 and 1991, cash transfers totaled nearly $1.4 billion.[14]

The Government of Egypt's Goals for U.S. Assistance

Clearly, the transfer of aid resources and their implementation do not occur solely on U.S. terms. The GOE is well aware of its geopolitical importance to the Arabs and Europeans, and especially to the United States. Sadat's turn to the United States in 1974 continued Egypt's history of trading a degree of independence for external resources. Furthermore, the political leadership risked less by obtaining foreign largesse in a time of superpower rivalry than by imposing the economic and political reforms necessary to stimulate new domestic wealth and political power in a growing, productive, private sector middle class.[15]

From the outset, the Egyptian leadership recognized the U.S. strategic political interests that lay behind the economic aid program, and it began viewing the aid as an entitlement almost from its inception. Indeed, this perspective maintained the rationale that Sadat had used to obtain extensive Arab aid during the 1970s. It has been apparent to Egypt throughout the assistance relationship that the U.S. administration's primary concerns—and those of most members of the U.S. Congress—are the security of Israel, the Middle East peace process, and Egypt's role in that process. Because Egypt sees U.S. aid as a quid pro quo for these U.S. objectives, when the United States tries to add other objectives such as policy dialogue toward economic reforms, many Egyptian government leaders react negatively. They maintain that Egypt met its part of the bargain when it entered the peace process. In fact, these leaders still feel shortchanged because the funds are provided for projects, whereas the Israelis receive straight cash transfers.

The U.S.-Egyptian relationship clearly demonstrates how aid levels (including even the cash transfer levels within the overall package) originally set to advance U.S. strategic political objectives cannot later have leverage value for encouraging changes in the recipient government's economic policies. The GOE chose to use its own resources in support of its priorities in a statist-oriented economy, while allowing aid donors to finance projects they favored. A 1985 GAO report also found important philosophical and practical differences between A.I.D. and the GOE over what the program should accomplish. While A.I.D. wanted to strengthen the Egyptian private sector, the GOE emphasized development of public sector industries. A.I.D. emphasized basic human needs, while the GOE wanted A.I.D. to concentrate on electrical power generation, water/wastewater projects, and other such infrastructure. All these differences caused delays and sometimes even confrontation.[16]

This remained the case in 1992. The GOE provided funding to support the government bureaucracy, including subsidization of state companies that operate with enormous losses. It also provided subsidized, though inadequate, social services in health, education, energy, and basic food items. There were few resources left for other broad development efforts.

PROCESS VERSUS PURPOSE

Setting the Level: 1974–1979

There have been differences within the A.I.D. mission in Cairo over the proper aid levels and their purposes in light of U.S. political objectives. The Cairo embassy in 1974 proposed a $70 million level, but the U.S. ambassador to Egypt, Hermann F. Eilts, did not want a large A.I.D. mission to administer the resources. He believed the embassy's economic staff could run the program.[17]

Aid levels escalated immediately. The U.S. government, through Secretary of State Henry Kissinger, approved the proposal but raised the level to $250 million. By FY 1975, the aid level had risen to $370 million. In 1976, the level reached $990 million.[18]

Ambassador Eilts has conceded that the administration had given no thought in advance to how much Egypt could absorb or how the money would be spent. The original intention was not to bring about major changes in Egypt. It was to manifest U.S. political support for Anwar Sadat's regime. According to Eilts, the State Department and the White House took the aid level "off the top of their heads. . . . It wasn't scientifically developed."[19] The rapid escalation in levels reflected the priority of U.S. political objectives and the political intent of the aid levels.

The record, however, does show that the State Department and Congress, through the GAO, briefly considered Egypt's capacity to use these funds according to sound development criteria. In May 1976, Congressman Lee Hamilton requested the GAO to review U.S. economic and food aid programs for Egypt following the 1973 Middle East war. The ensuing report came directly to the point:

> Levels of U.S. economic assistance to Egypt for fiscal years 1975–77 reflect U.S. political desires to demonstrate (1) equitable treatment of Israel and Egypt, (2) support of President Anwar Sadat's policy of moving away from military confrontation with Israel and toward economic development at home, and (3) satisfaction with the progress toward developing the second Sinai agreement.
>
> U.S. aid to Egypt is justified more on the basis of a political symbol of evenhanded support for stability in the Middle East than on the capacity of Egypt to effectively absorb and use the assistance available. Aid levels were increased from $370 million in 1975 to $990 million in 1976, even though U.S. policy makers believed that Egypt might not have the capacity to absorb increased project aid and that the actual impact on the economy would depend on Egypt's response to basic economic reforms being discussed with the International Monetary Fund. Moreover, administration officials believed that the United States was not in a position to link increased assistance levels to Egypt's movement toward economic reforms, even though reforms were recognized as essential to Egypt's economic recovery.[20]

Congressman Hamilton was concerned about this problem at the inception of the aid relationship. His expressed despair thirteen years later at the 1989 congressional hearing noted above is understandable, but it was also predictable given his and the Congress's unwillingness to require that U.S. political objectives be achieved through sound economic development using U.S. aid.

Thus, the aid program began and remained overfinanced. Waterbury observed, "It is known that Kissinger promised Sadat that the level of funding to Egypt would always be in rough parity with that of Israel. A chronic problem has been the inability of the Egyptian economy to absorb such high levels of aid. This, in fact, has placed a premium on moving aid funds as rapidly as possible, often at the expense of sound economic analysis or need."[21] But Egypt did require large-scale aid for postwar reconstruction and new power and water infrastructure—and there were plenty of U.S. businesses and other special interests who wanted access to the aid.

Barring an unexpected breakthrough in Arab-Israeli relations or serious political and economic cost-benefit analyses by a budget-conscious and courageous Congress, there is little prospect that the "U.S.-Egyptian honey pot"[22] will dry up soon. Moreover, because the billions of aid dollars provide significant subsidies for U.S. businesses in the power, water/wastewater, and agriculture sectors, as well as for universities across the United States, these special interests help sustain congressionally mandated aid levels despite the adverse effects these political and business-oriented linkages can have on attempts to apply sound development criteria to these resources.

Operational Objective #1: Spend the Money

U.S. political purposes and business interests are directly advanced through the transfer and expenditure process. Inevitably, the pressure to move high levels of aid led to large infrastructure projects, particularly in the power and water sectors. According to Ambassador Eilts, "We always had more money than we had projects. Instead of the program being designed by projects, we had an amount of money we had to find projects for."[23]

These early projects moved resources and provided significant additions to Egypt's power production capacity, and they helped resolve major water/wastewater problems. They were especially helpful in the Suez Canal cities, where the war had been most destructive. In the early 1980s, the breakdown of major portions of the Cairo wastewater system created major sanitation problems that threatened the political stability of the Mubarak government. The U.S. aid program extended wastewater project activities to address both sanitation problems and to support political stability. Unfortunately, parallel efforts to encourage the government to raise water rates and undertake new management approaches to operating and maintaining the new systems have had only marginal success at best.

Operations and maintenance concerns received little attention during the planning stages of these projects. A.I.D. applied its policy that the recipient country must be responsible for covering O&M costs. In Egypt, however, this policy was never viable because the need to expend high levels of assistance demanded major project activities in water/wastewater, irrigation, and power infrastructure projects that in turn created overwhelming O&M burdens. There were some training programs that included training in the United States for O&M personnel, but these were not coordinated with additional programs within the Egyptian bureaucracy to ensure that when the U.S. trainees returned they would be used effectively. The failure to develop new operations and maintenance capacities, including personnel, management structure and culture, budgets, and reliable funding sources, means that A.I.D. now has to provide budgetary support for O&M or risk embarrassing power and water plant breakdowns—some of which have already occurred.

A World Bank economist noted, "There was never any serious movement by Egypt to cover the costs of these operations through rates anywhere close to cost recovery. These weaknesses were the beginning of U.S. aid actually helping Egypt in self-destructive actions, destroying its economy. The U.S. is still trying to undo this damage."[24] Kissinger and Eilts, however, were concerned more about the political impact of these projects. Eilts recognized that this discouraged the A.I.D. staff in Cairo, who viewed Egypt's problems primarily in economic terms. "The [agency] people were interested in [projects in] the villages. But the political impact of that is not that much. What I wanted was things with political impact, things Sadat could point to, like a cement plant."[25]

The GAO found that the differences between the U.S. mission (both diplomatic and aid personnel), A.I.D./Washington, the State Department, and the GOE over how to achieve the program's political and economic goals intensified the pressures on A.I.D./Cairo to obligate ESF funds on high-visibility capital (infrastructure) projects that would "at least in the short run demonstrate U.S. support for the Egyptian government and its role in the peace process." Many A.I.D./Washington and mission officials believed many of these projects did "not have as high a priority/value for economic development as other possible programs or projects."[26]

The GAO found that the International Monetary Fund, the World Bank, and most senior A.I.D. officials all believed that Egypt had a unique "window of opportunity" to work on its major economic problems. A.I.D. emphasized the need for reforms, believing that securing economic reforms was "one of its main responsibilities." State Department officials, however, emphasized the overriding priority of the immediate political goal and believed that the goal was being met. "Although State officials agree with the need for structural changes in the economy in the long term, they believe that pushing too hard for these changes may raise political tensions."[27]

Even with pressure to spend money quickly and despite efforts to eliminate delays caused by the Egyptian bureaucracy's limited absorptive capacity, the Egyptian pipeline of obligated but unspent funds remained at or above $2 billion annually from 1987 at least through 1991. Ironically, the apparent intractability of this problem resulted in increased pressure to enlarge the cash transfer portion of the ESF portfolio. Cash transfers would meet political objectives, would decrease the pipeline, and would reduce project activities that create operations and maintenance requirements for the GOE —but they would not help stimulate a sustainable development process among the Egyptian people any more than had all the other assistance mechanisms.

The Project/Program Design and Implementation Process: Demands and Deadlines Versus Dialogue

The political context of the U.S.-Egyptian relationship impedes planning for a consistent development strategy, as well as negotiations between A.I.D. and the Egyptian government regarding the projects and the programming conditions for the aid resources.

The Country Development Strategy Statement initially allocated resources among sectors over a five-year period, but there was really no agreement among mission officials on an overall strategy. Each year a new debate on how to reallocate resources created an inconsistent development focus that sometimes emphasized long-term development benefits in such sectors as education, health, and agriculture and at other times placed priority on infrastructure projects in water/wastewater or on an electrical generating project.[28]

In 1986, A.I.D. and the mission moved to a three-year CDSS cycle with annual budget reviews. Nevertheless, many officials questioned this process simply because the political environment in both Egypt and Washington and frequent shifts in the program's short-term political priorities preclude predictability in planning and implementation for three- to five-year periods. Lack of guidance based on an existing, coherent, overall policy and program strategy, in turn, confuses planning staff and inevitably impedes project planning.

Project planning and implementation conditions for U.S. aid programs in all countries require that concessional financing must be tied to products and sevices with at least 50 percent U.S. content. While this requirement can be waived in exceptional circumstances, such conditions are necessary to obtain congressional support for any significant aid program. The consequences for development objectives can be severe. In Egypt's case, Weinbaum observed:

> Because U.S. financing is frequently available only for the purchase of capital equipment and higher technologies, investment choices can occur without full assessment of opportunity costs and may at times be inappropriate for Egypt's development needs and capabilities. Very seldom, for example, are projects designed to optimize the kind of labor-intensive approaches that can offer solutions to Egypt's serious urban unemployment problems. At the same time, the country is also locked by aid agreements into hiring high-priced foreign experts whose handsome salaries and other benefits are resented by their Egyptian counterparts.[29]

Moreover, even when the United States seriously tries to use the aid to encourage economic reforms that will help stimulate more Egyptian self-sufficiency, the GOE resists strongly. Some reforms, as with the cash transfer negotiations, call for reduced food subsidies, interest reforms, and price increases for agricultural products or energy. The Egyptians never fail to recall that IMF-imposed reforms caused the 1977 bread riots. They argue that new U.S.-proposed reforms could have similar consequences. Administrative reforms or efforts to promote privatization of public enterprises are especially volatile because they may weaken the power base of important government supporters. Consequently, the government leadership may raise objections with the U.S. ambassador, reminding him of the original quid pro quo political purposes of the aid resources. Furthermore, the leadership may point out that political instability undermines the government's capacity to deliver on its other political commitments to the United States.

In the policy dialogue arena, U.S. officials will eventually support a compromise by exaggerating minor reforms—or *intended* reforms—thereby making the policy dialogue appear successful. When facing difficult compromises on project-specific performance conditions, aid planners frequently use vague language in the passive voice that leaves unclear who will do what when. While these compromises facilitate completion of project documentation and obligation of funds, conflicts continue throughout project implementation simply because the planning process avoided clear delineation of responsibilities.

It is difficult to assess how much attempts to apply performance conditions may affect the political value of the original aid level, because the government's bureaucratic interests vary. Ministries that need U.S. aid for project activities may resent U.S. conditions, procedures, and contracting requirements. But they also realize, given the shortages and other priorities in the Egyptian budget, that without the aid resources there might be no project at all. In these cases, though a minister's interests may differ from those of the top leadership, that minister probably will not protest conditions so as not to risk strengthening those who prefer cash transfers. While cash transfers might serve the overall political objectives of the president of Egypt, they would hurt the minister and his or her bureaucracy's interests.

Evaluating project performance is also a difficult process in the highly political environment. Findings do not objectively highlight questionable performance or impact. Because the aid levels are politically mandated and linked to the aid levels for Israel, inadequate Egyptian performance could not result in a cut in Egypt's assistance allocation even if recommended corrections are not forthcoming. Moreover, any controversy, even only on a project basis, could be counterproductive politically. One official in the A.I.D. office in Cairo admitted that evaluations were often a waste of money. "Usually, the recommendations are not even followed by A.I.D. and very often these are given in a vacuum—they are not realistic given the *political* situation in Egypt, about which most American consultants know nothing."[30]

It is equally difficult to address adverse findings on the performance of U.S. contractors, including universities, because of the power these special interests have in the U.S. Congress or within the U.S. bureaucracy. Adherence to sound development criteria is often impossible in such situations. In one case, three consecutive project evaluations between 1979 and 1984 found that the Massachusetts Institute of Technology had failed to correct deficiencies that were impeding attainment of its project's objective: self-sustaining research capacity within the Egyptian university community. Recommendations from the first evaluation were repeated in two following evaluations. The A.I.D. project officer in Cairo who backstopped the project and participated in the third evaluation admitted that there was little possibility that MIT could fulfill its responsibilities. Nevertheless, the final project evaluation review committee in A.I.D./Washington decided to continue the project with MIT. A.I.D.'s administrative leadership was unprepared to invite additional congressional inquiries and pressure on behalf of the university. Nor did they believe the issues were worth the time and staff required to explain a termination of the contract.[31]

The Purposes and Actions of Other Public Agencies and Special Interests

Disagreements on the purposes of U.S. economic aid and on how best to use it in Egypt exist even within the U.S. foreign policy bureaucracy. The State Department has long preferred direct cash transfer. A.I.D. is not opposed to cash transfer if it actually results in meaningful economic reform. Until the GOE is prepared to make major reforms, A.I.D. argues that project and program approaches more effectively promote development. The State Department position reflects the GOE's argument that Egypt should receive equal treatment with Israel, which gets a direct cash transfer of its entire $1.3 billion annual grant. An additional argument is that Egypt's limited absorptive capacity impedes effective programming and implementation of a large project portfolio.

Both the State Department and the U.S. Department of Defense try to maintain access to key government officials so that they can ensure passage of U.S. naval vessels through the Suez Canal, military and political intelligence cooperation with the Egyptian government, and use of Egyptian territory for military exercises. Both ESF and military aid support these political and military objectives. Obviously, the president and the National Security Council give priority to these types of objectives.

Until they were forgiven as part of the coalition-building effort during the 1990–1991 Gulf War, the most serious threats to maintaining a close working relationship with the GOE leadership were requirements for repayments on Egypt's earlier military and economic loans. These repayments were for loans made prior to FY 1985; since 1985, all aid has been grant aid. Military loans outstanding exceeded $7 billion. Repayments on interest at market-level rates were increasingly hard to meet, given Egypt's chronic foreign exchange shortages. Moreover, payments on principal would have come due in the 1990s, and the Brooke amendment requirement of meeting repayment deadlines on U.S. loans threatened loss of aid.

Even a one- or two-week cessation of U.S. aid could seriously embarrass the Egyptian government and could draw attention to the vulnerabilities in the U.S.-Egyptian aid relationship. Such an event would also risk increased congressional and media awareness in the United States and could raise questions about the Egypt program, particularly the limited progress toward a self-sustaining economy. No one in the State Department or elsewhere in the U.S. government wants to risk an embarrassing assessment of how aid resources have failed to stimulate the type of economic, social, and political development necessary for self-sustainable peace in the Middle East.

Heroic, often high-tension efforts normally began when a payment deadline approached and Egypt's foreign exchange balance came into question. Whenever potential foreign exchange crises occurred, the first possible funding source was the ESF account. The State Department encouraged A.I.D. to make any of Egypt's remaining cash transfer funds available or even to consider converting funds from the pipeline of unexpended project funds. A variation of this situation occurred nearly every year from 1985 to 1990, and probably thereafter. Each time, A.I.D. had to set aside or loosen economic reform performance criteria that the Egyptian government had previously agreed to abide by. A.I.D. initially resisted, arguing that yet another compromise would undercut efforts to stimulate sustainable economic growth in Egypt. In the end, embassy policymakers found creative language to describe even the most token reform, or promise of future reform, so that the cash transfer could resolve the crisis of the moment.

U.S. Special Interests and Congress

U.S. special interests and Congress have also created problems for Egypt's and the U.S. government's development objectives. Many U.S. companies are nearly as dependent on the aid relationship as are the Egyptians. These businesses, including universities, often work through their representatives in Congress to pressure A.I.D. into undertaking their special projects. For example, in 1986, in the energy sector, a powerful New York senator who sat on the Foreign Relations Committee intervened with the A.I.D. administrator to obtain reversal of a policy decision that would have prohibited the funding of additional power plants until the Egyptian government implemented energy price reforms. A.I.D. had decided to shelve the upgrading of the Talkha power plant until reforms occurred. However, the likely contractor for the Talkha project was a major U.S. producer of power generators that had built the original Talkha plant. Working through the senator and with the additional lobbying of the Egyptian minister of energy—and A.I.D.'s always present need to obligate funds by the end of the fiscal year[32]—this company succeeded in obtaining a policy reversal. Later, it won the contract for the new generators.[33]

This policy reversal was inconsistent with sound economic development criteria. It compromised a previous agreement with the World Bank to hold back funding for power plants until the Egyptian government implemented necessary energy price reforms. Perhaps even more damaging, this triumph of a special U.S. business interest, aided by A.I.D.'s interest in supporting an Egyptian government minister who was important for other U.S. objectives, and the need to obligate funds, demonstrated to the Egyptians that the U.S. commitment to sustainable economic progress for Egypt had limits that could be manipulated in favor of other less painful purposes. If the U.S. government could not ask a U.S. business to endure a delay in its profits, how could it expect the Egyptian government to create even greater economic hardship for its people?

A.I.D. efforts to reduce PL 480 food shipments to Egypt run against the interests of the U.S. farmer. PL 480 food aid has enabled the GOE to avoid adjusting the price structure in order to increase domestic food production. Increased domestic prices would anger the urban population, which has the most direct impact on political stability. In 1961, Egypt purchased only 7 percent of its food requirements abroad. A decade later, imports had increased to one-fifth, but by 1983 agricultural imports from all sources had reached one-half of total domestic food consumption. In that year, Egypt was the world's third largest importer of U.S. wheat and wheat flour. The PL 480 program became the source for approximately one-third of the bread sold in Cairo.[34]

Although U.S. law required the secretary of agriculture to affirm that PL 480 food aid did not cause a substantial disincentive to farmers,[35] such findings were at times disregarded. An A.I.D. briefing paper on PL 480 food aid to Egypt prepared for former A.I.D. administrator Alan Woods in June 1987 suggested that Title I should be phased down because the imports had become a disincentive to local production and supported a costly system of food subsidies. The memo continued, "State, however, continues to press for the highest possible levels of food aid on the grounds that it increases overall levels and provides balance of payments support. This conflict has been played out against the background of strong popular opposition in Egypt to any change in food subsidies—a political issue State uses to support its position."[36]

The State Department finds the Department of Agriculture a strong supporter of this position. The benefits of shipping U.S. wheat surpluses on concessional terms to food-deficit countries include their value as indirect price supports for U.S. farmers, subsidies for the U.S. shipping industry, and savings to the federal treasury through reductions in costs for storing wheat lacking commercial markets. As Weinbaum concludes, "U.S. policy makers have made no effort to hide their long-term goals in the Third World of turning a dependence on American aid into a reliance on the United States for commercial grain purchases once a recipient country's economy had sufficiently strengthened."[37]

U.S. universities are another particularly effective special interest and a valuable element in the U.S.-Egyptian aid relationship for development purposes. Universities create training programs that bring Egyptians to the United States for short-term training or for long-term university education to the master's and Ph.D. degree levels. Unfortunately, universities often use their connections with Congress or the A.I.D. administrator to maintain their access to aid funds, even when their performance does not warrant extension of their contracts—as the experience with MIT, discussed earlier, illustrates.

These cases demonstrate how congressional pressure for specific projects benefit business interests in selected U.S. constituencies. Although the senator won a battle for his constituent, he undermined A.I.D.'s policy dialogue and World Bank efforts to obtain energy reforms in Egypt that would enable Egypt to meet its people's energy requirements without U.S. subsidies. U.S. farmers benefit from the PL 480 export opportunities, but they also seek advantages that ensure continued dependency of Egypt on U.S. food imports. U.S. universities can be effective development agents, but they create resentment when the recipient country cannot easily terminate contracts for nonperformance. In these cases, the A.I.D. contracts appear more to facilitate the U.S. universities' access to and information from the recipient country than to transfer knowledge and technology to that recipient.[38]

Business-congressional alliances, based on U.S. domestic political interests, have weakened U.S. policy dialogue objectives for reforms in other economic and social areas as well. When combined with the overriding foreign policy objectives, special interests inhibit a coherent policy dialogue process and stymie development assistance programs that would help Egypt create its own self-sustaining capacity. Yet, economic self-sufficiency is clearly a precondition for Egypt to contribute most effectively to lasting Middle East peace. All these factors cause the Egyptian power elite to question the integrity of the U.S. commitment to help stimulate a self-sustaining economy in Egypt. U.S. behavior encourages the Egyptians to believe that they can—and must—continue to trade on their geostrategic political position well into the future.

AN ASSESSMENT OF THE U.S.-EGYPTIAN ASSISTANCE RELATIONSHIP

U.S. economic aid to Egypt from 1974 through FY 1991 totaled over $17 billion. Military aid over this same period totaled another $16 billion.[39] This aid effort promoted several political objectives. While it is not possible to attribute success or failure in any objective to the provision of these resources alone, it is possible to describe the status of each objective at the end of 1991.

Attainment of Political Objectives

Peace. A.I.D. believes that the assistance program "has contributed importantly to U.S. foreign policy objectives. Peace between Egypt and Israel has been maintained, and Egypt has continued to be a full and supportive partner in the peace process."[40] Moreover, Egypt and Israel have succeeded in negotiating difficult issues—such as changes in the status of the Sinai, including Taba—that have further strengthened the peace process. Egypt and Israel differ on the Palestinian issue, but neither country is prepared to fight over the fate of the Palestinians. For the near future, preservation of at least the status quo between Israel and Egypt seems assured. Moreover, if the intensified U.S.-led diplomatic activity that began in March 1991 after the military defeat of Saddam Hussein results in meaningful negotiations for peace between other Arab states and Israel, Egypt and Israel will probably move beyond the current status quo into greater cooperation on economic issues.

Egypt would not have been able to stand apart and try to encourage greater moderation in the approaches Arabs chose for dealing with the West and with Israel without the substantial U.S. economic and military aid to replace the Arab support that Egypt lost after it signed the Camp David Accords with Israel. For this objective, the U.S. $16 billion ESF "investment" has provided a return. The return, however, remains limited, since the Camp David doctrine had intended, wrote U.S. Ambassador Atherton, that peace with Israel was to be a "point of departure for Egypt to lead other Arabs to negotiate peace. . . . Ten years later this scenario has yet to be played out."[41]

Ironically, Egypt's most important contribution to peace in the Middle East might have been its cooperation with Saudi Arabia and the United States in response to flagrant aggression by one Arab state against another Arab state: Iraq's assault on Kuwait on August 2, 1990. President Mubarak first tried to persuade Iraq's Saddam Hussein not to invade Kuwait. Even when Saddam invaded, Mubarak continued to work for an Iraqi withdrawal under an Arab face-saving formula that might have allowed Iraq to keep some of the disputed oil fields in Kuwait, along with some financial considerations. After initial hesitancy and when it became clear that Saddam was really annexing all of Kuwait, Mubarak took the lead among those Arab states who voted to condemn Saddam. He was also driven to a stronger stand by Saddam's call for the people of Saudi Arabia and Egypt to overthrow their governments.[42]

Mubarak rejected the posture of many Arab governments (namely, Jordan, Yemen, Sudan, Algeria, Tunisia, Mauritania, and Libya, as well as the PLO)[43] who either supported Saddam outright or became apologists for his aggression and sought to shift blame by arguing that Saddam merely reflected Arab anger with the West because of its continuing support of Israel. Finally, Mubarak committed nearly 40,000 Egyptian troops to the multinational force made up of U.S., European, and other Arab country troops that responded to Iraq's aggression.[44]

The United States rewarded Egypt generously for these efforts. President Bush encouraged and strengthened this commitment by promising and then attaining congressional approval for the forgiveness of Egypt's $7.3 billion military debt to the United States and for more military aid. Mubarak's efforts to pull together an Arab peacekeeping force "provided a critical patina of Arab legitimacy for the deep American military intervention in the Gulf, and deprived President Hussein of the argument that the conflict [was] simply between Iraq and the United States."[45]

The Saudis and other Gulf Arab states also erased Egypt's debts and promised more aid—rewards that the Cairo press, encouraged by the government, reported prominently. According to Tahseen Bashir, an Egyptian commentator and former government official, these benefits showed the "long-suffering Egyptian people that Mubarak's active role in the gulf, which may get Egyptians killed, is bringing economic rewards."[46]

Additional U.S. and Arab aid may have been necessary in this crisis because the nature of the military threat was so great, as was the cost to Egypt in terms of lost remittances from Egyptian workers in Iraq (about $3.5 billion per year), lower Suez Canal earnings, and reduced tourism income.[47] Nevertheless, it is also telling that Egypt's debt and economic weaknesses could have been so severe even after a seventeen-year aid relationship—over $32 billion in U.S. military and economic assistance—that such generous additional aid should have been necessary to compensate Egypt for the costs of cooperation in meeting a threat so vital to Egypt's own interests. Equally significant was Egypt's dependence on U.S. logistical support to get Egyptian forces to the front and on the Saudis and the United States to cover the maintenance costs of these troops in the field.

Reestablishment of a Leading Role in the Arab World. An underlying assumption from the outset of the U.S.-Egyptian relationship in 1975 has always been that "domestic [economic] progress [would] strengthen the Egyptian government's leadership role and the moderate forces in the Arab world."[48] While U.S. and Egyptian officials have had limited success over seventeen years in using the aid program to stimulate sustainable economic progress, there is no question that the aid program at least enabled Egypt to avoid economic collapse until other Arab states recognized again how important it was to reestablish their political and economic relationships with Egypt.

By the end of 1987, this process was well under way. All the other Arab/Muslim states in the Middle East—with the exception of Libya, Syria, and Iran—had sought to improve their ties with Egypt. The Arab League summit meeting of November 12, 1987, brought this process to a dramatic culmination. It lifted a prohibition on diplomatic ties with Cairo that had been in effect since the 1979 peace with Israel. Immediately following the summit, seven Arab states—Saudi Arabia, Kuwait, the United Arab Emirates, Iraq, Morocco, Bahrain, and Qatar—established formal diplomatic ties with Egypt. Moreover, for the first time, Israel was not identified as the major threat to the Arab Nation. Iran bore this mantle until Saddam Hussein transferred it to Iraq with his 1990 invasion of Kuwait.

The 1987 summit meeting publicly confirmed the process that had been evolving for the previous two years. During this time, many Arab states had been looking to Egypt for increased leadership and support. Two, Saudi Arabia and Kuwait, had already resumed provision of substantial financial support to Egypt, albeit ad hoc and very closely held. By 1989, Syria and Libya reduced tensions with Egypt and moved toward restoration of diplomatic relations. On December 27, 1989, Syria and Egypt resumed full diplomatic ties. Libya and Egypt completed the end of Egypt's exile from the Arab community when they restored diplomatic relations in 1990. More important, Egypt had begun taking active leadership of moderate Arab countries in an effort to form a consensus supportive of conciliatory policies by the Palestine Liberation Organization.[49]

Throughout these changing relationships, Egypt maintained its commitment to the peace process, despite provocations by Israel in its invasion of Lebanon and later bombing raids in southern Lebanon, and attempts by other Arabs to intimidate the Egyptian leadership. In early 1990, President Mubarak also tried to help relieve tensions between the United States and Libya.[50] Finally, in April 1990, Egypt began pushing for a halt to the Middle East arms race, citing the peace process with Israel and the Palestinians as "the master key" to this end.[51]

Clearly, the $17 billion in ESF support from 1974 to 1991 enabled Egypt to weather the political and economic sanctions imposed by its Arab neighbors. As the peace with Israel strengthened and Egypt began to regain its political and military strength, this display of courage began to benefit Egypt and the United States.

However, although the 1990–1991 Gulf crisis created an opportunity for Egypt to exercise leadership in forming the coalition of Arab states opposed to Saddam, the crisis and its aftermath revealed fundamental continuing constraints on Egypt's leadership capacity. The U.S.-Egyptian aid relationship, along with additional billions in revenues from oil exports, workers' remittances, tourism, Suez Canal revenues, and aid from other donors, had created neither a viable Egyptian economy less dependent on external largesse nor a viable, independent military force to enhance Egypt's political credibility as an ally for other Arab states in time of crisis.[52]

This latter point is important. One wonders, for example, what might *not* have happened on August 2, 1990, had Egypt been able to secretly warn Saddam Hussein that Egypt would come immediately to the aid of Kuwait—and, to emphasize the point, had deployed, under the guise of "military exercises," even one battalion of Egyptian troops to Kuwait in July 1990. It was precisely such a role that the Egyptian armed forces had begun to see as their primary purpose "in a period of peace with Israel." Writing in May 1988, Dunn noted that the armed forces "see their role to some extent to give Egypt the muscle required to exercise its strength in Arab councils, and also to deter any potential threat from its neighbors. . . . More controversial is the growing tendency in the Gulf to see Egypt as a potential savior. Egyptian advisers have been sent to Iraq, Oman, and probably Kuwait, but . . . combat troops are not likely to be dispatched to the Gulf except in the most extreme circumstances."[53] Dunn believed that Egypt was a potential "rapid deployment" contributor should the situation in the Arabian peninsula deteriorate. "Certainly Egypt would not permit—could not permit—a major conventional military threat to Saudi Arabia to go unchallenged."[54]

Despite this perception, when Iraq invaded Kuwait and threatened Saudi Arabia, Egypt's military forces clearly had no deterrent effect on Saddam. It became painfully obvious during the mobilization of coalition forces in Saudi Arabia that Egypt could not deploy and support its own forces. One month after the Iraqi invasion, only 2,000 Egyptian troops had arrived in Saudi Arabia—and these came with only their uniforms and weapons, but no transport. The *New York Times* quoted a U.S. official as saying, "[The Saudis] had to buy thousands of trucks to transport the Egyptians and other troops . . . [and the payments for the visiting soldiers were] on the order of billions."[55] Finally, U.S. Pentagon officials also acknowledged that, while they hoped Egypt would send two divisions including tanks, they did not want to divert any of the limited U.S. air- and sealift space then available to transport Egyptian forces. These same officials also had questions regarding the capacity of the Egyptians "to support such a large force in the field."[56]

Barely two months after the U.S.-led military defeat of Saddam's forces in Kuwait, another indication of continuing weaknesses in Egypt's leadership capacity in the Gulf was President Mubarak's announcement that Egypt would withdraw all of its nearly 40,000 troops from Saudi Arabia and Kuwait. This action revealed the depth of continuing rivalry among the Arab states and the realization that Egypt remains an economically weak state unable to project its military power without reliance on U.S.—and Saudi—logistic support.

Some analysts believe the Gulf states now prefer to rely on the militarily dominant United States, which proved its readiness to guarantee their security, "rather than weaker and less reliable Arab nations."[57] Moreover, Kuwait and Saudi Arabia probably resent the prospect of providing large cash grants to Egypt and Syria to support their troops, especially since these forces obviously could not provide an effective shield without U.S. naval and air support. One Gulf diplomat asked, "When you have a visible security link to the United States, who's going to attack you if they know the United States will come and protect you?" He added that the Saudis and Kuwaitis do not want massive Syrian or Egyptian forces on their soil.[58]

On the larger Middle East diplomatic front, Egypt's leadership also appeared to be less dynamic than it is often made out to be. In the aftermath of the 1990–1991 Gulf War, Egypt did not take an active leadership role in rallying other Arab states to support U.S. Secretary of State Baker's diplomatic effort between March and May 1991 to convene a Middle East peace conference. Indeed, the only real commitment to Secretary Baker was

Egyptian Foreign Minister Esmat Abdel Meguid's statement on April 10, 1991, that Egypt was "open to discuss any way to find a peaceful solution." This statement left questions about whether Egypt's intentions were, like Israel's, "to agree in principle to the idea of some kind of conference in order not to be blamed for the breakdown in the American-sponsored peace diplomacy while holding out all sorts of conditions and reservations that are being discussed privately."[59] Egypt become increasingly conscious of its responsibilities for negotiating on behalf of the Arab world, especially to the Gulf Arabs who have reportedly pledged considerable assistance to the Egyptian Central Bank: Saudi Arabia, $1.5 billion; the United Arab Emirates, $600 million; and the Gulf Cooperation Council, which is made up of the Saudis and smaller Gulf states, $1–2 billion.[60]

Progress in Egypt's reintegration with the Arab world bore the seeds of an ironic twist by enabling Arab donors to reenter aid relationships with Egypt, thereby enabling Egypt to delay or alter the scope of necessary economic reforms. Such delays could impede the economic policy dialogue process with the United States, the IMF, and the Paris Club and could undercut progress toward a self-sustaining economy. Nevertheless, Waterbury has suggested that Egypt's Arab donors might prefer to keep Egypt on the dole. The smaller (based on population) Arab states, and especially Saudi Arabia, might fear a prosperous Egypt that could sustain its rate of growth without massive external support. "Saudi Arabia wants Egypt as a client not as an independent neighbor that could forgo its friendship. The trick is to put enough resources in the Egyptian economy to prevent a major collapse, but not so much as to turn the economy around."[61]

In 1989, Egyptian President Mubarak began to behave in ways that were consistent with Waterbury's thesis. He warned that changes in Europe would require closer economic cooperation among Arab countries because he expects Western economic aid to Egypt to decline.[62] Nevertheless, economic constraints may not inhibit Egypt from seeking an expanded regional role. Such a role actually could help alleviate economic pressures because it attracts Arab donor support. Thus, Egypt could have the best of both worlds because, according to Atherton, it could use an expansion of its regional role "to help ease the economic constraints it faces now and over the years ahead."[63]

Democracy in Egypt. Egypt's progress toward a democratic political system is another U.S. political objective and an important component of the peace process. If President Sadat's achievement was to end Egypt's war with Israel, President Mubarak's could be stimulation of a process toward meaningful political freedom for the Egyptian people. Democracy in Egypt would increase the prospects for stable peace with Israel. History demonstrates that viable democracies do not initiate military aggression against neighboring democratic states.

Egypt has the freest press in the Arab world. It has an elected, legal opposition. Both of these things have generally been unheard of in the

Arab world. At the same time, however, Mubarak has also kept tight rein on the opposition, particularly Islamic Fundamentalists. Morover, the security forces continue to practice intimidation, detention, and sometimes torture.[64]

In the spring of 1987, President Mubarak called for new parliamentary elections after the Egyptian supreme court in late 1986 declared Egypt's election law unconstitutional. By his action, Mubarak enhanced the integrity and power of both the supreme court and the parliament. Nevertheless, in 1990, the supreme court again declared the election law unconstitutional. The court ruled that the 458-seat parliament, elected in 1987, was invalid because by limiting the number of independent candidates to forty-eight, the new electoral laws favored candidates on party lists. Remarkably, President Mubarak, acting at the height of the Gulf crisis, called for a referendum in October 1990 on the court's ruling that parliament be dissolved to make way for new elections. Diplomats said this action reflected Mubarak's belief that his performance during the Gulf crisis had created the necessary popular support to enhance the legitimacy of his National Democratic Party (NDP)–led government.[65] The general elections took place on December 1, 1990. Though the NDP maintained an unassailable hold on the parliament, many opposition candidates boycotted the elections or ran as independents, and the voter turnout may not have been as heavy as the government claimed.[66]

These constitutional challenges and changes have been consistent with the evolution of a democratic political process. Many U.S. policymakers and Egyptian development experts believe that, for Egypt, economic reform and developing democracy reinforce each other. Nevertheless, other observers question whether this process will succeed or is even appropriate for Egypt. Ann M. Lesch, a political scientist at Villanova University, notes that Egypt's political and economic elite are found primarily in the NDP and among entrepreneurs who have benefited from Egypt's limited economic "open door" policy begun under President Sadat. Lesch notes that while the NDP elite benefits from the party's monopoly of postions in the local councils and Consultative Council (*Majlis al-Shura*) and its predominate People's Assembly, that power base would crumble in a genuine democracy. "Thus the political and economic elite have an incentive to keep Mubarak in power so long as he fulfills their economic priorities and guarantees their perks."[67]

Many other writers have portrayed Egypt as a "pitiful, helpless giant" unable to take tough decisions, to administer its affairs, or to function coherently. They see Mubarak as diminished in power and legitimacy and "struggling to accommodate various demanding actors: external (the United States, the IMF), societal (classes, strata, associations), and state (the military, the central security forces, competing ministries, public companies)."[68] Michael C. Hudson of Georgetown University nevertheless believes that democracy does have a chance in Egypt. He notes that while Egypt's current experiment in pluralism clearly antedated the outbreak of reform toward democracy in Eastern Europe, "it seems plausible that outbreaks of democracy elsewhere can only have a positive reinforcing effect on Egypt's home-grown tendencies in that direction."[69]

A strong, democratic political process can directly stimulate relevant and realistic reform of the social-economic environment. To the degree that it continues and strengthens Mubarak's own legitimacy with his people, the democratic political process further strengthens Egypt's international position. The U.S. economic aid program has supported this democratization process, but only on the margins. Beyond transferring technologies, technical advice, and training, aid projects also promote ideas, including democratic principles and processes. Every Egyptian who comes to the United States as a participant trainee under an A.I.D. project becomes a witness to democratic processes and to their economic and social benefits. Some U.S.-Egyptian local development projects aimed at increasing local participation in the planning and allocation of financial resources according to locally determined priorities implicitly support a growing constituency for democracy in Egypt.

Attainment of Development Objectives

The FY 1990 Congressional Presentation asserted that Egypt's leadership in the peace process would become unsustainable unless Egyptians experienced economic and social benefits from the process and from the U.S. aid relationship.[70] Assessments of the development impact of U.S. aid reveal mixed results at best, depending on the measurement criteria. In January 1989, Washington State University Professor Roy Prosterman suggested that A.I.D.'s Egypt program should be a model for U.S. foreign aid. Prosterman contended that the Egypt program was a major demonstration "of what can be accomplished when enough foreign aid is spent on the right projects in one country."[71] The A.I.D. program has benefited millions of Egyptians in terms of basic health conditions, basic education, some higher education and research, and power and water/wastewater projects. Prosterman commended A.I.D. for steadily increasing funds on such basic human needs–related projects, touted its alleged success in promoting grassroots development, and called for more such large-scale development spending in other selected countries.

However, an Egyptian, Essam Rifaat, editor in chief of a government-owned financial weekly, *Al Ahram Al Iktisadi*, argues that most of the aid "goes right back to America. Sometimes it goes into the salaries of experts and into studies." He also notes the high cost of U.S. goods that must be shipped on U.S. bottoms. He criticizes the U.S. and Egyptian bureaucracies and, finally, notes that in some cases U.S. technology is not appropriate for Egypt.[72] Ahmed Abdul Salaama Zaki, who during the 1980s headed the Egyptian Office of Cooperation with the United States, A.I.D.'s counterpart agency in Egypt, echoed some of these charges: "Sometimes imports come with very high fees. Sometimes overhead [for contractors and consultants] is 100 percent of basic salary. We have to pay for their wife and dependents, a big flat and insurance."[73]

Handoussa criticized the amount of aid spent to rehabilitate basic infrastructure. Although investments such as doubling the number of telephone lines ($247 million), increasing rural electrification (from 19 percent of households in 1975 to 79 percent in 1985), or spending $764 million on the Cairo and Alexandria sewage systems were necessary, they also had "very high opportunity costs in forgoing industrial and agricultural expansion."[74] She blamed the anti–public sector bias of the Reagan administration for the redirection of U.S. aid away from the industrial sector. Other donors, such as the World Bank, were also reluctant to promote public sector efficiency. She believed such "condemnation of public enterprise has been a major contributor to unbalanced development, since ultimately neither public nor private enterprise was able to take up the challenge of self-sustaining growth."[75]

On balance, Prosterman's conclusions seem premature at best. They do not address the strains that U.S. aid has placed on the government's ability to create the new institutions and personnel infrastructure necessary to sustain and extend the aid programs. Like many others, Prosterman does not acknowledge that the Egyptians' expectations will remain unfulfilled if the aid declines and the Egyptian government cannot sustain the aid-initiated projects. Moreover, building elementary schools is easier than finding and retaining teachers who can provide relevant education. Nor does he consider that, despite years of family planning measures, Egypt's population growth rate has not begun a meaningful decline from the 2.8–3.0 percent level of the 1980s. Indeed, religion- and culture-based resistance has impeded implementation of a broad-based family planning program. All those lives that were saved through inoculations and oral rehydration therapy (ORT), which treats intestinal disorders in children, have only compounded the demands on the Egyptian socioeconomic system's capacity to provide relevant education, housing, and employment.

Even given these weaknesses, A.I.D. and the State Department can (and do) argue that A.I.D.'s previous efforts were neither ill-advised nor inappropriate. Much of the modernized infrastructure is necessary to stimulate the productive economy that Egypt so badly needs. The benefits of Egypt's oil boom and workers' remittances in the late 1970s and early 1980s and the massive external assistance resources, first from Arab states and then the United States, helped create economic growth even as they obscured the underlying weaknesses inherent in Egypt's statist economy.

The important issue today is that the country's precarious economic condition, including a permanent balance of payments crisis and a stifling, status quo government bureaucracy, undercut Egypt's capacity to maintain the new infrastructure and sustain the potential benefits of health, education, and agriculture programs developed with previous aid, and the technologies transferred with them. Currently, there is little evidence that the Egyptian government is able to sustain many of the aid-funded, large-scale infrastructure projects without some form of continuing U.S. operations and maintenance support.

The development process requires far more than foreign resources. In this sense, the U.S. economic aid program in Egypt cannot serve as a developmental model, except perhaps as for what not to do. Development occurs only when a country's sociopolitical-economic process and its institutions are able to grow continuously and meet the increased burdens created by, for example, all those infants who did not die because the health project aid was so successful. According to this criterion, Egypt has not established a self-sustaining development process even though it has enjoyed some modernization impact from the most massive infusion of economic assistance into one country in the history of foreign assistance, Israel excepted.

In many respects, Egypt before the Gulf crisis of 1990–1991 was worse off fiscally and monetarily than before the U.S. aid program began. When Iraq invaded Kuwait, Egypt was practically begging the international community for more resources to help pay the enormous $50+ billion debt it accumulated in the fifteen-year period during which the United States poured in over $16 billion in economic support assistance alone. The United States did not condition its aid programs in ways that would have required policies to promote cost recovery, institutional development, and fundamental economic reform. Had the United States maintained sound conditions, Egypt might not have amassed such a debt or found itself unable to sustain its development. Instead, the United States deferred too readily to the GOE's judgment on what types of reforms were politically feasible. "Politically feasible" in this case, as Lesch noted, meant doing nothing that would change the economic and political power base of the National Democratic Party and its supporters in Egypt's "corporate" state.[76] While questions of sovereignty and respect for the Egyptian government's ultimate responsibility do count, the United States must bear some responsibility—its political objectives notwithstanding—for poorly designed projects and for not demanding more in return for its aid.

CONCLUSION

Clearly, the $17 billion U.S. Economic Support Fund aid to Egypt has well served U.S. political objectives in the Middle East. It has helped strengthen the peace with Israel, though there was little probability that Egypt or Israel would have renewed hostilities again after the 1973 war. The aid helped create the opportunity for Egypt to play a leading role in the Arab world as the other Arab states began to recognize Egypt's vital importance to stability for all Arab states. U.S. aid has also helped, at least on the margins, to support democracy and has benefited U.S. trade interests with Egypt. With declining direct U.S. involvement, the long-term sustainability of these achievements still depends on the near-term contribution economic aid makes toward economic development objectives.

Unfortunately, Egypt has not effectively used U.S. economic aid resources to develop and expand its own human, natural, and financial resources and then to apply these resources for self-sustaining development. Instead, between 1976 and 1989, Egypt's economic conditions, disguised by oil revenue windfalls, weakened progressively despite U.S. aid. Today, Egypt's economy is stagnant and the country cannot carry its debt burden without considerable external assistance via direct cash transfers.

Since the mid-1980s, the United States, the IMF, the World Bank, and other major donors have steadily increased their pressure to stimulate economic and social reform in Egypt. Similar efforts in the 1960s and 1970s had virtually no lasting impact. The GOE continued to resist new efforts in 1989 and 1990, arguing that political instability would rise if the recommended reforms were carried out too swiftly. Until mid-1985, when some conditions accompanied the supplemental cash transfer for FYs 1985 and 1986, there had been no premium on performance toward specific economic and social goals. Indeed, the GOE had not fulfilled even its implementation responsibilities toward attaining the many different project-specific purposes and goals.

This lack of development has not occurred for lack of resources, whether domestically or externally derived. Moreover, the failure of the U.S.-Egyptian aid relationship to stimulate sustainable development raises questions about the reliability of the United States as a partner in efforts to obtain and sustain economic and political independence and security. Handoussa is correct in her observation that the United States must bear some responsibility for the success or failure of the aid program.

In this regard, it is especially regrettable that the U.S.-Egyptian aid relationship has not enabled the people of Egypt to experience measurable, sustained progress in the areas that most affect their daily lives. Certain types of democratization programs, for example, could have helped address the causes of social conflict within Egypt and enhanced the legitimacy of the Mubarak government with the people. The lack of such progress has allowed sociopolitical conditions to decline in ways that have encouraged the emergence and enhanced appeal of the Islamic Fundamentalists, as evidenced by their direct terrorist attacks on tourists in October and November of 1992 and their public criticisms of the U.S. aid relationship.[77]

In the aftermath of the Gulf War and with the new IMF Standby Agreement, Egypt has a new opportunity to develop its economic and political power, to become a meaningful political leader in the Middle East, and to move toward a new vision for itself. The new IMF agreement may be supported by the Gulf states with their own requirement that Egypt adhere to the reform package as a condition for receipt of the additional billions of dollars previously promised by these states. If such conditions exist, will they be applied by the United States and the Gulf states? Or, will the new resources, new donors, and Egypt's geostrategic value once again relieve the pressure on Mubarak and enable him to postpone or weaken the reforms so clearly laid out on paper?

Whatever the outcome of the Middle East peace process, the U.S. aid relationship with Egypt demonstrates the incompatibility between the development objectives of economic aid and the political objectives for which it is used. In Egypt, diplomacy that used economic aid to advance U.S. strategic interests has impeded use of those resources to stimulate self-sustaining development. Inadequately designed aid projects and acquiescence in Egypt's failure to take the tough steps that were necessary have contributed to its economic crisis. The overriding U.S. political purposes, including those of U.S. domestic special interests, have enabled Egypt to use the aid as a crutch from crisis to crisis.

In the end, the United States weakened its capacity to maintain its political objectives *without* continued, massive infusions of aid. Despite this negative, there remains a potential positive—that the profound changes in the region's political relations and power balances may provide new windows of opportunity for economic and political reform, thus stimulating development and enabling Arab states to do more with their foreign assistance or oil revenues than simply modernize their basic infrastructure.[78]

NOTES

1. Heba Handoussa, "U.S. Aid to Egypt: A Critical Review," in *The Political Economy of Contemporary Egypt*, ed. Ibrahim M. Oweiss (Washington, D.C.: Center for Contemporary Arab Studies, Georgetown University, 1990) p. 110. Handoussa draws on David A. Baldwin, *Economic Statecraft* (Princeton: Princeton University Press, 1985).

2. Ibid.

3. Congressman Hamilton expressed this concern during preliminary hearings on the aid program to Egypt. The primary witnesses were Richard Murphy, assistant secretary of state, and William Fuller, A.I.D. deputy assistant administrator for the Asia–Near East Bureau. Source: personal notes from hearing.

4. Paul Jabbar, "Egypt's Crisis, America's Dilemma," *Foreign Affairs* (Summer 1986), p. 965.

5. Alfred L. Atherton, Jr., "The Impact of Economic Constraints on Egypt's Regional Role" (Paper prepared for a joint Middle East Institute/National Defense University workshop, "U.S.-Egyptian Security Relations in an Era of Economic Constraints," May 17, 1988), p. 2.

6. John Waterbury, *The Egypt of Nasser and Sadat: The Political Economy of Two Regimes* (Princeton: Princeton University Press, 1983), p. 401.

7. A.I.D., *FY 1981 CP: Security Assistance Programs* (February 1980), p. 108.

8. Jabbar, "Egypt's Crisis," p. 962.

9. A.I.D., *FY 1976 CP: Middle East Peace and Security Supporting Assistance* (February 1975), p. 7.

10. A.I.D., *FY 1977 CP: Security Supporting Assistance Program and Middle East Requirements Fund* (February 1976), p. 13.

11. The Brooke amendment to the Foreign Assistance Act requires the cutoff of all U.S. aid to any country one year in arrears on interest payments due on U.S. loans.

12. The Paris Club is made up of the lenders (United States, Canada, Western European countries, and Japan) and Egyptian officials.

13. A.I.D., *FY 1990 CP*, Annex II: Asia and the Near East, p. 81.

14. This figure includes a special $500 million supplement for FY 1985 and FY 1986.

15. It is important to remember that President Sadat had changed Egypt's political orientation and then sought U.S. support to replace the loss of other Arab and Soviet assistance.

16. GAO, *The U.S. Economic Assistance Program for Egypt Poses a Management Challenge for A.I.D.* (Report to the Administrator, Agency for International Development, GAO/NSIAD-85-109, July 31, 1985), p. 8.

17. Edward Peck, retired foreign service officer who served as economic counselor at the U.S. embassy during this period. Conversation with author, May 1989.

18. GAO, *Egypt's Capacity to Absorb and Use Economic Assistance Effectively* (ID-77-33, September 15, 1977), p. 1.

19. Timothy M. Phelps, "An Aid Program Gone Awry," *Newsday*, May 26, 1987. This article created serious concern within A.I.D. Julia Chang Bloch, then assistant administrator of the Near East Bureau, ordered a review of the article for misstatements and preparation of a response letter to the editor. Notes on the margin of the report show that A.I.D.'s mission director in Egypt, Marshall "Buster" Brown, and the assistant administrator for external affairs, Thomas Blank, decided on July 16, 1987, to "leave this alone unless we get heat. We should not focus attention." It was agreed that the article contained a lot of truth, but much of it was old. Unfortunately, the quotes of previous A.I.D. and State officers made the article problematic. Any response would have had to acknowledge major problems; note the highly politicized environment; point out that it was too early to label the program a failure since few projects were complete; provide examples of successes (there were few); note that we had learned much from past weaknesses; and suggest that the aid relationship should also be judged on its political successes.

20. GAO, *Egypt's Capacity*.

21. Waterbury, *The Egypt of Nasser and Sadat*, p. 403.

22. A description provided by a ranking A.I.D. official who chose to remain anonymous.

23. Phelps, "An Aid Program Gone Awry."

24. Interview with a World Bank economist on condition of anonymity, August 1990.

25. Phelps, "An Aid Program Gone Awry."

26. GAO, *Management Challenge for A.I.D.*, p. 9.

27. Ibid.

28. Ibid., p. 11.

29. Marvin G. Weinbaum, "Dependent Development and U.S. Economic

Aid to Egypt," *International Journal of Middle East Studies* 18 (1986), p. 119.

30. Denis J. Sullivan, "Bureaucracy and Foreign Aid in Egypt," in Oweiss, ed., *The Political Economy of Contemporary Egypt*, p. 152.

31. Zimmerman, personal notes on conversation with the project officer and on the evaluation review held in the fall of 1984. Names of participants are withheld at their request.

32. This is the official reason for the policy reversal. However, A.I.D. could have reobligated funds to other projects had this not required congressional notification, with the probability that the senator involved would have put a hold on the funds.

33. Zimmerman, notes made while serving as desk officer for Egypt.

34. Weinbaum, "Dependent Development," p. 119.

35. Ibid., pp. 122–123.

36. Robert F. Zimmerman et al., "P.L. 480 Title I," *Woods's Briefing Book* (unclassified), June 16, 1987, item #10.

37. Weinbaum, "Dependent Development," p. 126.

38. See also Eric Pianin, "'Academic Pork' Fills Favored School Larders," *Washington Post*, September 23, 1992. This article briefly but accurately summarizes the nature of the problems university special interests create when they succeed in getting Congress to earmark funds for "politically influential universities." Massachusetts is one of the five most favored states. In the Egypt case, the Massachusetts Institute of Technology may not have had a special earmark from Congress for its project, but the effect is the same when A.I.D. officials won't challenge poor performance on a contract for fear of inspiring the university to use its political influence to retain the contract.

39. A.I.D., *U.S. Overseas Loans and Grants*, p. 13.

40. GAO, *Management Challenge for A.I.D.*, p. 10.

41. Atherton, *Impact of Economic Constraints*, p. 2.

42. John Kifner, "Arabs Vote to Send Troops to Help Saudis; Baghdad Isolated," *New York Times*, August 10, 1990.

43. John Kifner, "Badly Divided Arab League Votes to Return Headquarters to Cairo," *New York Times*, September 11, 1990.

44. Thomas L. Friedman, "Additional Troops Promised by Egypt," *New York Times*, September 9, 1990.

45. Thomas L. Friedman, "Baker Foresees a Long Stay for U.S. Troops in Mideast; Urges a Regional Alliance," *New York Times*, September 5, 1990.

46. Edward Cody, "Anger at Saddam, Financial Need Seen Motivating Mubarak," *Washington Post*, November 6, 1990.

47. John Kifner, "Gulf Price Tag for Egypt: $2 Billion Loss to Economy," *New York Times*, September 4, 1990.

48. A.I.D., *FY 1976 CP*, p. 7.

49. Alan Cowell, "Egypt and Syria Reopen Air Links," *New York Times*, December 12, 1989.

50. Caryle Murphy, "Mubarak Lends Bush, Gadhafi a Hand," *Washington Post*, March 27, 1990.

51. Caryle Murphy, "Egypt's Foreign Minister Urges Mideast Arms Ban," *Washington Post*, April 19, 1990.

52. Between 1981 and 1986, oil revenues totaled $13.9 billion; workers' remittances, $17.7 billion; tourism, $4.8 billion; Suez Canal, $4.6 billion. (Source: Sullivan, "Bureaucracy and Foreign Aid in Egypt", p. 129.) These resources enabled the GOE to increase subsidies covering bread and other food

items, fuel, electricity, and higher education for virtually the entire population. There is no way to calculate how much may also have been lost through corruption.

53. Michael Collins Dunn, "The Impact of Economic Constraints on Egypt's Military Posture" (Paper prepared for a joint Middle East Institute/ Institute for National Strategic Studies workshop on "U.S.-Egyptian Security Relations in an Era of Economic Constraints," May 17, 1988), p. 10.

54. Ibid.

55. Thomas L. Friedman, "Additional Troops Promised by Egypt," *New York Times*, September 9, 1990. David B. Ottaway, in another article, "Much of the Arab Force Still Far from the Front" (*Washington Post*, September 5, 1990), also reported that the slow pace of mobilization for the "Arab-Islamic forces" was partly due to "the fact that Saudi Arabia has had to arrange all the logistical support for them, coordinating everything from trucks and jeeps to food and other supplies."

56. Michael R. Gordon, "Combined Force in Saudi Arabia Is Light on Arabs," *New York Times*, September 5, 1990.

57. Caryle Murphy, "Egypt's Pullout Signals Discord with the Gulf," *Washington Post*, May 11, 1991.

58. Ibid.

59. Thomas L. Friedman, "Cairo Open to Baker's Meeting Proposal," *New York Times*, April 11, 1991.

60. Judith Miller, "Gulf Crisis Produces Surge of Egyptian Confidence," *New York Times*, November 11, 1990.

61. Waterbury, *The Egypt of Nasser and Sadat*, p. 421.

62. Caryle Murphy, "Egypt, Syria Resume Full Diplomatic Ties," *Washington Post*, December, 28, 1989.

63. Atherton, *Impact of Economic Constraints*, pp. 7–8.

64. Michael C. Hudson, "The Democratization Process in the Arab World: An Assessment" (Paper prepared for the 1990 Annual Meeting of the American Political Science Association, San Francisco, August 30–September 2, 1990), pp. 7–8.

65. "A Confident Mubarak Schedules Referendum," *New York Times*, September, 27, 1990.

66. Alan Cowell, "Mubarak's Party Far Ahead in Egyptian Legislative Vote," *New York Times*, December 3, 1991. Though the State Department's Egypt desk and the U.S. embassy in Cairo as late as May 17, 1992, had been unable to determine how the final returns affected the balance between opposition and government MPs, the parliament was meeting regularly and the government held a commanding majority.

67. Ann M. Lesch, "Egyptian Politics in the 1990s" (Paper for the Workshop on U.S.-Egyptian Security Relations in an Era of Economic Constraints, hosted by the Middle East Institute and the Institute for National Strategic Studies, May 17, 1988), p. 9.

68. Hudson, "Democratization Process," p. 8.

69. Ibid, p. 12.

70. A.I.D., *FY 1990 CP*, Annex II: Asia and the Near East, p. 29.

71. Roy Prosterman, "Egypt a Model for U.S. Aid to Other Lands," *Wall Street Journal*, January 6, 1989.

72. Phelps, "An Aid Program Gone Awry."

73. Ibid. Though these views are sometimes exaggerated, they explain why many Egyptian officials will try to shave these expenses by applying Egyptian

taxes or other fees to U.S. consultants or their companies who work on A.I.D.-sponsored projects. The consequent contracting disputes delay projects and create serious resentment all around.

74. Handoussa, "U.S. Aid to Egypt," p. 117. The Government of Egypt placed high priority on the sewage systems because the rising anger of the population affected by the flooding in Cairo's streets threatened political stability. In the industrial sector, a major obstacle was the notorious inefficiency of the state-run enterprises. Nevertheless, in the 1970s, the CIP program funded hundreds of millions of dollars ($504 million between 1974 and 1978, according to Handoussa) in raw materials and other supplies for these enterprises—with no impact on the low productivity and mismanagement that characterize this sector.

75. Ibid., p. 118.

76. According to Cantori, "Corporatism, not democratization or pluralism, is the operative form of political organization for Egypt. . . . [Many writers] depict the authoritarian regime incorporating the key functional socioeconomic organizations into a harmonious (and subordinate) relationship with the state. . . . The corporatist state enlists the core associations of society in a system that substitutes opposition in the liberal-pluralist sense with a system of state-led collusion with organizations that control social sectors such as labor, the professions, commerce, industry, and the academy." Quoted in Hudson, "Democratization Process," p. 8.

77. Chris Hedges, "As Islamic Militants Thunder, Egypt Grows More Nervous," *New York Times*, November 12, 1992.

78. The U.S. approach that maintained a balance between the Egypt and Israel programs had a precedent. During the 1970s, after Bangladesh became an independent state, the United States tried to allocate DA resources at balanced levels among Pakistan, India, and Bangladesh. These balances were only partially successful in helping the United States to retain some access and influence with these governments on diplomatic issues important to the United States. Ironically, two decades later, it seems clear that the previous aid has had little impact in terms of helping to eliminate the causes of conflict either within or between these three states—especially between India and Pakistan.

6

To What End? A Tour of Some ESF Countries in Asia, Africa, and Latin America

Chapter 5 reviewed the use of Economic Support Fund aid to attain major U.S. political objectives in Egypt and elsewhere in the Middle East. It generally illustrated the explanation in Chapter 4 of how political objectives and other U.S. special interests tend to affect the process for providing and implementing economic aid programs. This chapter extends the U.S. experience in Egypt through additional brief, country-specific reviews of the consequences of diplomacy that employed ESF aid to advance U.S. political objectives. The major focus will be the apparent impact of the ESF program on achieving the political and development objectives set forth in aid documents. Much of the discussion in Chapter 4 on the CDSS, CP, and program planning documentation and implementation process applies to one degree or another in each country.

As noted earlier, the U.S. government provides ESF to those countries in which the United States has the highest political and security interest. Perhaps the most successful uses of ESF aid as a political tool have occurred where U.S. diplomats could employ aid programs to encourage and sustain close political cooperation with political leaders in countries where ready U.S. access to military bases and communications facilities was necessary to contain the expansion of Soviet bloc efforts to extend political and military power into Africa, Latin America, and Asia.

U.S. aid to Pakistan in return for cooperation against the Soviets in Afghanistan, aid to Honduras in return for helping the contras resist the Sandinistas in Nicaragua and El Salvador, aid to Zaire and Liberia for their cooperation with U.S. efforts to monitor and resist Soviet/Cuban political and military activity in Africa, and aid to Egypt and Israel in support of the peace process in the Middle East are all examples of successful, aid-supported, short-to-medium-term U.S. diplomacy. The United States has also used aid to secure the political support of other countries for advancing U.S. objectives through international forums such as the United Nations; some-

---

The reader should note that unless otherwise specified, "economic assistance" in this and the remaining chapters refers to ESF program aid, often supplemented by PL 480 Food for Peace aid.

times aid has been cut when a recipient has actively opposed the United States in the United Nations.

All of these relationships have been essentially quid pro quo arrangements with existing governments and political leaders in recipient countries, though the aid documentation involved does not explicitly so state. Instead, the CDSS and CP language explains how the aid will support a series of development projects that will promote political stability in the recipient country. This stability, in turn, will enable the United States to pursue other U.S. political objectives with the recipient government's cooperation. The logic in these linkages appears essentially unassailable. The problem, however, is that in most cases the stability actually promoted is between the United States and recipient governments—usually specific political leaders—rather than between the recipient government and its people on the basis of increased legitimacy derived from development that benefits the whole society.

In certain countries, such as Oman or Kenya, ESF aid has facilitated U.S. access to sites for communication and intelligence purposes or ensured landing rights at airfields and seaports. The aid helps ease resistance to unpopular military bases or intelligence-gathering and -sharing agreements. Because the economic benefits to the general population from these agreements may not be significant, the aid levels help make the relationship politically palatable. In other cases, as in southern European NATO countries, the Mediterranean, and the Philippines where the United States has provided aid programs as a quid pro quo, U.S. bases also protected these countries or served their self-interest in other ways, including job creation and tourism.

In the base-related cases, ESF assistance has clearly succeeded in its quid pro quo function throughout the Cold War era, when U.S.-Soviet competition was often the determinant variable in decisions on how much aid to provide. Even though the aid program documentation does not describe the aid as rent money, that is essentially what it is, and media coverage of lease negotiations for the bases describes it as such.

Most of these apparent successes, however, are now proving to have been temporary, and successful primarily in terms of their Cold War function. The end of the Cold War makes it possible to examine the probability that aid relationships based on narrowly defined political-security terms frequently bear the seeds of future adverse political consequences—not only for the United States but even more for the recipients of the past largesse.

THE PHILIPPINES

The U.S.-Philippine aid relationship has been "special" far longer than any other. U.S. economic aid to the Philippines from 1946 through 1990 totaled

$4.1 billion, with $3.3 billion of this provided between 1962 and 1989, including $2.5 billion in grant aid. Direct, security-related economic aid was $1.427 billion of the total. Another $2 billion was provided in military aid from 1946 through 1990.[1]

Advancing U.S. Political Objectives

Through the mid-1980s the U.S.-Philippine aid relationship appeared to be one of the most successful. The outcome of the Vietnam War notwithstanding, Philippine bases and the political cooperation between the two governments through many administrations in both countries were vital elements in the successful resistance to Soviet and Chinese efforts to extend communism to Southeast Asia. Further testimony to the value of this relationship, even though the communist threat to the region had receded rapidly by the end of the 1980s, was the hope among virtually all of the other members of the Association of Southeast Asian Nations (ASEAN) that the United States and the Philippines would reach a new bases agreement. They believed a continued U.S. naval presence contributed to general political stability in the region and to their own dramatic economic and political progress.

Many Filipinos, however, viewed the bases quite differently. Moreover, it was the economic aid's quid pro quo linkage to the bases agreement that created much of the problem. The 1990–1991 U.S.-Philippine negotiations for extension of the agreements were especially rancorous. Many political leaders, led by a majority in the Philippine senate, in accordance with a provision in the Philippine constitution, demanded outright termination of the base leases when they expired in September 1991. The major issues were the level of compensation and an alleged U.S. failure to live up to previous commitments on assistance levels.

The bases agreement contained no explicit provision for base rental or other financial consideration. In a 1979 side letter, the U.S. president pledged his "best efforts" to provide specific levels of military and economic aid, rising from $20 million in 1979 to $50 million by 1984 and held at $95 million from 1985 through 1989.[2] For FY 1990, the United States was to provide $513 million in aid, of which $385 million was considered compensation for the bases. The Philippine government said this amount fell short of the level the United States promised at the base agreement review in 1988. At that time, President Reagan pledged that the U.S. executive branch would make its "best efforts" to provide $481 million per year in FYs 1990 and 1991. The State Department calculated the shortfall at $96 million.[3] The Philippine government put the shortfall at $225 million.

Unfortunately, rising Filipino nationalism and anti-American protests compounded the compensation issue. Anti-Americanism had become a serious problem during the early 1980s as Filipinos began to believe the bases agreements enabled the corrupt and increasingly dictatorial government of President Ferdinand Marcos to remain in power. Aside from the employment around the bases, most Filipinos appear to have experienced little measurable economic development benefits from the aid. Ironically, even though the United States played a major role in facilitating the transition from Marcos to the very popular Corazón Aquino in 1986, and then (using planes from the U.S. air bases) supported her when disgruntled military officers attempted a coup in 1990, these acts also convinced many Filipinos that the bases enabled the United States to infringe on Philippine sovereignty. The communists also took advantage of the anti-Americanism when they assassinated two U.S. servicemen on May 13, 1990, outside the major base at Clark Field.

These protests, the rancorous tone of the negotiating process, the diminished Soviet capacity to project forces into Southeast Asia, U.S. budget constraints, and increasing disappointment in the Aquino government's commitment to democratization encouraged many U.S. political leaders in the Congress and the administration to suggest that the United States do just what the vocal Filipino minority wanted: withdraw. The issue was resolved when a majority of Filipino senators reached agreement with President Aquino on a three-year withdrawal schedule that would have U.S. forces out by the end of 1994. U.S. officials had no plans to try to negotiate an alternative arrangement.[4] Moreover, after the forced abandonment of Clark Field following the eruption of Mt. Pinatubo in July–August 1991 and general dismay at the outcome of the bases negotiations, the United States accelerated its withdrawal plans, and completed withdrawal from the Subic Bay Naval Base on November 24, 1992.

A second objective of the four-decade aid relationship was to help the Philippine government defeat the communist insurgency that began in earnest after World War II. The United States remained committed to this objective and to the necessary aid during Marcos's presidency because of his "longstanding reputation as being pro-American and anti-communist."[5] The insurgency continued with varying intensity in different locales throughout the period. However, by 1990, though they could carry out assassinations at will, the communists no longer threatened the government.

U.S. economic aid did not play a major role in the Philippine government's effort to contain the insurgency and resolve its causes because the aid was not used effectively for development purposes. Indeed, as the Marcos government misused these resources, they probably served the political propaganda purposes of the communists. Ernest Preeg suggests that the nationalist sentiment against the bases added to their negative impact because radical leftists were able to portray all U.S. aid as base related. An alternative strategy to weaken support for the communists "would have been a more independent U.S.A.I.D. development program that brought more tangible benefits to the rural population. U.S.A.I.D. would likely have pursued such a strategy if its funding had not been linked to the bases agreement."[6]

Promotion of democracy has been a longtime interest of the United States in the Philippines—as the history of Philippine constitutions, political parties, and political institutions demonstrates—but the depth of commitment to this interest never equaled the commitment to retention of the bases or defeat of the communist insurgency. In fact, the higher-priority U.S. political objectives related to the military bases tended to deter all U.S. administrations from supporting democratization programs more actively because of fears about instability.

Advancing Development Objectives

The weakness of the Philippine economy and the political instability that followed the fall of the Marcos regime in 1986 suggest that the U.S.-Philippine aid relationship during the previous decade and a half of Marcos's rule had little positive benefit for sustainable development. Foreign investment had all but ceased in large part because of the notorious corruption of Marcos and his business cronies. The foreign debt burden had reached nearly $29 billion, and even in late 1989 total debt service for both foreign and domestic creditors was still 40 percent of the fiscal budget. Rural poverty remained pervasive and widespread, with over 60 percent of the population living below the poverty line.[7] Communist insurgency remained a problem in parts of the main island, Luzon, and in the Eastern Visayas on the island of Samar.

Preeg attributes the limited effectiveness of the U.S. aid program directly to the military base–economic aid linkage. The Marcos leadership group used the ESF-supported Rural Development Fund for their political patronage projects. A.I.D. should never have given this fund priority for U.S. resources. The highly visible patronage reflected negatively on the United States. "[Moreover,] U.S. policy-based budgetary support has been largely ineffective since the conditionality of the aid has little credibility in view of the non-economic objectives involved."[8]

The lost opportunities for advancing other political and economic development interests are more regrettable given the special historical relationship between the Filipino people and the United States since U.S. forces ended Spanish rule in 1898. Nevertheless, perhaps "better late than never" best described the opportunities that existed for the U.S.-Philippine relationship in 1991. The United States had facilitated the end of the Marcos regime and helped President Aquino remain in power, thereby creating an opportunity for the economy to regain growth momentum and for the redemocratization of the political process. A.I.D.'s FY 1990 Congressional Presentation contended that President Aquino's ascension to power in February 1986 and subsequent political and economic reforms had restored the confidence of domestic and foreign investors alike and turned around the economy. "After 11 consecutive quarters of contraction, gross national product grew by 6.4% in 1987 and by 6.8% in the first half of 1988. Inflation, once as high as 50%, registered 7.5% in 1987 and presently appears to be under 10%."[9]

The critical remaining question in 1992 was whether the United States would create a strong development-oriented relationship without a bases agreement to drive the aid level. Unfortunately, the answer was no. This missed opportunity reflects poorly on U.S. foreign policy, its aid programs, and the policymakers in the administration and the U.S. Congress who were responsible for the nature of the assistance relationship from 1947 to 1992.

Conclusion

In its relationship with the Philippines, the United States appears to have chosen not to actively and consistently pursue the development and democratization objectives of the aid program because U.S. policymakers feared such activity would create friction and lead to instability that could threaten the bases agreements. This sacrifice of historical, long-term U.S. political and development objectives to preserve the short-term strategic political objectives, which required access to the military bases, actually created much of the later resentment *and political instability* that undermined the U.S. capacity to protect its highest-priority strategic objective.

The most regrettable aspect of the anger and frustration in so many Filipino hearts today is that they actually believed the United States was committed to the high moral goals for democracy and development set forth by U.S. leaders and in aid program documents. The original 1947 Philippine constitution was almost a clone of the U.S. Constitution and was willingly adopted by the overwhelming majority of the Filipino people. Though there continues a strong fondness for the people of the United States throughout the Philippines, that fondness is today bittersweet. The visions Filipinos once shared with so many Americans for peace and prosperity within democracy for their country are further from fruition in 1993 than they appeared to be in 1947, even after four decades in a close assistance relationship that committed over $4 billion in economic aid toward those visions.

Herein lies a great irony of the rancorous end to the U.S.-Philippine political-security relationship. When that relationship began in 1898 after the United States drove the Spanish from the Philippines, the United States took political control because it was perceived to be in the U.S. national interest. Moreover, U.S. leaders defined that national interest more in terms of "manifest destiny"—to promote the American way of life, including democracy—than fear of a direct threat to U.S. security. Nearly one century later, the United States downgraded its special relationship with the Philippines at precisely the point when its capacity to promote the culmination of a return to democracy could not have been higher. Though a small aid program might be retained, it is highly unlikely that the commitment and imagination necessary to be *for* a new just cause—like democracy—in the Philippines will in no way equal the commitment made *against* international communism in the past.

ZAIRE

The United States maintained a close political and economic assistance relationship with the Government of Zaire (GOZ) for nearly three decades, from the early 1960s through the 1980s. Between 1962 and 1990, Zaire received over $1 billion in economic aid, including $289.9 million in Security Support Assistance/ESF and $413.9 million in PL 480 Food for Peace aid.[10] The FY 1984 Congressional Presentation said that U.S. aid would serve U.S. interests by (a) helping to maintain Zaire's stability, (b) helping to lay the groundwork for and assisting in development in key sectors, and (c) maintaining dialogue with the GOZ on policy and program direction. The aid program would "retain, strengthen or create essential human, institutional and physical development capacity [until] macroeconomic problems are alleviated and political/social constraints eased; and, in the meantime, achieve a measure of increased well-being as a result of the practical application of our manpower and institutional development activities, which in turn promotes stability."[11]

Advancing U.S. Political Objectives

The FY 1988 CP reiterated the link between Zaire's economic viability and U.S. interests: "The success of the Government's effort to create a stable economic environment conducive to growth and development is of critical importance to the political stability of Central Africa and to Western interests in the region."[12] Those interests were defined by the Cold War and the U.S. effort to contain Soviet influence in the region.

The U.S. military used the Kamina air base in the southern province of Shaba for joint exercises with U.S. Special Forces and Zairian troops for most of the 1980s and on three other crisis occasions, once in 1964 and twice in the 1970s. The U.S. Central Intelligence Agency also used the base to channel military aid to Jonas Savimbi's forces, who were fighting the Cuban/Soviet-supported Marxist government in Angola. As late as 1987, the Defense Department was reportedly trying to encourage President Reagan to reach a formal agreement with Zaire so that the Kamina base could be rehabilitated and become a permanent U.S. access point for southern and central Africa.[13] Finally, Zaire also usually sided with the United States during confrontations with Soviet-allied countries in the United Nations.

Throughout the 1970s and 1980s, Zaire's President Mobutu Sese Seko maintained his authoritarian rule in part by telling his people that his leadership was vital to the Western efforts to contain Soviet influence in Africa.

He used the aid relationship as evidence of U.S. confidence in him and thereby tried to enhance his legitimacy with his own people. When dealing with Western supporters who might be uneasy over the nature of his government, Mobutu used to respond, "Yes, I sit on my opposition, but I keep the Communists out."[14]

U.S. economic aid, both DA and ESF, for three decades provided balance of payments support and food imports, along with funding for Zairian government development project activities for its people. Zaire's cooperation enabled the United States to help Savimbi maintain his military pressure on the Cuban-Angolan forces until meaningful negotiations could begin, not only among the Angolan factions, but also with South Africa over the future of Namibia. The success of both negotiations eventually led to withdrawal of Cuban troops from Angola. This use of economic aid successfully promoted these U.S. political objectives.

Mobutu's claim to be a bastion against communism, however, became irrelevant as Namibian independence and peace talks between Angola's adversaries indicated that the U.S.-Soviet proxy war was coming to an end. With the exit of Cuban forces, peace in Angola seemed only a matter of time. Access to Zaire's airfields became less important. These changes led to decreased economic aid and enabled bilateral donors to apply greater pressure for internal economic, fiscal, and political reform, particularly on human rights issues.

Advancing Development Objectives

Interestingly, the end of the superpower conflict has created an opportunity to address hidden issues and could enable political democracy to emerge in Zaire. The Congressional Presentation has always included such political change among U.S. development goals. Many observers believe that President Mobutu's initial 1990 moves toward limited multiparty democracy were an attempt to encourage continued economic aid to his government, which had come under increasing criticism for human rights abuses and economic mismanagement. Critics in Congress, including David Obey (D-Wisconsin), Stephen Solarz (D-New York), and Howard Wolpe (D-Michigan), were determined to reduce Zaire's future aid from its FY 1990 levels of $4 million military aid and $60 million economic aid. Finally, on November 3, 1990, the Congress cut all military aid to Zaire.[15] Without the need for access to Zaire's airstrips and intelligence facilities, Congress could justify only limited basic needs–oriented aid.

Even though relations had cooled markedly by the end of the 1980s, in 1991 Zaire still had one of the largest Peace Corps contingents in the world, and A.I.D. intended to provide $23 million in development assistance during FY 1992. This aid would be channeled through nongovernmental organizations, rather than the Mobutu government, for basic rural health, family planning services, food production, and marketing projects.

The FY 1992 CP also addressed the limited developmental impact of the U.S.-Zairian assistance relationship over the previous two decades. It noted that while Zaire's economy had continued to decline over the years, 1990 had seen unprecedented deterioration. All indicators showed an economy in rapid decline, with "no bright spots on the horizon. The economic situation is one part of the broader problem of ineffective governance and political stability in Zaire. . . . Under current circumstances, and in keeping with Congressional intent, A.I.D. has shifted its focus to those projects having the greatest impact on the basic human needs of the people of Zaire, with particular emphasis on activities carried out by private voluntary and non-governmental organizations."[16] All other projects were phased out.

Although the aid cutback was appropriate in light of the extent of government repression and failure to use previous assistance effectively, the aid that would continue had even less capacity to encourage change in Mobutu's behavior. The dilemma was that even by providing only aid that meets basic welfare needs, the United States was still enabling the Mobutu government to avoid many of its own responsibilities. Welfare-oriented aid does not promote development defined as including the empowerment of people. Previous aid, though it included change-oriented projects, also may only have helped serve the "welfare" needs of the regime leadership because the GOZ never carried out many of its responsibilities for change. Whatever hope for change that may have existed with the previous aid has now been replaced by aid that will help meet only the welfare needs of the people until the existing regime finally collapses—but this aid itself helps to delay that collapse.

The past association of the United States with Mobutu left a widespread belief among the public that the United States was still Mobutu's prime supporter and therefore an obstacle to political change. Etienne Tshisekedi Wa Mulumba, a leader of the opposition Union for Democracy and Social Progress, charged that "[Mobutu] has been a lackey for the Americans for so many years, I think it is difficult for them to give him up. I wish the United States would try to do more to help."[17] The answer to this plea came in September 1991 when U.S. planes carried French and Belgian troops to Zaire to protect the evacuation of foreign nationals threatened by rioting Zairian government troops.

Government corruption and mismanagement had led to economic collapse and forced the government to delay paying its soldiers. Their response was to mutiny and to begin looting the very people, including foreigners, they were supposed to protect.[18] In the Cold War environment, the Western response would have been some form of special aid, probably an ESF grant in cash, that would have at least enabled the government to pay its military and civil employees. These resources would have restored the semblance of stability even though the rot would have continued.

This time they and other international aid agencies, including the IMF, refused to provide assistance unless Mobutu established a coalition government with his opponents and appointed Etienne Tshisekedi as prime minister. But Zaire's economic and political condition had become so weak that even this compromise seemed unlikely to have much immediate impact on the chaos across the country.[19] It didn't. Mobutu continued to hold power, using every apparent compromise to buy time for himself while his country slid into economic and social chaos.

Prospects for a new constitution and an honest process for transition to a new government based on new talks between government and opposition leaders in April 1992 were threatened by Mobutu's insistence that he retain control over the army and the national treasury pending the elections—elections that he intended to participate in himself.[20] Nevertheless, Mobutu's representatives and the opposition led by Etienne Tshisekedi began drafting a new constitution in August 1992 while Mobutu clung to his waning power from his yacht on the Congo River.[21] His days do seem numbered. The question is whether, when he does fall, there will be more bloody civil conflict. That has been the case in so many of the states that received U.S. economic and political support as long as they could serve U.S. political objectives, but who are no longer essential players in the emerging post–Cold War world.

LIBERIA

U.S. assistance to the Government of Liberia (GOL) from FY 1980 through FY 1986 totaled approximately $434 million: ESF ($200 million), DA ($83 million), PL 480 Title I food aid ($85 million), and military aid ($66 million). The 1980 aid level was $24 million. Interestingly, after the Liberian military staged a coup in 1980, U.S. economic aid increased, reaching $78 million by FY 1985. The FY 1980 CP, prepared prior to the 1980 coup, stated that it was "in the U.S. interest to insure that Liberia remains independent from external influence [and] has a viable economy and that development and progress towards equity proceed at an acceptable rate."[22]

The "external influence" was Soviet activity in Africa. The linkage of development to Liberia's capacity to resist those possible influences was also clear. In the FY 1981 CP, this wording changed slightly. The United States no longer sought to "insure" progress towards a viable economy and equity but considered "the viability of Liberia's economy and its progress toward equitable development [as] important to the United States."[23] Neither of these CPs made any reference to the political situation in the country. The second statement, however, reflected less U.S. confidence in its capacity to help "insure" such progress. Sergeant Samuel K. Doe had come to power via the 1980 coup.

Advancing U.S. Political Objectives

A.I.D.'s FY 1985 Congressional Presentation noted that the United States had been Liberia's closest friend, citing cultural and historical ties dating to the arrival in Liberia of former slaves from the United States during the country's founding in 1847. Equally important were U.S. rights at the airfield and port, the most important concentration of U.S. facilities in Africa, and one of sub-Saharan Africa's largest blocks of U.S. private investment. "U.S. short-to-medium term objectives are to foster economic and financial stability and to support a return to stable, democratic, civilian rule by 1986. Over the longer term, the U.S. believes that a government committed to political, economic, and social justice can best assure peace and stability."[24]

This statement includes competing political objectives: the medium-to long-term U.S. political interest in helping to develop a Liberian government committed to political and social justice, including respect for human rights, and the immediate U.S. political objectives related to the naval base and communications facilities that were so important to containing Soviet efforts in Africa. Not unlike the Philippines, also a country with which the United States had unique historical ties, the conflict between these different political objectives usually resulted in actions that served the immediate security-related political objectives at the expense of the democratic, human rights, and development objectives of the ESF program.

A 1987 GAO report on the Liberian government's misuse and mismanagement of U.S. aid noted the political considerations underlying the assistance program: a large U.S. diplomatic communications center and Voice of America transmission and relay stations; U.S. access to strategically located port and airfield facilities in the country; and moderate, pro-Western positions by the Liberian government on international issues.[25] The GAO report clearly confirmed that high-priority U.S. political objectives drove the assistance program, creating pressure to move the resources as quickly as possible: "A.I.D. records indicate that its Liberia Mission was under a great deal of pressure from the U.S. embassy to quickly provide large amounts of ESF assistance to the new Liberian Government in an effort to promote economic and political stability. We believe that the urgency to disburse ESF funds contributed to some of the control problems encountered in the initial programs."[26]

While the State Department and the Reagan administration relied on U.S. economic assistance to promote immediate U.S. strategic objectives, dissatisfaction with the Doe government's human rights record finally led Congress to reduce the aid level to $59 million in FY 1986. Through the 1980s, the United States had successfully used economic aid to obtain the Liberian political leadership's cooperation against the spread of Soviet-inspired instability in Africa. But that aid was not creating conditions for continued political stability in Liberia.

Advancing Development Objectives

Liberia's plight after the Cold War is possibly more tragic than that of Zaire following years of nearly identical assistance policies. Until the end of the 1980s, U.S. economic aid had supported U.S. monitoring and containment of Soviet-Cuban activities in Africa. Ironically, the end of the Cold War may have relieved the United States of paying the consequences for its previous failure to apply sound economic and political development criteria because of the higher priority given to short-term political-security interests.

The 1987 GAO report to Senator Edward M. Kennedy (D-Massachusetts) found diversion and misuse in the PL 480 and ESF aid to Liberia dating back to 1980. The report noted the Liberian government's failure to implement responsible fiscal and economic policies and its inadequate accountability for development programs. Although the United States had improved controls over most of its assistance to Liberia, the GAO found that, for foreign policy reasons, the U.S. government had been "reluctant . . . to enforce certain conditions designed to promote fiscal and economic reforms. For example, in late 1984 and early 1985, ESF was disbursed in an effort to promote presidential and legislative elections in the country, even though conditions designed to promote accountability and fiscal discipline were not met."[27]

The elections were held in 1985. While most observers believed the elections were highly rigged and a farce, the administration told Congress, "There is now the beginning, however imperfect, of a democratic experience." Many U.S. diplomats were bitter over the acceptance of Doe's fraud. "It was one of those rare times when U.S. foreign policy could have made the difference," said one senior diplomat who served in Monrovia during the election. "We funded the election. We supervised the voting, and then when Doe stole it, we didn't have the guts to tell him to get his ass out of the mansion."[28]

In contrast to the evidence on the misuse of ESF resources, the GAO found that A.I.D. could avoid misuse of DA resources by not disbursing through the Liberian government. Nevertheless, the effectiveness of these development resources was limited because the Liberian government could not meet its obligations to provide the necessary counterpart funds in local currency to cover local costs. A.I.D. could not rigorously apply sound, development-oriented approaches with either the ESF, DA, or PL 480 resources because of the constraints imposed by U.S. foreign policy considerations. ESF resources were not used to help stimulate economic and social progress, nor were DA resources and PL 480–generated local currency effectively employed. The GAO attributed the reduced effectiveness of A.I.D. projects to the misuse of funds in the PL 480 special accounts; and U.S. Treasury Department staff reported that even World Bank projects suffered because the Liberian government failed to meet its counterpart funding obligations.[29]

By the middle of 1990, the Liberian failure was apparent to the world. Even though Congress mandated cuts in U.S. aid levels to less than $10 million per year following the GOL's failure to make the necessary fiscal and economic reforms, it could not repair the damage caused during the original aid arrangements. The aid relationship had afforded Doe some legitimacy. The aid relieved him of the necessity to undertake economic, political, and social reforms that could have strengthened his legitimacy and helped ensure his political survival. Doe's government collapsed after an eight-month struggle with guerrillas, who numbered only 200 when they invaded Liberia on December 24, 1989. They finally reached his palace and killed him on September 9, 1990.

The United States never intervened, either to save Doe or to prevent the continuing slaughter by Doe's army or the forces of the two guerrilla factions. The guerrilla force had split in February 1990, each faction charging the other with corruption. A senior unidentified State Department official explained that the United States would not intervene because it could find no one among any of the parties in the conflict "to be people we can stand up and support. They have all said various things about democracy but none of them have any proven democratic credentials."[30]

This is an interesting position in light of the immediate support, including increased economic and military assistance, that the United States had given Doe when he came to power via a coup in 1979. Responding to the U.S. decision not to intervene in 1990, Claude Ake, a Nigerian political economist at the Brookings Institution, accepted the fact that the United States no longer had overwhelming interests in Liberia. But he cited special historical considerations such as Liberia's role as one of the most reliable U.S. allies. He saw "an opportunity to make Liberia a sort of showcase of American involvement in the Third World. That opportunity was not realized. From that point of view, America does have some interest in setting things right."[31]

Blaine Harden, writing in the *Washington Post* on June 3, 1990, eloquently answered the question this chapter asks: To what end?

> In the years 1980–85, Washington gave [Doe's] government $500 million. . . . For five years the American taxpayer subsidized one-third of government spending under Doe. What Americans ended up buying was neither stability nor democracy. They paid for a brand of temporary legitimacy that has become a specialty of African Big Men: guns to coerce loyalty, money to rent it. . . . Repeatedly, [Doe] outfoxed the State Department. . . . He promised to return to his barracks, which he did not. He promised a free and fair election, which he rigged. He promised financial discipline, which he faked. For his every promise, the U.S. government rewarded him with aid. For his every betrayal, the U.S. government accepted another promise. Finally, under pressure from human rights groups and Congress, the cycle of Doe's bad faith and American generosity broke down.[32]

Throughout the assistance relationship, A.I.D. and the State Department refused to face the reality before them. All Congressional Presentations asserted that U.S. and other donors' intentions, along with Liberian promises of action, likely would be implemented. Each CP claimed that time was necessary for additional aid to have its impact. This is a standard practice, repeated for years in other programs, including Egypt's.

Conclusion

By the time the rot in the Doe regime had reached the point where civil disorder cum insurgency was about to undermine the U.S. political relationship with the government, the end of Soviet involvement in Africa had all but eliminated the U.S. need for ready access to Liberian intelligence, communications, and port facilities. The tragedy was that the earlier compromises, combined with the end of the Cold War, contributed indirectly to the loss of hundereds of innocent lives in the 1990–1991 Liberian civil war.

Moreover, the United States was aware of these aid program compromises and their consequences for the development objectives of the aid. In the Liberian experience, the political and economic stability most important to the United States was a stable political relationship with the host government. The U.S. State Department and the Department of Defense used the economic and military aid programs to ensure the steady transfer of U.S. funds. The embassy's objective was to quickly move money to the Liberian government so that it could resolve immediate balance of payments problems and other foreign exchange requirements. This type of rapid response helped maintain cordial relations with the Liberian leadership and thereby preserved uninterrupted access to the U.S. facilities involved.

Pursuit of this objective, however, prevented sound development and management approaches to implementation of the aid programs, thereby facilitating increased corruption in the GOL as some leaders used the resources for their own purposes. At the same time, these leaders could use the existence of the aid relationship as evidence that the United States had confidence in their integrity. In this way, U.S. aid helped enhance the legitimacy of a Liberian government that was actually opposed to the long-term U.S. interest in a return to stable, democratic government.

SOMALIA

As the tragedy in Liberia played itself out on the west coast of Africa in early 1991, an almost identical tragedy was under way on the east coast, in Somalia—which had also received hundreds of millions of dollars in U.S. military and economic aid when it was the cornerstone of U.S. efforts to counter Soviet policy in the Horn of Africa. The United States provided

$706.6 million in economic aid, including $162.1 million in security supporting aid (SSA) and ESF, and $313.1 million in PL 480 Food for Peace, between 1962 and 1989. Military aid added another $199.3 million.[33]

The FY 1984 Congressional Presentation based United States interests in Somalia on humanitarian, developmental, and political considerations, which would be served by "providing assistance to lessen the refugee burden of the Government of the Somali Democratic Republic (GSDR), and in providing resources to assist Somalia in realizing its economic potential, particularly in agriculture, which is vital to the country's security. Economic assistance also contributes toward rapidly improving relations between the United States and Somalia, and further encourages close cooperation in an area of the world strategically vital to the United States."[34] The aid program sought to help increase food production, develop Somalia's human resources, improve its institutional capabilities, and encourage movement toward a market-oriented economy.

Advancing U.S. Political Objectives

The stongest U.S. support for Somalia began in the mid-1970s after Soviet-backed Mengistu Haile Mariam seized power in Ethiopia in 1974 from U.S. ally Haile Selassie. With this increased aid, the United States gained access to Somalia's air bases and the seaport of Berbera near the southern entrance to the Red Sea; and Somali Major General Siad Barre was able "to fight a catastrophic war with the Soviet-supported Ethiopia over the disputed Ogaden region in 1977–78."[35]

On January 5, 1991, in a scene that resembled the U.S. departure from Vietnam in 1975, more than 250 U.S. citizens and other foreigners were rescued by helicopter from the lawn of the U.S. Embassy in Mogadishu. Over 1,500 people had died during a week-long urban battle in the streets of this capital. During the previous three and a half years, Siad Barre's war against rebels in the northern part of the country had cost an estimated 50,000 lives.

This event brought to an end another chapter in the U.S. Cold War policy in Africa and ended the twenty-one-year authoritarian rule of Siad Barre, whom the U.S. had backed until Congress stopped all military aid and placed limits on other aid in 1989.[36] Ironically, barely four months after the collapse of Siad Barre's government in Somalia, the Soviet-backed Ethiopian dictator Mengistu had to flee to Zimbabwe. The incoming Ethiopian government, headed by the vice president, asked the United States to help negotiate peace with the rebels.[37]

Both of these leaders had been able to survive because the Soviet Union and the United States provided the aid that enabled them to secure their personal dictatorships while serving as proxies for the purposes of their superpower patrons. The United States gained access to a strategic port on the Horn of Africa, and U.S. economic and military aid enabled Siad Barre to contest the Marxist government in Ethiopia, at least until it was clear that the Soviets were themselves tiring of supporting Mengistu. The decade-plus effort to use economic aid in support of other military aid to these ends can thus be considered successful.

Advancing Development Objectives

In a statement on Siad Barre's fall that echoed almost precisely those made about the fall of Doe in Liberia, Representative Howard Wolpe observed, "It is a clear failure of American policy and we should bear some of the responsibility. We established a strong security relationship [with Somalia] and transferred millions in weaponry, while we totally disregarded the internal policies of the regime, the human rights violations that occurred over time. . . . Now what you are seeing is a general indifference to a disaster that we played a role in creating."[38] Peter J. Schraeder, of Loyola University in Chicago, also suggested the collapse of the Barre government was a "textbook example" of the consequences of U.S. policies that provided support to a country "solely for external reasons while ignoring that country's internal problems."[39]

U.S. policies and programs for Somalia were driven primarily by the perceived Soviet threat to the Horn of Africa. The consequences provide another example of the costs of pursuing a political-security objective with economic aid. In these circumstances, the ESF aid tends to encourage leaders such as Siad Barre to depend for support more on external sources than on his country's people. U.S. government officials reject such criticisms. They view Somalia's plight as simply another example of an African leader wasting an opportunity to use the aid for development purposes. *Washington Post* reporter Neil Henry quotes one such official as saying: "This is a sovereign country we're talking about. They have chosen to spend the [aid] that way, to hurt people and destroy their own economy, and now they are reaping the consequences."[40]

This type of argument, however, ignores the fact that the United States chose to continue providing the aid even when it knew—as the GAO reports on Liberia clearly demonstrate—that the recipient government was not using the aid for development purposes. While it is proper to retain hope and set development goals as stated in the Congressional Presentation, there can be little justification for continuing to provide aid in the face of its outright misuse in ways that, indirectly at least, help sustain a government that is destroying its people. Though this direct a link is never accepted for the record, the bottom line is that the continued aid was needed to advance immediate U.S. strategic purposes in the Horn of Africa, and those interests counted more than the long-term development of the people and the peace that might ensue therefrom.

Conclusion

As this book goes to press, the horror in death and destruction continues in Somalia. Armed marauders from different clans fight over foreign emergency food aid. Andrew Natsios, an A.I.D. humanitarian relief official, described the situation as the most "unspeakably tragic human suffering he had ever seen."[41] The *Washington Post* saw this tragedy as the handiwork of Somalia's "armed and powerful."[42] Keith B. Richburg in a dispatch to the *Washington Post* added perspective: "Just over 30 years after it officially became an independent nation, Somalia essentially has ceased to exist. . . . Can the state that was once Somalia ever be pieced back together?"[43]

The tragedy of Somalia is the handiwork of more than its own marauders and former leaders. It is also a demonstration of how using ESF aid for short-term U.S. political objectives often precludes any prospect that the aid can be used to promote sound development, most especially in programs that might help to resolve the causes of conflict within a given state. The developmental orientation of the CP language is always hopeful about the future. It should be. But the other reality is that the CP language obscures the costs to the Somali, Liberian, and Zairian people—including their lives—of advancing U.S. political objectives with economic and military aid. In fact, neither A.I.D. nor the State Department undertakes such human cost–benefit analysis as a routine part of the aid policy and programming process. At best, these issues will appear only in GAO reports, and even these reports often do not address all factors that may affect the application of foreign aid, whether for political or development objectives. Some of these factors include earmarks or other special efforts that individual members of Congress have applied either to support or obstruct A.I.D. programming in these countries.

Perhaps, however, had U.S. diplomatic and aid officials tried as early as 1984–1986 to determine the potential humanitarian costs of not applying the strictest development criteria while providing ESF and other economic aid resources, the tragedy that befell Somalia in 1992 might have been averted. At least, the U.S. government and its taxpayers might have been spared the ironic twist of events that began in January 1991 with U.S. Marines rescuing U.S. diplomats from the roof of their embassy in Mogadishu and, less than two years later, saw the U.S. government, under United Nations authority, using U.S. combat troops, under U.S. command, to reenter Somalia to deliver food and other humanitarian aid to a refugee population dying at the rate of 1,000 per week.[44]

Yet another ironic footnote to these Cold War experiences and their consequences began to emerge even before we had reflected on their lessons. The headline in the *Washington Post* on April 30, 1992, read: "U.S., Seeking New Friends, Turns to Botswana." In this article, David B. Ottaway noted that "the United States, having lost many of its traditional allies in sub-Saharan Africa in a wave of political turmoil sweeping this continent, is turning to this relatively stable, democratic southern African nation in its search for new friends and military partners." The Voice of America inaugurated a new short-wave transmitter outside Selebi-Phikwe to replace the one it lost in Liberia. A small contingent of U.S. paratroops had recently conducted a two-week training exercise. Ottaway continued: "With the collapse of its alliances with Liberia, Zaire, Sudan and Somalia, the United States has had to turn elsewhere to forge new relationships and find new sites for its military and other activities."[45]

Botswana at this point in its history has a stable economy and is a functioning democracy. Though senior U.S. officials deny that the United States wants to establish a special relationship with Botswana, this may be what is happening. Botswana's president, Quett Masire, commended the United States for helping his country "call South Africa to order" in the mid-1980s. Masire and his people want friends outside the region "to protect us in the event of the need for protection."[46]

HONDURAS

During the decade-long U.S. effort to pressure the Sandinista government of Nicaragua to abide by their 1979 agreement to restore democracy and not interfere—through guerrilla war—in the affairs of neighboring countries, the United States provided $1.4 billion in economic aid to Honduras. The Congressional Presentation for FY 1984 noted that the United States shared with Honduras a reliance on the free enterprise system and a respect for democratic government. Moreover, the unsettled political and social situation in Central America made preservation of Honduras's relative stability of great importance. The CP asserted that following the honest and peaceful election of November 1981, "the United States [had] an excellent opportunity for effective development collaboration."[47]

Advancing U.S. Political Objectives

The United States developed in Honduras an extensive network of military and intelligence facilities that were exceeded only by those in Panama. The United States provided substantial covert support for the Nicaraguan contras, who operated from Honduran bases, causing Honduras to become known as the "USS Honduras." In return for its cooperation, Honduras received high levels of ESF and military aid, including U.S. training for its forces.

This aid relationship created pressures on the Sandinistas that hindered their efforts to spread their revolution to other countries in Central America, including Honduras. The U.S.-supported opposition also bought time until the other governments in the region, led by President Oscar Arias of Costa Rica, were able to compel the Sandinistas to cooperate in a Central American solution to a Central American problem—albeit a problem exploited by both superpowers.

Had there been no U.S. resistance to the Sandinistas' efforts to export their Marxist revolution after they reneged on the democracy provisions of the 1979 agreement removing the Somoza dictatorship, it is highly unlikely that El Salvador or Honduras would have survived the insurgencies. Most certainly, the opposition to the Sandinistas in Nicaragua would never have been able to compel the Sandinista leadership to risk an election, much less for this opposition to win the election themselves. On these counts, U.S. economic aid successfully served overriding U.S. security objectives in Central America.

Advancing Development Objectives

This ESF aid, however, had little apparent impact in terms of its economic development objectives. At the end of the 1980s, Honduras remained one of the poorest countries in the Western Hemisphere. According to the FY 1991 CP, Honduras's most serious problems included an overvalued exchange rate, a large fiscal deficit, increasing inflation, lack of foreign exchange, and decreasing private sector confidence. Significant aid from the major donors, including the World Bank and the IMF, did not materialize in 1989 because the Government of Honduras (GOH) failed to reach agreement with donors on its economic adjustment program. Finally, the CP noted, "Given the pressures of a hotly contested election year, the GOH lacked the political will to undertake needed measures."[48] Moreover, the government was in arrears on payments owed to international financial institutions and some bilateral donors. Even A.I.D. did not forward $70 million in ESF resources for balance of payments support in FY 1989 because of the government's failure to apply a sound reform program.

What happened? How is it possible that Honduras could have been in such economic difficulty after its $1.4 billion aid relationship with the United States? The answer appears in large measure to lie in the nature of the relationship and the high priority given to its political-security purposes. Many Hondurans felt that the ESF aid hurt more than it helped because it far exceeded the government's absorptive capacity and flooded the economy. According to Victor Meza, director of the Honduran Documentation Center, a think tank in Tegucigalpa, "[The aid] created the mind-set [among officials] of an international beggar. The aid allowed Honduras to avoid needed reforms."[49]

Though the end of the confrontation with the Sandinistas meant less U.S. aid for Honduras, President Rafael Leonardo Callejas's government reportedly considered the new situation "wonderful." Gilberto Goldstein, Callejas's private secretary, observed, "As a new government, we can now concentrate on development."[50]

U.S. officials have often expressed U.S. interest in working with governments that are committed to building a stable democratic political process. In its FY 1992 CP on Honduras, A.I.D. stated that the United States remained "strongly committed to this close neighbor and staunch ally in its efforts to stabilize its economy and strengthen democracy."[51] The CP noted that the Honduran government was progressing on both these fronts and that it had "initiated a program of sweeping economic reforms."[52] These reforms cut subsidies and tariffs and implemented new laws to end discrimination against foreign businesses, thus making it easier for U.S. businesses to compete in Honduras and helping increase imports of U.S. products.

Nevertheless, the United States appears far less interested in a new aid relationship for development purposes than it was to one based on countering communism in Central America. While Honduras works on its democracy and tries to reform its economy, the United States has drastically cut its economic aid program for FY 1993 by 62 percent from the 1987 level, while proposing a 45 percent increase in aid to Peru. Poland was to receive nearly twice Honduras's level, though Poland's per capita GNP is over two times greater than Honduras's. Rosemary Piper of the Hudson Institute in Indianapolis concluded, "Everyone knows that the cut in U.S. aid has less to do with the shape of the Honduran economy than a shift in U.S. priorities from the 1980s' preoccupation with countering the communist threat in Central America to the 1990s' concerns of drug interdiction and Eastern Europe."[53]

The 1992 U.S. presidential election also became a distraction, leading the Central American nations to believe that they had been "abandoned" at a critical point in time—their transition to viable democracies—by a Bush administration fearful of raising any serious foreign policy issue during the campaign. Honduras was among the nations most affected by such U.S. disinterest after the end of the Cold War precisely because, as U.S. officials who had been involved in Honduras during the 1980s admitted, "little attention was paid to Honduras's development through the years of plenty, as long as U.S. contra policy was allowed to go forward."[54] Honduran President Rafael Callejas in the fall of 1992 was still struggling "to break the dependence that [U.S.] aid had brought." He told the *Washington Post* that his country "was virtually bankrupt when he took office." And he concluded, "Most of the U.S. money came to sustain the wrong policies. . . . We lost a decade."[55]

Conclusion

Few would dispute that the new U.S. priorities are important. But why when new opportunities for real development emerge in those countries that have been such loyal allies in the past does the United States shrink from the "debt of honor" to support former allies, most especially when they have made a new commitment to democracy? The lesson seems to be that if we follow the aid, we again find U.S. short-term political interests overriding the longer-term political interest in building a sustainable peace based on economic, political, and social development in the lands of our former "staunch allies." Both Poland and Honduras need U.S. aid, and the United States should help. It should also carefully consider which country is currently best prepared to absorb and benefit from different types and amounts of aid.

ELSEWHERE IN CENTRAL AMERICA

A 1989 GAO report on the ESF programs for Costa Rica, Belize, Guatemala, El Salvador, Honduras, Panama, and Nicaragua noted the impact of U.S. political objectives on the effectiveness of ESF economic stabilization efforts. The report found that U.S. efforts to promote stabilization and adjustment were relatively successful in Costa Rica, Belize, and Guatemala because their governments had not only recognized the need for, and were committed to, reforms, but had also developed internal support for the reforms.[56] In addition, except for Guatemala, the programs of the IMF and the World Bank complemented those of the United States. The report also noted that "the United States did not have competing political or security interests that overrode its economic objectives."[57]

War and U.S. sanctions during the 1980s, in contrast, undercut ESF programs in Nicaragua and Panama. In El Salvador and Honduras, the ESF programs might have stemmed economic declines, but they had not achieved stabilization and adjustment for reasons precisely the opposite of those cited for success in other countries. The Honduran and El Salvadoran governments faced domestic opposition to reform, lacked other donor support for stabilization and adjustment programs, had not undertaken necessary reforms, and—most compelling—"U.S. political considerations overrode A.I.D.'s imposition and enforcement of strict conditionality related to economic reforms."[58]

PAKISTAN

The United States–Pakistan assistance relationship provides a final, major example of the successful use of economic aid to contain the extension of another country's military and political power. The changes in levels and the rationales over time, however, also reflect changing priorities for conflicting political objectives. This aid relationship clearly demonstrates how the priority of short-term U.S. political objectives compromised commitment to economic and social development, even when the aid was a multiyear commitment to promote development of a politically important country.

U.S. economic aid to Pakistan between 1962 and 1989 totaled $6.528

billion, which included $1.797 billion in security-supporting (ESF-type) aid and $2.479 billion in PL 480 Food for Peace aid.[59] During 1987, at the height of efforts to maintain pressure on the Soviet forces in Afghanistan, the United States developed a multiyear $2.28 billion economic aid package for FY 1988–FY 1993. Three million Afghan refugees complicated U.S. efforts to strengthen and support the social and economic development of Pakistan. The FY 1990 CP asserted: "A massive repatriation effort will be required, followed by an uncertain level of reconstruction in Pakistan, especially in rangelands and watersheds where refugees have lived. Continued uncertainty over Afghanistan leaves Pakistan understandably nervous about future aid levels. The pledge of $1.6 billion in economic assistance during FY 1982–FY 1987 was largely met, and it is just as important the stated commitment of $2.28 billion over the period FY 1988–FY 1993 be realized."[60]

Advancing U.S. Political Objectives

This aid commitment was designed to strengthen Pakistan's economic and political stability through broad-based economic growth and an improved social environment. Ten key concerns were (1) balance of payments, (2) domestic resource mobilization, (3) energy supply and demand, (4) agricultural productivity, (5) population growth, (6) infant mortality, (7) literacy, (8) quality of key institutions, (9) development in "lagging areas," and (10) narcotics production and use.[61]

This multiyear commitment was possible because all the major actors—the State Department, Treasury, OMB, and Congress—cooperated toward the primary U.S. political goal of bringing about Soviet withdrawal from Afghanistan. Pakistan had become the frontline state in this effort. The United States also provided high levels of military aid to the Pakistani military and the Afghan guerrillas, who were the instrument of force against the Soviets. In return for this assistance commitment, Pakistan agreed to "do the needful" in supporting the Afghan guerrillas. The decade-long effort to keep the pressure on succeeded in preventing the Soviets from consolidating their initial military gains and finally helped impel their negotiated withdrawal after Mikhail Gorbachev came to realize the futility of continued Soviet involvement. At the start of the FY 1988–FY 1993 commitment, this outcome still seemed a long-term political goal. The early accomplishment of this objective, however, created an opportunity in September 1990 for other U.S. political interests to override the earlier U.S. commitment toward "a strong and prosperous Pakistan," in the words of the CP.

The issue of Pakistan's nuclear program resurfaced. It had been a major issue in 1978–1980. With the passage of the Symington amendment to the Foreign Assistance Act, Congress prohibited new allocations of aid because of concern that Pakistan was trying to develop a nuclear weapons capacity. Though the Symington constraints remained technically applicable in the early 1980s, they were set aside via annual messages to Congress from the administration that in essence "certified" that there was no clear evidence that Pakistan was actively pursuing a nuclear weapons program. Congress willingly and routinely accepted these certifications in order to cooperate with the U.S. decision to actively resist the Soviet invasion of Afghanistan. All parties recognized that Pakistan's cooperation was vital for the support of the Afghan resistance movement.

Successful attainment of this U.S. political objective, however, cleared the way for the previous political objective—particularly as Congress defined it—to resurface as a top priority. Representative Stephen J. Solarz, chairman of the House Foreign Affairs Subcommittee on Asian and Pacific Affairs, in a letter to President Bush on September 19, 1990, urged that all military and economic aid be cut off. Solarz asserted that Pakistan had continued to ignore U.S. demands to curtail its program to develop nuclear weapons. Noting Pakistan's past role in funneling aid to the Afghan rebels, Solarz acknowledged: "For over a decade there has been a temptation to look the other way. We have now reached the point where continuing to certify [that Pakistan does not have a nuclear weapon] would deprive us of what tattered shreds may be left of our nonproliferation policy."[62] Solarz apparently did not accept the argument in the FY 1990 CP regarding the nuclear issue, which stated: "The Pakistan government is well aware of U.S. concerns and legislation. The U.S. assistance program seeks both to advance non-proliferation and to support Pakistan's courageous stand on Afghanistan. It is premised on a belief that a close and reliable partnership gives Pakistan an alternative to the development of nuclear weapons in meeting its legitimate security needs."[63]

In other words, the CP was arguing that the new U.S. political objective could be achieved if the United States–Pakistan aid relationship continued and supported Pakistan's development into a strong and prosperous state; moreover, the existence of a close United States–Pakistan relationship would enhance Pakistan's sense of security and obviate the need for a nuclear deterrent of its own. The key was a credible U.S. commitment to help Pakistan's development and to create conditions for a stable peace. U.S. credibility was a problem, however, because of the U.S. tendency to reduce aid and switch priorities whenever its short-term security objectives changed.

In this case, the clear U.S. manipulation of economic aid for changing U.S. political objectives provoked bitter reactions in Pakistan. Anti-Americanism increased, intensified by the election campaign in which Benazir Bhutto's opponents accused her of "playing to a Congressional lobby in Washington bent on interfering in Pakistan's internal affairs."[64] All military and economic aid to Pakistan was suspended on October 1, 1990, because President Bush could not certify that Pakistan's nuclear program was peaceful.[65]

A central theme reportedly ran through Pakistani newspapers and in letters to the editor: Why only Pakistan? "When the United States' interest in Pakistan has been minimal, our nuclear program has proved to be the bugbear," a long editorial in the sober independent newspaper *Dawn* observed. "This approach . . . smacks of cynicism when compared to the tolerance displayed by the U.S. toward other aid receiving countries such as Israel, Brazil, and India. . . . Public opinion polls support Islamabad's belief that it has the right to develop a nuclear deterrent so long as India, which detonated a device in 1974, has one."[66]

Advancing Development Objectives

The Pakistan case illustrates that even the strongest long-term commitment of economic aid for development goals seen as necessary to achieve one vital political objective can be overridden when another, shorter-term political objective has been achieved. Moreover, this override occurred even though achieving the original development objective was still necessary to attain the new political objective: nuclear nonproliferation. The people of Pakistan had hardly begun to experience the development impact of the long-term aid package. "A strong and prosperous Pakistan" appears to have had hardly any priority in the U.S. multiyear commitment.

Interestingly, by early 1991, it was apparent that the United States would retain the drastic cuts in the aid program even if Pakistan were exonerated from nuclear suspicion or given a presidential waiver on the congressional requirement. The administration, in its final FY 1991 budget request, asked for only $220 million instead of the $564 million in the original FY 1991 request—and if Pakistan did not pass the nuclear proliferation test, it would get nothing. Other political priorities took precedence. The first was the intention to develop closer ties with India, and the second was the need to find resources to support new opportunities in Eastern Europe.[67]

Conclusion

U.S. economic aid served U.S. containment objectives against the Soviets in Afghanistan. Indeed, this was probably the most successful of all U.S. efforts to use economic aid for U.S. political-security purposes, because it also contributed in turn to the chain of events that led to Soviet withdrawal from Eastern Europe, and eventually to the collapse of the Soviet empire itself. However, manipulation of aid to somehow force Pakistan to adhere to U.S. nuclear nonproliferation objectives has not worked; and, because this manipulation is so obvious and open to charges of double standards, it may even have unnecessarily exacerbated United States–Pakistan relations. Given the magnitude of the military-political success against the Soviet Union in which Pakistan played such an instrumental role, this fickle treatment of a U.S. ally seemed particularly hypocritical.

SUMMARY

Clearly, U.S. diplomacy has successfully used economic assistance resources, especially ESF, to advance an impressive array of short-term U.S. political objectives in country-specific programs in virtually every region of the world. In addition to the role that ESF assistance to Pakistan played in the Soviet decision to withdraw from Afghanistan, ESF and DA resources together were a major factor in maintaining U.S. access to intelligence, communications, and air base and port facilities in Zaire, Liberia, Somalia, and Kenya that were vital to U.S. containment of Soviet and Cuban activities in East and Central Africa. ESF aid was essential in sustaining the U.S.-Philippine bases agreements, particularly after the U.S. withdrawal from South Vietnam made possible Soviet access to the massive U.S.-constructed base at Cam Ranh Bay there. Successful resistance to Cuban- and Sandinista-supported guerrillas in Central America would have been impossible without the cooperation of Honduras and El Salvador, both of which received large ESF transfers. Finally, over $17 billion in ESF and PL 480 aid to Egypt and $18 billion in ESF for Israel have sustained the Middle East peace process with these two countries and created an opportunity to extend it to other Arab countries.

These successes are only the most obvious. Many observers and even more U.S. officials in the State Department, A.I.D., OMB, the Departments of Agriculture, Treasury, Defense, and Commerce, and the U.S. Congress would agree that these successes were worth the price. Perhaps. But there were other costs in the sacrifice of longer-term political, economic, and social development goals that are increasingly apparent. In the words of a cliché that seems all too appropriate: Other chickens—which could only be satisfied with real development success—are beginning to come home to roost in the last decade of the twentieth century: massive refugee migrations sparked by violent civil war, ethnic conflict, and economic chaos; environmental degradation; the international drug trade; and massive debt for nearly all countries in the Third World and many richer countries. All four of these problems are directly related, each in its own way, to the failure of foreign aid to fulfill its role in the development process, not only in economic terms but, most important, politically.

Aid resources alone, even if applied in accordance with sound development criteria, would not have been the determining factor in any country's development process. But this fact does not override the reality that, however limited the development impact of U.S. aid resources might have been, the United States made little or no sustained effort to ensure the consistent application of its aid toward the development objectives so clearly stated in every Congressional Presentation and program document.

NOTES

1. A.I.D., *U.S. Overseas Loans and Grants*, p. 81.

2. Ernest H. Preeg, "Neither Fish Nor Fowl: U.S. Economic Assistance for Non-Economic Objectives in the Philippines" (Draft paper, Center for Strategic and International Studies, October 1990), pp. 7–8.

3. Robert Pear, "U.S. May Give Up One of Its Bases in the Philippines, Officials Say," *New York Times*, May 14, 1990.

4. "Philippines Agree to Three-Year U.S. Pullout," *New York Times*, October 3, 1991.

5. Preeg, *Neither Fish nor Fowl*, p. 10.

6. Ibid., p. 15.

7. A.I.D., *FY 1990 CP*, Annex II: Asia and the Near East, p. 215.

8. Preeg, *Neither Fish nor Fowl*, pp. 4, 36. The Rural Development Fund was a special ESF account for Philippine pesos generated from the sale of $20 million given directly to the Philippine government in 1979 as part of the side letter agreement on the U.S. bases agreement. The pesos would build schools, rural markets, and secondary roads. Imelda Marcos controlled the funds, which supported projects in areas where Marcos supporters would benefit most directly.

9. A.I.D., *FY 1990 CP*.

10. A.I.D., *U.S. Overseas Loans and Grants*, p. 138.

11. A.I.D., *FY 1984 CP*, Annex I: Africa, pp. 382–383.

12. A.I.D., *FY 1988 CP*, Annex I: Africa, p. 398.

13. David B. Ottaway, "Defense Department Seeks to Renovate Base in Zaire," *Washington Post*, February 21, 1987.

14. Jonathan C. Randal, "Peace in Neighboring Angola Seen Diminishing Zaire's Importance to the West," *Washington Post*, May 10, 1990.

15. Clifford Krauss, "U.S. Cuts Off Aid to Zaire, Setting Off Policy Debate," *New York Times*, November 4, 1990. See also Neil Henry, "Mobutu Holds onto Power as Zaire Crumbles," *Washington Post*, May 14, 1991.

16. A.I.D., *FY 1992 CP*, Annex I: Africa, p. 422.

17. Henry, "Mobutu Holds onto Power."

18. Keith Bradsher, "West Reluctant to Quell Zaire Unrest," *New York Times*, September 27, 1991.

19. Keith Richberg, "A Rich Man in Poor Standing," *Washington Post*, October 3, 1991.

20. Kenneth B. Noble, "Zaire Resumes Constitutional Talks," *New York Times*, April 14, 1992.

21. Kenneth B. Noble, "As the Nation's Economy Collapses, Zairians Squirm Under Mobutu's Heel," *New York Times*, August 24, 1992.

22. A.I.D., *FY 1980 CP*, Annex I: Africa, p. 340.

23. A.I.D., *FY 1981 CP*, Annex I, Africa, p. 328.

24. A.I.D., *FY 1985 CP*: Annex I: Africa, p. 242.

25. GAO, *Liberia: Need to Improve Accountability and Control over U.S. Assistance* (Report to the Honorable Edward M. Kennedy, U.S. Senate, GAO/NSIAD-87-173, July 1987), pp. 1–2.

26. Ibid., p. 4.

27. Ibid., p. 2.

28. Blaine Harden, "End of the Line for One of Africa's Worst Tyrants," *Washington Post*, June 3, 1990.

29. GAO, *Liberia: Need to Improve Accountability*, p. 5.

30. David Hoffman, "U.S. Explains Reluctance to Intervene," *Washington Post*, July 31, 1990.

31. Ibid.
32. Harden, "End of the Line."
33. A.I.D., *U.S. Overseas Loans and Grants*, p. 130.
34. A.I.D., *FY 1984 CP*, Annex I: Africa, p. 199.
35. Neil Henry, "Somali Civil War Slaughter a Legacy of Cold War Feuds," *Washington Post*, January 8, 1991.
36. Ibid.
37. Clifford Krauss, "Ethiopia's Dictator Flees; Officials Seeking U.S. Help," *New York Times*, May 22, 1991.
38. Henry, "Somali Civil War."
39. Ibid.
40. Ibid.
41. "Somalia: 'A Man-Made Tragedy'," editorial, *Washington Post*, September 17, 1992.
42. Ibid.
43. Keith B. Richburg, "Can Battered Somalia Be Pieced Back Together?" *Washington Post*, September 24, 1992.
44. Michael R. Gordon, "Somali Aid Plan Called Most Ambitious Option," *New York Times*, November 28, 1992.
45. David B. Ottaway, "U.S., Seeking African Friends, Turns to Botswana," *Washington Post*, April 30, 1992.
46. Ibid.
47. A.I.D., *FY 1984 CP*, Annex III: Latin America and the Caribbean, p. 203.
48. A.I.D., *FY 1991 CP*, Annex III: Latin America and the Caribbean, p. 166.
49. Wilson Ring, "Honduras Still Feels U.S. Role," *Washington Post*, June 2, 1990.
50. Ibid.
51. A.I.D., *FY 1992 CP*, Honduras, p. 782.
52. Ibid.
53. Rosemary Piper, "Shifting Policy on Honduras," *Washington Times*, commentary, May 7, 1992.
54. Douglas Farah, "Central America Feels Abandoned by Bush at Crucial Time," *Washington Post*, November 22, 1992.
55. Ibid.
56. This finding seems premature in Guatemala's case, since the first real steps toward ending the thirty-year guerrilla war did not begin until April 1991. All previous efforts had been little more than public statements of intentions while the killings, totaling more than 100,000 violent deaths into 1991, continued. Lee Hochstader, "Guatemalans Taking Initial Steps toward Resolving Long Rebel War," *Washington Post*, May 15, 1991. Even these steps may not bear fruit.
57. GAO, *Central America: Impact of U.S. Assistance in the 1980s*, pp. 39–42.
58. Ibid.
59. A.I.D., *U.S. Overseas Loans and Grants*, p. 26.
60. A.I.D., *FY 1990 CP*, Annex II: Asia and the Near East, p. 203.
61. Ibid., p. 204. Note: The lagging area initiative consisted of road building and irrigation to improve living conditions and basic infrastructure in provinces such as Baluchistan and the Northwest Frontier Province adjacent to the Afghan border.

62. Michael R. Gordon, "End to Pakistan Aid Is Sought Over Nuclear Issue," *New York Times*, September 25, 1990.

63. A.I.D., *FY 1990 CP*, Annex II: Asia and the Near East.

64. Barbara Crossette, "U.S. Aid Judgment Upsets Pakistanis," *New York Times*, October 16, 1990.

65. Susumu Awanohara and Salamat Ali, "Devalued Ally," *Far Eastern Economic Review* (February 14, 1991), p. 10.

66. Ibid.

67. Ibid.

7

The Relationship Between Development Assistance and Political Objectives

Economic Support Fund resources, supplemented on occasion by the PL 480 Food for Peace program and some Development Assistance, have clearly advanced U.S. short-term political objectives. This study has focused on the considerable tension and contradiction between the long- and short-term political objectives and the long-term economic and social-political *development* objectives of U.S. foreign policy. Several interrelated lessons bear further consideration in this chapter:

- The sustainability of most U.S. political and security objectives, including peace, ultimately depends on the effectiveness of economic assistance as a development tool, not on a quid pro quo for political-security cooperation.
- Using economic aid as a quid pro quo to advance short-term U.S. political objectives undermines application of development-oriented criteria and conditions in the planning and implementation of programs and projects intended to help stimulate sustainable economic, social, and political development.
- Earmarks, often driven by the potential domestic political impact of U.S. special interests, can also compromise the allocation and implementation of economic assistance programs for development purposes.
- Attainment of U.S. foreign policy objectives can be enhanced when the people of a recipient country experience benefits from the achievement of development purposes of the economic assistance.
- When recipient countries' leaders use the assistance relationship with the United States to advance their personal political interests, they undermine prospects for its long-term development impact—and for the sustainability of U.S. diplomatic achievements.

SUSTAINING U.S. POLITICAL OBJECTIVES ONCE ACHIEVED

One of the clear lessons of the 1990–1991 Gulf crisis is that relying on dollar-based, quid pro quo diplomacy to advance U.S. political objectives, especially for security and peace, by preserving the status quo is costly and not effective over the long term. This lesson has been apparent for years; it has been unheeded, and there is much evidence that it continues to go unheeded today in Europe and the Middle East.

In the Middle East, Africa, and Latin America, it cannot yet be said that U.S. economic aid has helped promote the type of social, economic, and political change that empowers people as individuals and in groups to control their own destinies—and to have the political power in their own countries to constrain their governments from engaging in war with other countries or against their own people.

While there are more opportunities to promote such change in Africa, Asia, and Latin America today than ever before, U.S. aid and attention are increasingly diverted elsewhere: against drug traffickers in the Andes, for example, or toward economic and political reforms in the former East bloc states. Though the latter clearly merit U.S. help, they are still unprepared to effectively absorb for development purposes the enormous resources now allocated to them.

In the Middle East, there is little change in either the amounts or the nature of aid allocations. U.S. ESF aid continues to do more to sustain the status quo—in effect, maintaining the conditions of and capacity for conflict—than to create the conditions for reconciliation of conflict between and within the states of the region. Moreover, at this writing it seems clear that past use of over $97 billion in economic and military aid between 1962 and 1990 to promote U.S. interests in the Middle East[1] still was not enough to obtain the quid pro quo political and military cooperation it was supposed to ensure when requested from Congress in countless hearings over the previous thirty years. Perhaps these difficulties and the continuing practice of using enormous resources to obtain (buy?) cooperation reflect weaknesses in our credibility as a reliable ally, as well as the specific causes we are perceived to be serving.

U.S. diplomacy can most readily achieve the diplomatic and military cooperation it seeks when the credibility and integrity of its causes are so compelling that it need not use ESF cash transfers and aid projects, PL 480 food transfers, Commodity Credit Corporation loans, military assistance programs, or other aid as quids pro quo. In the Middle East context, we also clearly need to reexamine some aspects of U.S.-Israeli policies and practices, particularly in terms of how they may affect the integrity of other U.S. objectives and our capacity to obtain Arab cooperation toward creating the conditions for long-term stable peace in the Middle East.

A major lesson from the Gulf War is the United States' need for Arab friends and allies who welcome a U.S. presence—political, social, economic, and perhaps even cultural. The reality that cannot be ignored is that in the 1990 Gulf crisis, the U.S.-Israeli relationship and past policies had become a constraint that required "dollar diplomacy" to convince most Arab members of the coalition to swallow hard and accept a U.S. military presence in the Saudi desert.

The danger in late 1992 was that the opportunities created for the peace process throughout the Middle East—by the military defeat of Saddam Hussein of Iraq and the election of Yitzhak Rabin in Israel—could still be lost in the inertia of a status quo based on the existing political and territorial divisions. When the 1992 Israeli elections brought to power a new government more interested than its predecessor in reconciliation with its Arab neighbors, the peace process appeared to be regaining some momentum. Israel's new prime minister, Yitzhak Rabin, froze political settlements and offered the prospect of trading land for peace with the Palestinians and Syria. At this point, any perceived Egyptian unwillingness to cooperate with Israel, however much it might be caused by apparent Israeli intransigence, will increase pressure from Israel's supporters to strengthen the current U.S.-Israeli alliance. The U.S. aid relationship with Egypt will then have failed to achieve its most overriding political objective just when it appeared the opportunity for real reconciliation was at hand.

Ultimately, the conditions for peace in the Middle East must rest on sustainable social, economic, and political development, not diplomacy that relies on resource transfers that merely subsidize modernization of twentieth-century Arab feudalism. Reconciliation among the countries and peoples in conflict in this region, and elsewhere, is not going to occur without strong, sustained political and social development within each country of the sort that empowers people to control their personal destinies and to participate in decisions that affect the political and economic destinies of their countries. Thus, for example, sustainable peace depends on development of opportunities for the Arab people to create wealth by their personal imagination, initiative, and labor rather than to rely on revenues from oil controlled by their governments and shared as an act of grace.

Few of the governing elites in the Arab world are prepared for such changes in the structure of power throughout their societies, even after the Gulf crisis so clearly exposed the fragility of their states. Moreover, oil revenues provide a secure base for modernization, because they enable a government to effectively limit or control the extent of foreign penetration of the existing political-social structure.

These political realities are also evident in Egypt, which has been able to count on U.S. aid along with its more limited oil reserves, tourism, and Suez Canal tolls to maintain its statist, social welfare–oriented political and economic structures. Yet, while it is expected to be a major player in creating and maintaining an Arab coalition that can ensure the peace in the aftermath of Saddam's defeat, Egypt remains economically and politically fragile. Its current high political profile is based solely on the temporary benefit of having been available and willing to cooperate with the United States and Saudi Arabia in the successful confrontation with Iraq—cooperation that was amply rewarded with debt relief and promises for, as yet, untold further aid from the United States, the Saudis, and the Kuwaitis. Egypt's power, thus, remains compromised by its economic frailty, even after seventeen years in an aid relationship with the United States that has included nearly $17 billion in ESF economic aid. Moreover, the reemerging Islamic Fundamentalists who in November 1992 were working so well to meet emerging needs of earthquake victims in Cairo, while their cohorts were attacking tourists in southern Egypt, provide ample evidence of political weakness in the Mubarak government.

The challenge for the United States is to encourage serious dialogue among and with all the Arab states about the differences between modernization and development, particularly the development of people that creates the conditions for stable peace within and between all countries. In this dialogue, while the United States must be sensitive, respectful, and very clear that it does not seek to impose its vision of a developed society on the Arab countries, it must also press behind the scenes to encourage promotion of the basic rights of all the people, including women, in Muslim societies. The Arab governments must define their interests and objectives in any development process, and, most important, state whether they even want any non-Arab countries to participate in an Arab development process. The United States should stand ready to be as cooperative as possible with clearly defined development goals.

This discussion has concentrated on the Middle East because, for example, this region has received almost as much aid ($97.2 billion) as Latin America, Africa, and East Asia combined, both ESF and DA ($98.1 billion).[2] The Middle East, moreover, is where the United States has made most use of ESF aid to promote its political objectives. The lesson discussed here, nevertheless, also applies to other regions; the difference is one of scale.

THE COMPATIBILITY OF POLITICAL AND DEVELOPMENT OBJECTIVES

Foreign service officers in A.I.D. and the State Department have long debated whether stimulation of long-term economic, social, and political development is a prerequisite for sustaining the political stability necessary to achieving U.S. foreign policy objectives. Some officers responsible for advancing specific U.S. political objectives argue that attaining short-term objectives does not depend on a country's economic development progress; rather, it depends on stable government-to-government relations.

It is frequently easiest to advance short-term political objectives in a country where the government leadership finds itself economically and politically vulnerable and needs U.S. economic aid. In these cases, the aid is normally linked on a quid pro quo basis to U.S. political objectives. However, when a country receives substantial aid that is perceived as directly related to a particular U.S. political objective, U.S. leverage with the recipient government declines over time as the aid comes to be seen as an entitlement.

The U.S. aid relationships with Egypt and Israel, the largest recipients, and a host of other U.S. aid recipients (including especially ESF countries) demonstrate the direct relationship between aid levels and the importance of U.S. political objectives in any given country. As noted, the more critical the U.S. political objective, and the higher the relevant aid level, the less leverage the United States has with the recipient government. The recipient government will resist additional U.S. efforts to attach economic reform conditions to the assistance, because it believes this aid is a quid pro quo arrangement for recipient government cooperation in advancing a U.S. political objective.

U.S. readiness to use ESF assistance in quid pro quo arrangements often becomes a substitute for dialogue, supposedly the essence of diplomacy. If U.S. political objectives have a compelling enough logic, it should be possible to advance them successfully through dialogue without large amounts of aid. Moreover, if U.S. economic aid were applied for development purposes—as opposed to large infrastructure for modernization purposes—projects could focus on empowering people, and aid levels should then be considerably lower, fluctuating according to need, opportunity, and performance over time. Such aid would reward positive political and economic reform efforts in a country, lessening the need to worry about high aid levels to make U.S. bases more acceptable or to leverage unpopular reforms to which leaders were not committed. Most important, from the perspective of U.S. political objectives, the people in such recipient countries might directly *experience* long-term development in their own lives, making the security aspects of the relationship acceptable. Examples of such positive results are discussed in Chapter 8.

This perspective seems like an echo from 1952 in India, where U.S. Ambassador Chester Bowles tried with little success to argue that U.S. economic aid should be used first to assist governments committed to the development of their people: "Bowles's strong belief in democratic values went hand in hand with his preference for aid to popularly based Third World governments over help to authoritarian ones, especially right-wing regimes. He was convinced that only governments enjoying strong public support would be able to create the climate of popular enthusiasm required for successful economic development."[3] Bowles also opposed using aid as a quid pro quo for obtaining military agreements between the United States and Asian governments. He was convinced that efforts to use aid "as a weapon to bring about significant changes in the international political or security positions of recipients were futile. They would either be rebuffed or, if accepted, would have limited value, because the pliant recipient government was unlikely to be able to bring its people genuinely to accept the changes."[4]

Using aid first to promote real development, especially toward the empowerment of people, would require that U.S. policymakers and aid practitioners maintain long-term perspectives even when trying to advance short-term political objectives. This is necessary because some aid efforts could create short-term strains in the relationship. For example, where political change toward democracy is occurring, even though such change is a long-term U.S. objective, it may be increasingly difficult to advance other, short-term U.S. objectives. This was the case in Thailand after the 1973 student uprising and subsequent elections created a democratic political process. Intense criticism of the close U.S. ties with the Thai military leadership, coupled with the threat of large, student-led protests during 1974, made it impossible for the United States to continue using the Thai air base at Uttapao. Thus, the United States lost a stopover point for U.S. aircraft supplying the U.S. base at Diego Garcia in the Indian Ocean. While Thai military leaders were willing to cooperate with this U.S. objective, they could not do so overtly at that time because students could easily observe U.S. planes taking off or landing.[5]

The U.S. embassy's political reporting process also became more difficult as more parties and interest groups participated in the emerging political process. It was no longer possible to rely on a few well-placed military officers or civilian bureaucrats to advance U.S. interests. There was greater need for those U.S. diplomatic and aid personnel having language capacity and social-cultural understanding to provide accurate analyses of the forces at work. Such expertise was in short supply.

The return to democracy in the Philippines following the fall of President Marcos also led to increased protests against U.S. military bases. In both of these countries, the aid relationship with the United States had clearly not been experienced in personal, developmentally positive ways by enough of the population to encourage them to resist those who highlighted negative aspects of the political relationship.

Many short-term political objectives—such as access to intelligence and communication facilities, military bases, passage of U.S. aircraft and naval vessels, or support for the United States on an issue before the United Nations—do not depend on a country's economic or political condition or the impact of any U.S. aid thereon. Providing a specific level of aid, however, does ensure U.S. access to the recipient government and the possibility that the leadership will cooperate with the United States on certain ad hoc issues. The 1989 A.I.D. study recognized that "economic growth–oriented development objectives have to function in uneasy tandem with other U.S. Government objectives and with their own, distinctly separate targets in host countries. While foreign aid is supposed to both influence policy and move money within a fixed time limit, in reality, the latter consideration generally drives the program."[6] It drives the program precisely because moving the money has the most direct impact in favor of the political objectives the United States may be pursuing.

Additional evidence that U.S. economic aid is allocated primarily on the basis of political objectives and interests is apparent in the number of countries that have clear development needs and opportunities yet receive only small amounts of aid. Bangladesh is an example today. India has always received less aid than would have been useful in responding to the development opportunities in its struggling democracy. Many countries in Africa provide other examples, including some that were priority recipients during the Cold War but for whom aid is being cut even when the opportunities for using aid for development purposes may never have been better. Though less aid for some countries may reflect these countries' limited capacity to use resources effectively, such considerations have seldom come into play when major political interests are involved.

Countries that have demonstrated their incapacity to use aid for development ends yet have continued to receive high levels of aid, even when they defied efforts to make such aid more effective, include Egypt, Liberia, Somalia, Honduras, and Zaire. The Philippines under Marcos also was notorious for its corruption and failure to use resources effectively. Mozambique and Ethiopia received aid even in the face of clear evidence that such aid could not serve a real development purpose. In these cases, the recipient government's political and economic failures created human suffering so massive that the U.S. public, who respond to pathetic scenes of starvation with little or no regard to the political causes of the disasters, have driven U.S. political leaders into "doing something" to show that they are not insensitive to suffering people. The sad reality is that even direct humanitarian aid to people who are suffering can actually help relieve the burdens of those leaders who created the disaster in the first place. Somalia, in October 1992, created a different dilemma, because the emergency food being flown in to fight mass starvation actually added to the violence as marauding clans hijacked food shipments almost at will.

The types of political linkages found in the Philippines, Zaire, Liberia, Somalia, Egypt, Israel, Honduras, El Salvador, Pakistan, and other countries that have received high levels of ESF aid can also have negative political side effects in other countries where the United States has few political interests. Countries whose aid is limited see the political linkages clearly. They see that these linkages are the real criteria for obtaining significant assistance and that the economic conditions in nonstrategic countries mean very little to the United States. Thus, the reaction of nonstrategic countries is often indifference to the United States, even when they receive a few million dollars of nonpolitical DA money.

In strategically important countries receiving high ESF levels, the United States has tolerated poor economic and political performance as long as stable government-to-government relations are maintained. Later, when political interest declines, so do the aid levels—as the Pakistan, Zaire, Somalia, and Liberia cases so clearly illustrate. Usually such declines have negative consequences, but not always. In Zaire, the decline of U.S. strategic interest might actually have created conditions more favorable to the development of political democracy. This U.S. objective was not pursuable during the Cold War, because the U.S. requirement for intelligence and transport facilities placed a special premium on stable political relations between the U.S. government and the Mobutu government. However, the new opportunities to use economic aid to support the democratization in Eastern Europe are a siren song that obscures such possibilities in the once important Third World.

Ultimately, foreign policy objectives such as self-sustainable peace, basic human rights, and free trade—all of which contribute to the security and well-being of the United States—depend on the progress other nations make toward responsive political systems and self-sustaining economies. Success in these areas will help sustain the earlier gains for shorter-term objectives, and facilitate as well the diplomatic dialogue that may become necessary in advancing future U.S. objectives. Maintaining gains for short-term political objectives ultimately becomes more difficult when the longer-term development objectives are not being attained. Clearly, this has been the case in Liberia, the Philippines, Zaire, Kenya, Jordan, Honduras, Pakistan, and Egypt.

THE PRICE OF EARMARKS

Earmarking high levels of aid for high-priority countries creates serious problems for other country programs. Egypt and Israel combined receive $2.2 billion in ESF every year; other major ESF recipients—the Philippines, El Salvador, Honduras, Pakistan, Turkey, and, most recently, Panama and Nicaragua—were allocated a total of $1.397 billion in FY 1990.[7] Economic aid from all sources (PL 480, ESF, DA, Peace Corps, international financial institutions) available for the rest of the world totaled approximately $7.2 billion.[8]

When U.S. foreign aid levels are cut for domestic budgetary reasons, the DA recipients are the major losers. These countries quickly learn not to rely on the United States as a long-term participant in their development process. Though not easily measurable, the quiet resentment following the loss of funds for long-planned projects is a political loss for the United States. Ultimately, if the momentum lost on the development process leaves a given country less able to meet debt repayments or otherwise move out of dependency relationships, there are also financial costs for the United States.

Perhaps the most adverse effect of politically based earmarks is that recipients take the aid as an entitlement and use the aid level as leverage against the United States. Any cut in the level can lead to a reduction in the recipient countries' commitment to help the United States. In some cases, as in Israel and Egypt, the earmark becomes so sacred that it cannot be cut, even when the recipients are not fulfilling their part of the bargain. Even worse, the recipient's performance is not open for discussion and evaluation because the issue is too politically sensitive for the recipient or because of U.S. domestic political concerns. Thus, with each passing year, the value of the aid for promoting U.S. interests lessens, while the value of its retention for the political purposes of the recipient increases.

The linkage between the Egyptian and the Israeli aid programs illustrates both the risk of political suicide and how the U.S. political process can impede development of sound foreign aid policy. In January 1990, Senator Robert Dole proposed that the Bush administration be permitted to obtain additional resources for Eastern Europe by cutting several ESF recipients like Israel and Egypt by 5 percent.[9] Dole's proposal drew immediate fire from the Israeli government, the America-Israel Public Affairs Committee (AIPAC), and many of Dole's colleagues in Congress.[10] The capacity of the president and the State Department to respond to new opportunities to support democracy in Eastern Europe was thus constrained by other players: Israel, AIPAC, and many members of Congress who know well the power of AIPAC and its capacity to affect their own political interests in getting reelected.

AID AND PERCEIVED DEVELOPMENT BENEFITS

If the recipient country's leaders and the general population perceive that U.S. economic aid *is* accomplishing its stated development objectives, opportunities to advance U.S. political objectives increase. A.I.D.-supported training programs, which development specialists refer to as "participant training," may be the aid tool best suited for advancing both development and political objectives.

Participant training has a potential forty-year payoff. It creates a cadre of contacts who can participate in policy dialogue with the United States as these former trainees move up in their government's hierarchy or elsewhere in the society's social structure. Because they are in the best position to experience the impact of U.S. development assistance in their own lives or in their countries, these people become valuable interlocutors even when they disagree with the United States on a given issue. Indeed, they can become the fabric that forms a safety net during periods of strong political disagreements. As these former trainees gain political importance, their capacity to help advance U.S. political or development objectives increases.

India is a classic example in this regard. The United States and India have long had strong political disagreements, yet over the decades U.S. dialogue with the Indian leadership and cadre throughout the government and wider society has continued to flourish. The dialogue is substantive because each treats the other as a colleague, rather than donor or recipient.[11]

In fact, the U.S.-Indian assistance relationship has had some success in both development and diplomatic terms precisely because the development efforts have been *experienced* by so many Indians. For over twenty-five years, the Indians chose to maintain closer diplomatic and military relations with the Soviets than with the United States. Nonetheless, with only brief interruptions, the United States was able to maintain an economic aid program with DA resources that focused on agriculture research and production, university support, health projects, and rural development. Participant training was a major element throughout.

The most spectacular success occurred in the agriculture sector when the United States, using emergency food shipments, helped the Indian government overcome the threat of mass starvation in the mid-1960s and then began long-term cooperation to improve agriculture research and extension programs. In August 1982, when I escorted three women from End World Hunger, a private U.S. PVO, to a meeting with the Indian ambassador to the United Nations, he told them that the Green Revolution actually began in India with the U.S. aid program, adding, "But we don't give you enough public credit for that."[12] The "credit," nevertheless, was expressed in the continued, quiet cooperation between U.S. and Indian diplomats in the United Nations Second Committee—the development committee—even during periods of tension when the Indian government often appeared to be more interested in serving Soviet political interests in other UN forums.

Participant training (PT) programs can be fully useful for diplomatic purposes only when contacts are maintained over the years. However, U.S. diplomats have generally failed to maintain follow-up procedures for strengthening personal relationships with the returned participants. Follow-up can be complicated, expensive, and subject to creativity-stifling audit problems. The constant rotation of U.S. personnel to other assignments also impedes retention of contacts. Then there is the problem of disregarding the selection criteria and using the PT program to reward a given minister's relative. In such cases, the compromises are usually explained as necessary to maintain good working relations with key host government officials.

The issues of most importance regarding the PT programs' future effectiveness include the capacity of LDC institutions to make use of the trainees' skills after they complete their training, the relative cost per trainee, the difficulty of integrating the trainees into U.S. institutions, and the need to continue U.S. support to the trainees when they return home.

Despite these problem areas, the benefits of participant training are worth the investment. If advancing political objectives must remain the primary purpose of U.S. foreign aid, A.I.D. should reallocate more resources from infrastructure to participant training programs. Granted, power plants form an essential base for productive economies in developing countries, but multilateral assistance institutions can meet these needs even in ESF recipient countries. Transferring bilateral aid resources through large, costly infrastructure projects is less effective over the long term for advancing political objectives than are less expensive training activities. Moreover, as discussed earlier in the case of Egypt and other countries, A.I.D.-funded, large-scale infrastructure projects have already created insurmountable recurrent-cost mortgages for countries with limited foreign exchange or tax revenues. Finally, training programs are more effective development tools because they are inherently empowering.

THE IMPACT OF RECIPIENT'S POLITICAL OBJECTIVES ON AID PROGRAMS

The recipient government's own diplomatic, political, and development objectives for accepting economic aid affect the aid's usefulness for advancing either U.S. political or development objectives. While obvious, as we have seen in Egypt and elsewhere, failure to take the recipient's objectives into account usually means that U.S. political objectives, even if achieved for the short run, will not be sustainable or will cost more than necessary. Moreover, advancing development objectives will become even more difficult, if not impossible.

In their assistance relationship, the United States and Egypt pursue often contradictory political and development agendas. For the United States, the political objective has moved beyond the mere cease-fire to a condition in which Israel and Egypt actively cooperate with each other on political and development issues. The historical record suggests that while both parties have sought a comprehensive peace settlement, the Egyptians—especially when Israel was unwilling to even discuss the possibility of relinquishing some control in the West Bank and Gaza—have been prepared to settle for an absence of war. This has also been Israel's approach. Both states continued to receive their congressionally mandated ESF assistance with no reductions in levels. The record shows even wider divergence on development objectives between the United States and these countries, both of which retain statist, socialized, and massively welfare-oriented economies dependent on U.S. economic and military aid.

From this perspective, and in light of the consequences of their last military confrontation, U.S. economic aid has only marginally influenced the political or economic policies of either Egypt or Israel. Certainly, Egypt was not going to launch another assault on Israel, even if it had received far less U.S. aid. Perhaps the aid resources could have induced greater activism toward comprehensive peace. However, at least until the 1992 elections that brought to power Yitzhak Rabin, who is more willing to explore possibilities for real peace with the Palestinians and Arabs, this possibility was undermined by Egypt's suspicion that Israel had no intention of giving up its "Greater Israel" concept. Moreover, after the 1990–1991 Gulf crisis, Egypt had better prospects for renewed financial assistance from previous Arab benefactors.

In Egypt, U.S. compromises of sound development-oriented criteria do not appear to have harmed the GOE's short-term foreign and domestic political objectives. If anything, U.S. willingness to ignore performance conditions in the economic reform policy process has enabled the GOE to avoid implementing the economic reforms. Cash transfers, the commodity import program, and U.S. help in obtaining IMF support have enabled the GOE to continue the subsidy-driven social contract with its people. Ultimately, these U.S. compromises hurt Egypt, but so far the government has chosen short-term political stability over long-term political-economic viability.

Israel's political agenda also differs from that of the United States. In 1981, for example, the Israeli deputy minister of finance was asked if he could ever see circumstances when the aid program would decrease. He allegedly replied, "What aid program? It's not an aid program; it's a narcotic and we are hooked. Do you think I fought in 1947 for my country to become a dependent of your country? That's ridiculous. But this escalator will go down when we tell you. You won't tell us."[13] The minister suggested that Israel's priority was paying off its military debt. The ESF resources enable Israel to pay its military debt, while freeing up resources to establish settlements in the West Bank. The U.S. objective is to advance the cause of peace by encouraging greater Israeli flexibility in trading land for peace in the West Bank, Gaza, and the Golan Heights.

The U.S. assistance relationships with Egypt, Israel, Liberia, Zaire, the Philippines, and other countries have clearly demonstrated that trading sound development criteria for short-term diplomatic objectives will exact its price at a later date, not only in terms of development lost but also by threats to previous political arrangements.The leaders of recipient countries, including elements within government ministries, also use the aid to sway domestic power balances.

This was clearly the case in the U.S.-Liberian aid relationship (and the others discussed in Chapter 6). Throughout the 1980s, the U.S. government transferred economic assistance resources to the government of Samuel K. Doe, with the stated intention of supporting that government's economic and political stability. However, the United States compromised its own development criteria for planning and implementing development projects by continuing to provide aid even when GAO reports and U.S. officials knew they were being misused and having no development impact. Thus, stability through development was not possible. Instead, key leaders in the Doe government used the assistance for personal economic gain and to enhance their political power vis-à-vis other groups in Liberia. The U.S. government's earlier compromises made this diversion easier.

The lesson Liberia teaches so clearly is that recipient countries' leaderships will often readily use their countries' geopolitical strategic value to obtain foreign aid, fully intending to use it to further their personal viability, even if other sectors of the society remain undeveloped as a result. Some may argue that these risks are inherent in any assistance effort and that political objectives do not leave the United States with the option of withholding assistance. The rationale becomes: Since the political constraints cannot be avoided, work within them toward developmental changes, at least on the margins, and accept the Liberia case as an exception.

This study demonstrates that such rationales nevertheless have a negative effect, even for the political objectives that drive the aid relationship. In the new international political environment and given the lessons offered in the cases discussed earlier, recipient governments should no longer be permitted to influence U.S. aid programs in ways that undermine the programs' capacity to stimulate sustainable development.

A major theme in this study has been that foreign economic assistance can most likely play a significant role in stimulating self-sustaining economic and social development in those countries where the political process is conducive to change in the nature, scope, and structure of a country's social and political power. The past thirty years of effort clearly demonstrate that without unwavering political will in the highest echelons of developing countries' governments to undertake uncomfortable changes, foreign aid cannot stimulate self-sustaining, growth-oriented economic and social development. That political will depends upon the agendas that evolve from the political processes in each country.

NOTES

1. A.I.D., *U.S. Overseas Loans and Grants*, pp. 13, 18, 19, 20, 21, 29, 30, 31, 121, 136. This total includes aid to Egypt ($33.8 billion), Israel ($42.7 billion), Jordan ($3.2 billion), Tunisia ($1.76 billion), Morocco ($2.36 billion), Lebanon ($577.6 million), Syria ($582.3 million), Yemen Arab Republic ($490.9 million), and Turkey ($11.6 billion). While part of the aid to Turkey related to its status as a member of NATO, Turkey is also a key player for U.S. policy in the Middle East, as the confrontation with Iraq demonstrated.

2. Ibid., pp. 35, 69, 89. Total economic and military aid for these three regions between 1962 and 1990 was $98.1 billion. Moreover, much of this aid was DA rather than ESF.

3. Howard B. Schaffer, *Chester Bowles—New Dealer in the Cold War,* an Institute for the Study of Diplomacy Book (Cambridge: Harvard University Press, 1993), chap. 4.

4. Ibid.

5. Zimmerman, journal notes in Bangkok, 1974.

6. A.I.D., *Development and the National Interest*, p. 113.

7. A.I.D., *FY 1990 CP*, Near East and Latin America annexes.

8. A.I.D., *U.S. Overseas Loans and Grants*, p. 4.

9. Helen Dewar and Al Kamen, "Cut in Aid to Israel Proposed," *Washington Post*, January 17, 1990.

10. Jackson Diehl, "Israeli Leaders React with Alarm to Proposal That U.S. Aid Be Cut," *Washington Post*, January 18, 1990.

11. Richard Brown, interview with author.

12. Zimmerman, personal journal notes, August 1982.

13. Robert Berg, interview with author.

8

To What End? Aid for Peace and Development

This chapter assesses the use of aid to promote broader U.S. foreign policy objectives concerned with peace, human rights, and political, economic, and social development. How well have U.S. economic assistance programs—in particular Economic Support Funds—met the political and economic development challenges set forth by Presidents Roosevelt and Kennedy and Ambassador McGhee? In 1963 Kennedy articulated a vision for U.S. aid, stating that a major objective should be to

> achieve a reduction and ultimate elimination of United States assistance by enabling nations to stand on their own as rapidly as possible. Both this nation and the countries we help have a stake in their reaching the point of self-sustaining growth—the point where they no longer require external aid to maintain their own independence. Our goal is not an arbitrary cutoff date but the earliest possible "takeoff" date—the date when their economies will have been launched with sufficient momentum to enable them to become self-supporting, requiring only the same normal sources of financing to meet expanding capital needs that this country required for many decades.[1]

Major criticisms of U.S. foreign aid have been that it concentrates too much on the Middle East, overemphasizes military sales, puts too many resources into bilateral ESF programs and not enough into multilateral institutions, and focuses too much on immediate political objectives. Echoing the expectations of Roosevelt, McGhee, and Kennedy, Representative Lee Hamilton argues that

> the purpose of the U.S. development program should be sustainable, broad-based economic growth in developing countries. When economic development benefits only the few, it cannot be sustained. Providing broad-based economic growth energizes all levels of the economy, from small farms and micro-enterprises to large establishments. This objective includes improving the capacity of the poor to participate in development. We must do what we can to alleviate the worst aspects of poverty. This means helping the poor to become productive members of society. . . . The objectives should also include increasing economic and social pluralism. Development is about justice as well as economic growth.[2]

Development is also about peace—peace based on resolution of the causes of conflict. Economic and social development creates the conditions for sustainable peace because it motivates people involved in conflict to reconcile their differences. How well has ESF aid promoted U.S. political-security objectives by helping to create the conditions of peace rather than by maintaining the absence of open warfare? How well has U.S. economic aid promoted respect for human rights and the development of social, political, and economic institutions and processes that most effectively ensure basic human rights? This chapter will address these questions on a global scale, though country-specific examples will emerge as appropriate.

PEACE

Promotion and maintenance of peace is the most effective way to ensure the security interests of the United States. Thus, peace, even if unstated, has always been the major immediate and long-term U.S. foreign policy objective. The United States has provided billions of dollars in economic assistance to this end, particularly with ESF resources, in the Middle East and Central America. This section will address the relationship between development and peace in these two regions and try to determine how well U.S. economic aid has helped to create the conditions for sustainable peace.

The Middle East

From the 1960s through the 1980s, U.S. diplomacy in the Middle East relied on military and economic assistance to maintain a U.S. political presence, ensure military cooperation when necessary, and promote expansion of the peace process between Israel and its Arab neighbors. Between 1962 and 1990, the United States provided Israel and Egypt $77.155 billion in economic and military aid, of which $33.814 billion was economic aid. Lesser amounts for Jordan, Tunisia, Morocco, Yemen, Oman, Syria, Turkey, and Lebanon totaled over $20 billion, of which $9.7 billion was economic aid.[3] The United States also provided trade credits, favorable terms for access to U.S. technology and food exports, military training programs, and sales of modern weaponry (tanks, fighter aircraft, and early warning aircraft) to Saudi Arabia, Kuwait, the Gulf Emirates, and Iraq.

Total aid to the Middle East equaled approximately 34 percent of all U.S. bilateral foreign military and economic aid for countries receiving U.S. aid between 1962 and 1990. Economic aid to the Middle East alone exceeded the combined total for Latin America and Africa and was more than double that for all of East Asia. Indeed, economic aid to Egypt and Israel exceeded the totals for any of these other three regions.[4]

The allocation of ESF resources in 1982, for example, illustrates U.S.

political-security priorities. To support the Middle East peace initiative, the United States allocated fully 72 percent of all ESF resources to that region.[5] If there is any region in the world in which to assess the effectiveness of using U.S. economic aid, most especially ESF, for advancing U.S. political objectives, including creating the conditions for peace, it has to be the Middle East.

The fundamental threat to peace in the Middle East, as elsewhere, has always been the underdeveloped social, economic, and political condition of the people in the feudal monarchies, military dictatorships, and struggling semidemocracies. Iraq's condition prior to its August 2, 1990, invasion of Kuwait provides a classic example. While Iraq's leadership modernized the economic infrastructure, it also maintained totalitarian control over an exceptionally underdeveloped and fragile political process. This weakness impelled the drift to war. In addition, Iraq's eight-year war with Iran resulted in enormous debt and a shattered economy. Saddam Hussein needed increased oil revenues to control the police-state apparatus which, in turn, protected his political position. Invading Kuwait was a means to this end—and an opportunity to pursue his messianic visions. The initial fearful reaction of other Arab states revealed their similar political weaknesses, especially their dependence on oil revenues to meet their peoples' social welfare needs.

From 1980 through 1990, the United States sought to use Iraq as a counterweight to revolutionary Iran. During this time, Iraq traded with U.S. farmers; received cooperation from U.S. intelligence agencies, including satellite-derived information during its war with Iran; sold oil to U.S. refiners that helped finance the Iraqi military buildup; and received only muted White House criticism of its human rights abuses and war crimes.

The U.S. decision in 1983 to remove Iraq from its list of countries supporting terrorism gave Iraq access to federal subsidies and loan guarantees. Between 1982 and 1990, Iraq purchased crops and livestock worth $5.5 billion, using federally guaranteed loans, agricultural subsidies, and its own hard cash. Moreover, subsequently declassified documents indicate that Iraq may have diverted some of these resources to purchase arms and high-tech equipment to support its own nuclear weapons program.[6] Finally, Iraq also obtained some $270 million in government-guaranteed credit from the Export-Import Bank to buy other U.S. goods, even though it had repeatedly failed to make loan repayments on time.[7] Throughout this period, the United States cooperated with Iraqi intelligence agencies in hopes of getting information on terrorist activity.

All of this cooperation, including the decision not to press Iraq for its human rights atrocities, was part of the attempt to expand U.S. influence with Saddam Hussein and to prevent an Iranian rout of Iraq during their eight-year war, which ended in 1988. After the war, administration officials believed that economic and political ties created the only opportunity to modify Saddam Hussein's behavior. The White House also argued in the months preceding Iraq's assault on Kuwait that those who wanted trade sanctions against Iraq would hurt U.S. farmers and business people without having any impact on Saddam's behavior. Some members of Congress from agricultural states also lobbied strongly against sanctions and for increased trade.[8] As late as October 1989, the Bush administration issued National Security Decision Directive #26, which proposed selling some military goods to Iraq as a "means of developing access to and influence with" the Iraqi military. The directive argued that normal U.S.-Iraqi relations "would serve our long-term interests in promoting stability in both the Gulf and the Middle East."[9]

In August 1990, Edward W. Gnehm, deputy assistant secretary of state for Near Eastern and South Asian affairs, explained that, being a global power, the United States was obligated to develop the closest possible relationships with countries that may affect U.S. strategic interests. In Iraq's case, the United States held "a reasonable expectation that Saddam Hussein might well want to develop closer ties to the West. He had an oil-based economy that was tied to the West. He had a technology base with Western interests. . . . There were lots of things that didn't work, but we hoped to be able to weave him into the fabric of Western nations. And we never tried to build that relationship with an extended hand without pointing out these problems with the other hand. I can only say it failed."[10] Deputy Secretary of State Lawrence Eagleburger repeated this theme during congressional hearings in May 1992: "It is clear that policy did not work. We tried. Because we tried does not mean that we created a Frankenstein monster. He was his own monster. We tried to contain him. We did not succeed."[11]

While these rationales are typical, almost standard operating procedure for a policy that focuses on obtaining and preserving stability above all and with whatever form of aid works best under existing circumstances, they still offer a revealing perspective. One could argue the "reasonable expectation" case only in the absence of, or indifference to, analysis of the nature of the Iraqi political-social process, including particularly the manner in which Saddam Hussein controlled and applied that power. Given the previous U.S. experience in Iran with the fall of the shah and the debate over how political analyses have been carried out and conveyed to decisionmakers, it is difficult to believe that U.S. intelligence analysts were unaware of the nature of power and its application in Iraq. Far more likely is the probability that circulation of such analyses would have been contrary to the prevailing company line and could have undermined the assistance policies.

Senator Alfonse M. D'Amato (R-New York) suggested this probability: "We were so desperate to believe we could convert him that we were taken completely in, and the State Department was a willing accomplice to it, because they wanted to believe too."[12] The hearings in September and October 1991 on the nomination of Robert Gates for director of the Central Intelligence Agency also raised the issue of politically influenced intelligence analysis—or simply discouraging analysis of the unthinkable.[13] During the 1992 presidential campaign, Democratic vice-presidential candidate Albert Gore, Jr. attacked President Bush, charging "his poor judgement, moral blindness, and bungling policies led directly to a war that should never have taken place. . . . The path leading us to that war and the path which the President followed after are deeply shadowed in profound error, in duplicity and in amoral disregard for our most basic values as a nation. . . . Coddling tyrants is a hallmark of the Bush foreign policy."[14]

Other countries followed similar practices. For example, Kuwait and other Arab oil producers, including Saudi Arabia, also provided tens of billions of dollars in economic aid to Iraq during and after the Iran-Iraq war to persuade Iraq that peaceful cooperation offered benefits preferable to war.

The uncomfortable reality, Gore's comments notwithstanding, is that the history of diplomacy reveals many examples of such "coddling" of dictators —and they cut across all U.S. administrations and appear in the diplomatic practices of many countries. This reality should not, however, continue to justify, or even simply explain, such diplomacy. The costs are clearly too tragic.

The fundamental issue is more than skewed intelligence processes, the desire to believe certain things in the face of other realities, or even duplicity. U.S. foreign policy toward Iraq, including its heavy reliance on the use of agricultural credits, intelligence exchanges, favorable trade policies, and economic aid, was fully consistent with a policy that gives priority to the stability of the moment, using whatever resources are available for that end. The net effect of all the U.S. behavior-modification, dollar-based diplomatic efforts was to buy the absence of war, or in Eagleburger's words, "to contain" Saddam. None of these efforts could create the conditions for sustainable peace based on reconciliation between peoples and states in conflict. It should hardly be surprising that these efforts failed to prevent an act of war and the rape of a nation of 600,000 people. Moreover, the behavior of U.S. regional allies and sometime friends during the Gulf crisis raises serious questions regarding the history and purposes of U.S. aid to nearly every country in the Middle East.

A major purpose of this aid, including over twenty years of U.S. military sales and aid to Saudi Arabia (although paid for by the Saudis), has been to ensure timely, unquestioned quid pro quo political and military cooperation in response to precisely the kind of threat that Iraq created. Why, then, was it necessary for the United States in 1990 to seek to provide additional tens of billions of dollars in aid and debt relief to cobble together an alliance of states whose own self-interest should have compelled them to welcome unhesitatingly and unconditionally the thousands of young Americans who came to camp among the sand dunes and protect Arab lives and treasures?

We can begin with Egypt. The U.S economic and military aid program to Egypt from 1974 through 1990, which totaled over $32 billion, contributed to the peace process between Israel and Egypt by improving their political relations and by encouraging Egypt to remain a moderate political voice in the Middle East. However, the U.S.-Egyptian aid relationship has not stimulated a social-economic development process with benefits throughout Egyptian society and demonstrable to the rest of the Arab world. A measure of these failures is Egypt's debt burden. After this aid relationship began, Egypt's debt skyrocketed from approximately $2 billion in 1974 to nearly $55 billion in 1990.

The lack of a generally positive experience among the Egyptian population with the U.S. role in Egypt contributed to President Mubarak's initial hesitancy to identify himself with the United States when responding to Iraq's invasion of Kuwait. Mubarak knew full well that any attempt by Saddam Hussein to appeal to pan-Arabism, the United States versus the Arabs, or to the struggle between rich and poor could strike positive chords among many Arabs, including intellectuals, throughout the region. Not having experienced U.S. aid in their "just cause"—for dignity and a better quality of life—the masses of Palestinians and other Arabs remained receptive to appeals from Saddam Hussein for his "just cause" against the United States and its ally, Israel.

Even journalists, academicians, professionals, and other intellectuals, many of whom were educated in the United States, reportedly believed that Saddam Hussein's action against Kuwait was an assertion of Arab dignity. Some observers suggested that many of these intellectuals, at a minimum, would have liked to see the United States "humbled . . . in the sands of the Arabian desert."[15]

Egypt's cooperation with the United States came less from any sense of obligation for past U.S. aid than in response to Defense Secretary Cheney's promise of more military and economic aid, relief on Egypt's $7 billion military debt to the United States, Saudi requests, expectations of additional Saudi aid later, hopes for other debt relief, and Saddam's attempts to incite civil conflict in Egypt, Saudi Arabia, and the other Gulf states.[16]

On the basis of $14 billion in U.S. and allied debt forgiveness alone, Egypt received about $300,000 per Egyptian soldier for the nearly 40,000 troops it eventually sent to Saudi Arabia. Yet, the Government of Egypt refused to allow Egyptian soldiers to directly attack Iraq, and it maintained this stance when the time came to use force.[17] During the first weeks after the invasion, Egypt was reportedly still willing to back a proposed payoff to Saddam if he would withdraw from Kuwait. The concessions considered included a share of the oil fields and continued Iraqi presence on Bubiyan Island, which controls access to Iraqi ports. An unidentified Egyptian revealed that "the Egyptian strategy was to use the buildup against him, and then turn at the last minute and offer him a way out, a face-saving so he [would] not go away empty-handed."[18] Trying to ensure that Saddam would not go away empty-handed was fully consistent with Egypt's own approach to U.S. economic and military aid in return for maintaining peace with Israel, and with U.S. dollar diplomacy in the Middle East over the previous seventeen years.

The early behavior of Saudi Arabia also reflected the weakness of using arms transfers as a means to deter hostile nations from waging war. During the most blatant act of aggression, the Saudis wavered. The United States undertook heroic behind-the-scenes diplomacy, laced with additional promises of future arms transfers, to entice the Saudis to collaborate in their own defense. However, such sales created uneasiness among the Israelis, who demanded additional U.S. assurances and offsetting military aid.[19]

Why were the Saudis, who had received so much U.S. military equipment in the past, still unable to match Saddam? In addition to Saudi concerns about Arab brotherhood and a far more limited manpower pool, Israel had successfully opposed every U.S. effort to strengthen Saudi Arabia militarily. Thus, the arms transfers were always limited in both quantity and quality. These transfers were as much for diplomatic purposes—to "buy" access to Saudi facilities in the event of war—as to create a credible Saudi military force that might deter a potential aggressor.

Israel's supporters in the U.S. Congress continue to exercise a veto over the nature of U.S.-Saudi military cooperation, even while many of those same supporters bemoaned the Saudis' inability to play a bigger role in facing down Saddam Hussein. The Bush administration and the Saudi government decided in early January 1991 not to push for more arms transfers for fear of activating the Israeli lobby in the United States and a battle in Congress during the national debate over Gulf policy.[20]

Jordan's behavior was even more telling. Despite twenty-seven years of U.S. economic and military aid totaling over $3 billion,[21] Jordan's King Hussein became an apologist for Saddam Hussein. Thousands of Jordanians signed up to fight for Saddam, and on August 12, 1990, King Hussein publicly accused the United States of creating an "explosive situation" in the Middle East.[22] Three months later, he used even harsher language, attributing the goals of the United States and its Western allies to "their desire to control our destiny and the Arab nations' resources. Their blatant and shameless conduct must confirm to us that their real motives are far from being the hollow claim to uphold legitimacy and defend principles." He criticized the failure to act against "Israeli aggression while assuming the role of international defenders of international legitimacy and human rights in The Gulf. They maintain this double-standard attitude with the least regard for principles."[23]

Defying the United Nations Security Council resolution imposing trade sanctions on Iraq, King Hussein continued for several weeks to permit Iraq to import through Jordan's port at Aqaba everything from food to chemicals. Moreover, Jordan's military reportedly provided reconnaissance aid to Iraq and may have helped train Iraqi troops to use Hawk missiles captured in Kuwait.[24] And after Saddam's forces were routed, U.S. Navy Rear Admiral Mike McConnell, director of intelligence for the Joint Chiefs of Staff, confirmed that arms supplied to Jordan with January 1991 shipping dates were found stockpiled in former Iraqi-held facilities and bunkers in Kuwait.[25] Throughout 1991–1992, Jordan continued to defy the UN sanctions by turning a blind eye to Iraqi trade through Jordan and the port at Aqaba.[26]

In response to Jordan's early support for Saddam, Congressman Stephen J. Solarz threatened a cutoff in U.S. aid in order to get the king to cooperate. Solarz suggested that the king's "whole relationship with the United States hinged on making the sanctions effective. . . . Given the interests we have in the Gulf, it's inconceivable that we'd be prepared to maintain relations as we have in the past if he subverts the sanctions meant to bring the aggression to an end."[27] President Bush took a different tack. He offered more aid to Jordan if it would honor the embargo and make a U.S. blockade of Aqaba unnecessary. In both approaches, the United States demonstrated the blatant use of economic aid for political objectives.

The Jordanian case illustrates the ineffectiveness of such manipulation when the aid does not address the political-economic conditions that provide the tinder for war. A.I.D.'s FY 1990 Congressional Presentation had praised Jordan's commitment to the Arab-Israeli peace process, directly linking political stability to economic growth and development: "Jordan realizes that regional stability is essential for economic growth. Only through political stability and cooperation can Jordan and the region play a more vital political and economic role in world affairs. . . . Jordan must remain economically and politically strong while maintaining ties with other moderate Arab nations and the West, particularly the United States. The United States Government, with similar strategic objectives in the region, has a vested interest in a stable Jordan and must support the GOJ by providing a substantial economic assistance program that promotes sustained economic growth."[28]

Nevertheless, over thirty-five years of U.S. aid had not ensured that Jordan could stand as a reliable ally during the greatest threat to Middle East peace since the Arab-Israeli war of 1973. U.S. aid could not buy this friend, yet some members of Congress proposed terminating aid to force compliance, while the president promised even more aid as a reward for cooperation. Clearly, Jordanians resent aid that creates dependencies that later can be used to coerce cooperation with the United States.

Because of these weaknesses, other factors easily overrode the political objectives of the U.S.-Jordanian aid relationship. U.S. economic aid did not enable Jordan to reduce its dependence on Iraq for much of its oil and for most of the trade that flows through the port of Aqaba. Large numbers of the Jordanian people, 60 percent of whom are Palestinian, had not experienced enough benefit from the U.S.-Jordanian aid relationship to overcome their susceptibility to Saddam's pan-Arabist appeals. Instead, they appeared to believe that Saddam's assault on the rich Kuwaitis would yield more benefits to them than the existing U.S. relationship. For Jordan's Palestinian population, U.S. ties and policies toward Israel overrode the aggression of one Arab state against another. They quickly accused the United States of applying a double standard in its Middle East policies, noting that there had been no blockade of Israel when it invaded Lebanon in 1982, nor had the United States cut even one dollar of its aid to Israel. Most Arabs recognize that even though Israeli policy in the West Bank violates UN resolutions demanding Israel's withdrawal from the Occupied Territories, the United States has not applied any sanctions against Israel. All of these factors obtain throughout the Arab world, even though much of its leadership supported the U.S.-led reaction to Saddam Hussein.[29]

Throughout the crisis, Tunisia, also a longtime recipient of U.S. economic assistance, opposed the U.S. deployment of troops to Saudi Arabia. Only Turkey and Morocco, after initial, limited hesitation, rallied to oppose Saddam's aggression.

The U.S.-led coalition finally prevailed in a remarkably short, carefully implemented six-week air and 100-hour ground campaign that ended on February 28, 1991. The United States had taken the lead from the outset. Through highly skilled diplomacy, it gathered from its allies among the Arabs, the Europeans (primarily Germany), and the Japanese enough financial support for a military effort to reinforce its diplomatic efforts in the United Nations to build an anti-Saddam coalition with its NATO allies and many Arab states (including at least one enemy, Syria). Saddam's forces were battered and forced to withdraw from Kuwait.

Peace, defined as the absence of war between states, had returned to the Persian Gulf by the end of May 1991. Iraq is supposed to pay reparations to Kuwait. It is supposed to remain under UN-imposed sanctions and supervision, probably until Saddam is at last forced from power. Finally, Iraq's nuclear and chemical weapons will be destroyed. This victory was a major example of the successful use of economic assistance, along with military aid and force, to advance U.S. political objectives.

But serious weaknesses surfaced in the commitment under United Nations auspices to make Saddam pay for his aggression and prevent him from ever becoming a threat again. Jordan continued to facilitate leakage in the trade sanctions until mid-1992. Moreover, even the Arab League's secretary general, Esmat Abdel-Meguid, an Egyptian, suggested that sanctions against Iraq be eased in order to relieve the suffering of the Iraqi people.[30]

Thus, in many ways this success had only restored the peace of the status quo ante in most of the Middle East—a peace bought by economic and military aid but not built on conditions that could be sustained without that assistance. Moreover, by the fall of 1992 there were reports of Iran's renewed effort to modernize its military and technological power base, even while continuing to deny empowerment to its people. Peace, defined in terms of the personal security, basic welfare, and viable opportunities for common men, women, and children to improve their own lives, remained only a distant dream.

Central America

In contrast to the Middle East, U.S. aid to Central America during the 1980s was more directly *intended* to foster the long-term conditions for peace, and the types of projects more directly reflected the intended purposes. This region, which former U.S. ambassador to the United Nations Jeane J. Kirkpatrick once described as "the most important place in the world for the United States today," received over $9 billion in U.S. economic and military aid in the 1980s.[31] Costa Rica, El Salvador, Guatemala, Honduras, Nicaragua, Panama, and Belize combined received $1.2 billion in 1985 alone.

Economic aid supported development of local organizations in agriculture and labor, strengthened government institutions, repaired damages from insurgent warfare, and bought time while diplomatic and military efforts created the opportunity to end regional conflict. Democracy and market economies are developing in every Central American country. It is possible that these opportunities would not have evolved without U.S. economic aid to Honduras and El Salvador, but the evidence shows that the assistance has not yet stimulated *sustainable* progress for either democracy or economic growth.

While President Reagan's policies became "the first time in the history of U.S.–Central American relations that the colonels knew that the U.S. didn't want them running their governments"[32] and led to elected civilian governments at least nominally replacing most military dictatorships that began the decade, little else seems to have changed. Despite billions of aid dollars throughout the 1980s, the sad state of education, literacy, and housing remained about where it was when the decade began.[33] Health care has improved to some extent, with the necessary help of U.S. aid for significant parts of the relevant government programs.

Human rights abuses still occur, and the feudal nature of social structures in Central America will continue to impede democratic development for the immediate future. Maintaining fundamental government programs and buying time were probably all that the aid could have achieved, given that the recipient governments had to deal with serious, subversive military and political destabilization efforts supported from Nicaragua and Cuba. Within this reality, U.S. aid efforts helped create the opportunity for sustainable peace, but that peace has to be built on sound political, economic, and social development. There were new opportunities for carefully targeted, imaginative, and less expensive economic aid programs. With the end of the Cold War and its most violent manifestations in the region, the real question in 1990 was whether these programs would be forthcoming.

Few observers expected they would be. The 1991 economic aid request to Congress for these countries totaled only $840 million. Central America's plight was no longer a mobilizing cause for the politicians, interest groups, and academics, who once built careers and multimillion-dollar organizations on both sides of the struggle during the 1980s by appealing to the hearts, minds, and pocketbooks of the American people.[34]

This type of priority change parallels that which Pakistan, Zaire, Liberia, Somalia, and other nations are experiencing as the compelling force once called the Cold War recedes. Though inspired by legitimate domestic political and social grievences, the insurgencies had been opportunities for external superpower competition.[35] They are winding down in the early 1990s because these external players now have to address new priorities. The remaining question is whether these new priorities will include helping to create opportunities for better lives in the villages that were once part of the superpower battlefield.

HUMAN RIGHTS

The United Nations community generally recognizes three categories of human rights: economic, social, and political. Economic rights include the rights to work, to change jobs, to relocate in order to obtain remunerative employment, and to campaign for safe working conditions and fair wages. Social rights include the rights to education, basic health care, and adequate food and nutrition. Political rights include the right to free speech; the right to organize political groups; free and fair elections; and access to information.

U.S. economic aid has helped developing countries' governments meet social rights in basic education and health for millions of people, especially when U.S. resources have been readily available to support these project purposes. This aid has built schools and health clinics; trained teachers, nurses, doctors, and health workers; provided medical supplies in rural and urban areas; and improved access to food and nutrition through PL 480 food aid programs and other agriculture-oriented projects. Aid programs have also helped create new employment opportunities through the creation of large-scale infrastructure projects, the opening of rural areas with road projects, support for small-scale enterprise programs, farmers' cooperative organizations, vocational training programs, and labor organizations.

The open question is whether these gains can be sustained and, more important, whether individual human potential can be more fully realized. Success depends on continuing advances in peoples' political rights and the impact of this on developing political processes, as well as on recipient governments' commitment of their own resources to replace the foreign aid that has been so instrumental in the social-economic welfare areas.

The political process in all countries is the major determinant in creating a human rights environment conducive to the development of people. It also sets the parameters within which foreign aid can be applied to such ends. Throughout the thirty-year period from 1960 to 1990, the United States was reluctant to address political development issues directly, though it was often involved in projects that in one way or another affected the development of democratic institutions. A.I.D.'s primary instruments for promoting human rights were private voluntary organizations, which removed A.I.D. from the onus of everyday involvement in this sensitive area.[36]

U.S. economic aid programs that have at times promoted institutional development in ways that stimulate responsive government include Title IX (Utilization of Democratic Institutions in Development) and the Human Rights Initiative: Encouraging Development of Civil and Human Rights. Congress created the Title IX program because a majority supported the idea that development required changes in human institutions. Section 108 of the 1969 Foreign Assistance Act (FAA) encouraged A.I.D. to support participatory institutional development in the social, economic, and political domains. The Title IX program supported university research and training projects aimed at incorporating development of social and political institutions into A.I.D. projects. Under this initiative, Stanford University conducted research on effective participatory methods; Northwestern University looked at modernization and sociopolitical participation; the Fletcher School at Tufts University provided training in the social and political aspects of development; and Yale University examined the role of law and legal institutions in development.[37]

The United States became most directly involved in human rights programs when Congress amended the FAAs of 1974 and 1978 to provide that A.I.D. should program resources for political rights–oriented project activities. Congress became most committed in the 1970s to application of human rights principles in the conduct of U.S. foreign policy because of frustration over its inability to constrain executive power during the Vietnam War and by former Secretary of State Henry Kissinger's practice of realpolitik during the 1973 coup in Chile. Congress chose to use the power of the purse to obtain leverage in the foreign policy process. Aid legislation tied the provision of U.S. economic and military aid to judgments on human rights and "gave Congress the initiative in pressing selected issues of human rights into the policy process by threatening to deny U.S. aid to countries shown to engage in 'a consistent pattern of gross violations of human rights.' "[38]

Section 502(b) of the 1974 Foreign Assistance Act attempts to tie foreign aid to developing country adherence to human rights. In accordance with this act, the Carter administration established human rights initiatives aimed at enhancing individual integrity through civil and human rights projects. The Reagan administration, however, narrowed the focus to strengthening democratic institutions as the best guarantor of individual human rights. This approach excluded "economic rights" from the general human rights arena. Rights pertaining to individual work and production were "left to the ebb and flow of the market place rather than to the rule of law."[39]

Rev. J. Bryan Hehir, Joseph Kennedy Professor of Christian Ethics at Georgetown University, contends that the United States requires a human rights policy on political and moral grounds. He notes that "when the United States provides military and economic assistance to a government accused of 'gross and systematic' violations of human rights, the provision of the assistance *de facto* implicates the United States in the charge against the government. The degree of moral responsibility will vary with the kind and amount of aid provided as well as with the degree of dependence the government has on U.S. support." U.S. foreign aid legislation requires public examination of the moral responsibility the United States incurs by giving aid. "Looked at in this way, human rights policy is not 'an intervention' or principally a 'punitive' measure by the United States into the affairs of another country, but a scrutiny of its own policy." Thus, the purpose of human rights conditions is "not to tell others what to do, but to establish the conditions under which the United States will cooperate with another government."[40]

A.I.D. issued its formal Policy Determination on Human Rights after Congress added Section 116(e) to the FAA of 1978. This directive specified that A.I.D. should "carry out programs and activities that will enhance adherence to civil and political rights. Such activities are appropriate for a developmental organization because the United States recognizes that the engine of economic growth is personal liberty."[41] Section 116(e) authorized not less than $3 million for studies and programs that would promote civil and political rights. Interestingly, the policy determination held that civil and political rights could not be separated from economic policies or development.[42]

Consistent with this view, A.I.D. support includes projects for (a) research and discussion of civil and political rights, (b) adherence to the rule of law through a legal framework conducive to civil and political rights, (c) free and democratic electoral systems, (d) development of democratic principles and institutions that promote human rights, and (e) development of human rights organizations. The A.I.D. human rights program for Asia and the Near East began in 1979. Through FY 1987, A.I.D. had obligated $5.6 million for human rights–related projects, out of an annual foreign aid budget that averaged at least $6 billion per year in economic and military aid for these regions.

A.I.D. distributed these funds through various foundations and organizations to support strengthening of legal systems and to increase access to justice. The Asia Foundation's human rights program for Asia includes projects to improve the skills and human rights orientation of lawyers and judges, as well as the other types of projects listed above. Beginning in 1985, America-Mideast Educational and Training Services (AMIDEAST) managed a four-year, $685,000 project that provided education and training for legal professionals—lawyers, judges, prosecutors, law professors, and magistrates—in Egypt, Jordan, and Morocco.

A.I.D. has focused its most in-depth investment in democratic and human rights initiatives in Latin America and the Caribbean. These programs began in the 1960s under Title IX and included legislative development projects, local government, civic education, and leadership training. In 1985, Congress authorized another project, the Regional Administration of Justice project, that has since expanded beyond Central America to incorporate six South American countries. This project seeks to strengthen national legal and judicial systems. Its funding increased from several hundred thousand dollars in 1985 to $11.8 million in ESF through 1986.[43]

The U.S. approach in Africa, at least up to 1989, was more piecemeal than its approach toward the other regions. The Human Rights Fund for Africa includes small grant projects for thirty countries in activities such as seminars and conferences, educational programs, local research, scholarship programs, and assistance to local organizations.

U.S. support for efforts in the human rights area is a delicate process because the aid programs are on a government-to-government basis. Obtaining recipient government cooperation for assistance to human rights organizations is difficult. First, the human rights organizations, both domestic and foreign, are likely to have been long opposed to the recipient government because of its alleged human rights abuses. Such opposition would probably have created hard feelings and mistrust on both sides—and certainly not contributed to a willingness on the part of the government to see its opponents funded by a foreign government, even if it permits such organizations to exist.

Second, having to accept aid for the purpose of improving alleged human rights violations or weaknesses is more than embarrassing; it compromises a government's integrity and legitimacy both domestically and internationally. Moreover, conflicts of interest on these issues and on the project implementation process can create tensions that could impede government-to-government dialogue on other diplomatic and development objectives. For these reasons, even indirect aid efforts through PVOs must be handled with discretion.

Two types of long-standing A.I.D.-sponsored project aid that could have significant impact on human rights in the political arena are participant training and local government decentralization projects. Participant training programs, whether funded by A.I.D. or through PVOs, provide training in law and public administration. Moreover, all training in the United States exposes the participants to the U.S. political process. Any participant who watches evening television news programs or simply scans the front page of a major newspaper will likely find an issue that involves basic human rights. These visitors will also witness how the U.S. political process—including its free press, the interest groups involved, the political parties, Congress, and the courts—addresses rights issues.

The impact of such training experiences on a participant's view of human rights issues in his or her country is difficult to measure. Nevertheless, there is undeniable impact. The author recalls an instance in Thailand in December 1974. One of the primary student leaders in that country, Seksan Prasertkul, returned from a short visit to the United States. During his interview at Don Muang Airport in Bangkok, he commented on the U.S. political process. Seksan observed, "The Watergate scandal shows that American democracy works. It did not prevent the political corruption that occurred, but the political and legal systems could bring even the President to justice."[44]

Local government and decentralization projects affect human rights and the political process by creating and strengthening local government administration and providing opportunities for local participation in the planning and implementation of development projects. These skills and this experience are necessary prerequisites for the day when local government entities can raise and spend their own revenues. Moreover, spreading the idea that the people should have a say in how their governments spend money in their villages and provinces advances human rights.

Again, an incident in Indonesia in the spring of 1980 illustrates this point. A.I.D. and representatives of several Indonesian government ministries were reviewing a joint evaluation of the Luwu Area Development project, which was under way in the island province of Suluwesi. A member of the Suluwesi Provincial Assembly attended the evaluation discussion at A.I.D. offices in Jakarta. He told the central government representatives that his assembly had sent him to the meeting to ensure that the local people's views on the Luwu project's strengths and weaknesses were presented and discussed. Indirectly, but clearly, this project was beginning to have an impact on the Suluwesi people's capacity to secure greater responsiveness from the central authorities in Jakarta.[45]

U.S. officials and the U.S. contractors who work on development projects can also affect human rights in the political arena. Many of these officials maintain their own small libraries in their homes, which often contain books and other literature that are full of information, ideas, and political theories. The children of host country employees of the A.I.D. mission or friends of U.S. employees will frequently have opportunities to borrow these books. At the least, these activities help spread concepts of political freedom and organization, thereby advancing U.S. diplomatic objectives related to the promotion and protection of basic human rights.

How effective are these U.S. efforts to use economic aid to advance U.S. diplomatic objectives in the human rights area? Beyond anecdotal indications of impact, have U.S. human rights activities resulted in measurable improvements? The simple answer is either "no" or "we do not know."

Because there were so few evaluations of these activities, the 1990 A.I.D. report on the agency's democratic and human rights initiatives based much of its findings on interviews of A.I.D. officials previously or presently involved in democratic initiatives work. Such interviews, which permitted the documentation to be cross-checked, uncovered information that was not available in other A.I.D. reports. Some A.I.D. officials noted that a significant limitation of the written documentation is that it tended "to gloss over certain realities because of the political sensitivities surrounding the topic of democratic initiatives *as well as the level of A.I.D. interest in these initiatives*"[46] (emphasis added).

The 1990 A.I.D. evaluation focused on legal institution-building efforts because A.I.D. considered these the strongest programs. The evaluation used four effectiveness criteria—management organization, including monitoring and evaluation; institution-building effectiveness; improvements in human rights; and sustainability—to assess the aid projects in each of the three geographic regions. Following are the findings:

- *Management Organization*: The evaluation was inconclusive due to A.I.D. mission inattention to monitoring and the absence of an effective management communication system. Another serious drawback was the lack of identifiable program performance indicators and evaluation factors. At least one interviewee believed these weaknesses reflected a lack of A.I.D. commitment.
- *Institution-Building Effectiveness*: The evaluation found limited impact on legal reform in Asia and the Near East. It concluded that transforming judicial systems in Latin America may be ambitious. In Africa, legal reform was limited and probably not intended to have much impact.
- *Improvements in Human Rights*: The evaluation observed no significant change in Asia and the Near East, found too many external variables in Latin America to permit measures of improvement, and determined no measure of change in Africa.
- *Sustainability*: Sustainability is perhaps the most telling part of the evaluation. In Asia and the Near East, it concluded that the programs were financially unsustainable given the lack of government support. Moreover, most organizations were unsustainable. In Latin America, questions of financial absorptive capacity and uncertain financial viability of national institutions arose after A.I.D. support ceased. In Africa, it was unclear that sustainability was the intended outcome.[47]

These summary findings are neither surprising nor conclusive. The evaluation did find case-specific positive impact in different projects, but as with all projects, some people always benefit while the aid program is implemented and foreign funds are available. The real test is whether a program continues when the U.S. aid ends. On this score it is too early to tell.

In terms of lessons learned, the evaluation found that the transfer of the substance and processes of democratic development was more important than the transfer of the forms of some preferred democratic system. It also contended that A.I.D. had to make a strong commitment to carry out democratic initiatives. "As is true for much of what is done in the name of development, individual A.I.D. officials must share corporately in the conviction that democratic institution building is the 'right' thing to do."[48] Equally important was the lesson that the host country or some group within the society should initiate democratic efforts. Intermediary, nongovernmental organizations are the ideal entities to administer country human rights activities.

Finally, "human rights activities require a low profile. . . . The human rights area is rife with potential to become politicized and emotionalized. . . . The success of legal institution building efforts results not from the degree of publicity they engender but the number of people whose rights are positively affected and the extent to which these efforts penetrate the institutions they are intended to serve."[49] Another lesson might be that democracy is itself an evolving political process, even in the United States.

In many countries, the United States has been unable or unwilling to engage in such aid programs. Particularly during the Cold War, the United States infrequently used letters of protest or withheld economic aid when human rights violations occurred. In important ESF recipient countries, three considerations usually overrode any public U.S. protest. First, the alleged violations were either random or lacked clear proof. Second, the country in question—read Liberia or the Philippines—was important to the United States because of high-priority political interests, which would be threatened by U.S. intervention. Finally, using aid for human rights activities requires host country cooperation.

In its conclusion, the report emphasized the importance of pursuing human rights policy without damaging other important U.S. interests. Most A.I.D. officials believe it is impractical to turn the aid flow (whether ESF or DA) off and on in response to human rights conditions, because doing so disrupts other aspects of the long-term development process. In many cases, particularly during the Cold War period, the only viable approach was to respond to human rights conditions through normal diplomatic channels, behind closed doors and with no public fanfare. "Probably the most appropriate response is for A.I.D. to continue to support the 'positive' aspect of human rights activities by supporting developmental activities, while allowing the State Department to respond to human rights violations, as is their current responsibility under the law."[50]

This latter approach was standard practice into the late 1980s. But it was inadequate for responding to unexpected opportunities to support a positive human rights change in a country previously prohibited from receiving U.S. aid. The aid programming processes, including congressional reporting requirements, were and remain too inflexible. There are no unearmarked "opportunity funds." All funds are programmed into projects. Taking funds even from projects that have large pipelines of unused funds requires agreement from the recipient government and from many different A.I.D. offices, as well as a congressional notification of such a reallocation of funds. Obtaining new funds to respond to unexpected opportunities would still require following the annual Congressional Presentation process. Finally, designing an appropriate project activity would take a year under the best of circumstances. Political priorities are changing, however, as the next section discusses.

POLITICAL AND ECONOMIC DEVELOPMENT

Assessing the economic and political development impact of any type of U.S. economic aid is difficult because of the many different variables in the development process. If development does not occur in a given situation, it is difficult to prove that one actor—in this case the United States through its assistance programs—by pursuing other, nondevelopment objectives, was not supportive of development, or even in part undermined development objectives. The many definitions of development, including confusion between modernization and development, also make assessment of impact difficult. These reasons can easily stifle any attempt to evaluate impact or to criticize any type of completed assessment. Despite these difficulties, some assessment is necessary. This section continues the assessments begun in previous chapters based on the definition of development suggested in Chapter 3.

The United States has clearly stated development-related objectives in all Congressional Presentations for foreign economic aid and has argued that attainment of these objectives will advance U.S. political objectives. It is also useful to remember that the United States since 1946 has expended over $222.3 billion in foreign economic aid *with development rationales*.[51] As noted in earlier chapters, A.I.D. itself began an honest effort in 1989 to assess the effectiveness of foreign aid in terms of its development-oriented objectives.[52] After a quarter of a century, does the evidence show that "America [has] applied the dynamism and realism to its official development programs that have been the keys to development success for ourselves and other individual nations? Is today's U.S. foreign aid fostering healthy development towards independent prosperity—or simply postponing the day of reckoning for governments unwilling or unable to take the politically painful steps needed for their own development?"[53]

Based on a general scan of the so-called underdeveloped world, it seems clear—even if only defined by the capacity of people throughout a given society to improve their welfare—that economic, social, and political development has not occurred in a way that reduces the amount of poverty and suffering in many parts of Africa, the Middle East, Asia, and Latin America.

Ambassador Millicent Fenwick addressed this issue at length after her 1984 trip to Africa. Appalled at the continuing starvation and hunger she had witnessed, she charged that "foreign aid as now administered has demonstrably failed as a bulwark against hunger, despite the expenditure of enormous sums of money. Development aid from all sources to the African states was over $20 billion in only two years—1980 and 1981—and yet in 24 African countries, with an estimated population of 150 million, some 25 to 30 million are at risk today. If the planning were adequate, such suffering would not occur except in an emergency. Present plans have not worked."[54]

The 1989 A.I.D. study also found that only a handful of countries that started receiving U.S. aid in the 1950s and 1960s had graduated from dependent status. It argued that an open-ended maintenance program for developing countries was never envisioned by the pioneers of development policy. On the contrary, where development has occurred, economic growth has been the key. And this growth has been "largely the result of individual nations making the right policy choices and making the most of their internal human and natural resources. . . . Direct U.S. development assistance, overall, has played a secondary role and has not always succeeded in fostering growth-oriented policies among recipient states."[55]

Neither Ambassador Fenwick nor the A.I.D. study, however, get to the question of why the aid plans haven't worked. It is difficult to say that the planning has been inadequate, though in many cases this may be a major factor, when so often the development-oriented plans have not been allowed to work without persistent interventions in favor of the political objectives for which the aid was provided in the first place. The Congressional Presentation clearly delineates development rationales and objectives at the time the administration requests resources from Congress. It ought to be possible to determine whether, even when aid is used to pursue high-priority political objectives, the United States has successfully encouraged reforms and project activities that stimulated a country's capacity for self-sustaining development.

Foreign Aid and Social-Political Change

The past thirty years of experience includes project-specific cases where the United States has successfully applied aid to create institutional capacity, at least in the short term, that can be useful in the development process. But the United States does not consistently allocate and apply aid in ways that persuade developing countries to commit additional resources and to make the larger social, political, and economic changes that will promote a national environment conducive to sustainable development. Diplomatic necessities have consistently overridden development necessities in too many politically important countries.

The United States has regularly provided balance of payments assistance to promote political stability. Unfortunately, such assistance, particularly in countries of political importance to the United States (like Egypt and Liberia), has basically relieved only short-term fiscal stress for the recipient governments, thus enabling them to avoid painful economic and fiscal reforms and maintain the status quo.

Development, particularly political development, can lead to rapid change. Change creates instability. Instability is a virtual anathema for the diplomatic process, which requires stable government-to-government relations, a degree of predictability, and confidence that diplomatic agreements can be sustained. As democratization of the political process takes effect, the internal debate in the recipient country can create pressures that affect U.S. security and economic interests. The tensions in these areas are inherent, especially when a given economic assistance program does not appear to work.

In the past, there may have been a subconscious reflex against applying politically oriented development aid that risked promoting instability. Building roads and power plants, for example, is far less destabilizing than creating legal aid organizations or autonomous labor unions. Large infrastructure projects are also highly visible manifestations of the aid relationship, which serves U.S. diplomatic objectives.

Thus, policy dialogues that aim at the redistribution of power will be unsuccessful unless the U.S.-proposed reforms are relevant to the types of power structure changes that the recipient government leadership has already decided to strive for. For example, in its effort to promote democratization in South Korea, the United States provided strong support to the cooperative movement. U.S. experience had shown that cooperatives promoted local-level power, responsibility, and organizational, planning, and implementation capacities. Cooperatives were an empowering process that would support democratization. In Korea, however, the cooperative movement was a parastatal organization designed to serve the government's interests in the rural areas. It was and remained a very strong organization for political control, despite the contrary efforts of U.S. aid at a time when many felt the United States almost owned the country.

Nevertheless, when the Koreans decided to develop local capital for investment in industry with export potential, they did accept U.S. advice on interest rate reforms. The reforms attracted considerable capital to the banks, which then used them for development purposes. In this case, the Koreans accepted the U.S. advice because it enabled them to achieve objectives they had already committed themselves to.[56]

Despite the limitations created by the differing political agendas of the United States and its aid recipients, there is substantial project-specific evidence that the aid can benefit at least the project participants, even when applied primarily for political purposes. Projects create new capacities, either through the transfer of knowledge and skills in participant training programs or the building of irrigation systems, roads, and power plants. The issue then becomes the recipient country's capacity to maintain or even enhance these gains without further support from foreign donors. In cases where U.S. political objectives determine whether or not there is any aid, does the recipient government seek such self-sustainable development?

Institutional Development

U.S. aid projects that have built linkages with recipient country institutions, particularly universities and other research institutions, probably offer the best prospects for long-term development impact. The Asia Foundation (TAF) has created successful, regionally focused university linkage mechanisms using A.I.D. funds (approximately $8 million in FY 1986–FY 1988) and direct annual grants from Congress ($9.5 million in FY 1986).[57] Private companies and foundations also support TAF activities, which include population and family planning, support for democratic initiatives, and linkages between U.S. and Asian business interests. TAF has a population project in Bangladesh, a training program in Malaysia for headmasters from schools in the Maldives, and a human rights project under Section 116(e) of the Foreign Assistance Act, which supports the Bangladesh Institute of Law, a Sri Lankan legal aid project, the Sri Lanka Law Mediation Project, Indonesia University Legal Outreach, and PVO Legal Services in Indonesia.

During the 1960s and 1970s, a series of A.I.D. agreements focused on institutional development with the Korea Institute of Science and Technology (KIST), Seoul National University, Korean Development Institute, Korea Standards Research Institute, Korean Atomic Energy Research Institute, and the Integrated Development Center at Soong Yung Waa University. These efforts are now self-sustaining. For example, A.I.D. invested $12 million in KIST. By 1980, five years after this funding ended, KIST was receiving support from government and private industry contracts and from an Asian Development Bank loan.[58]

The Southeast Asia Ministers of Education Organization (SEAMEO) was another successful institution-building effort. From 1967 through 1979, the United States provided $21.6 million to support several different SEAMEO projects that established six regional institutions: the Regional Center for Tropical Biology (BIOTROP), the Regional Center for Educational Innovation and Technology (INNOTECH), the Regional Center for Education in Science and Mathematics (RECSAM), the Regional English Language Center (RELC), the Regional Center for Graduate Study and Research in Agriculture (SEARCA), and the Regional Project for Tropical Medicine and Public Health (TROPMED).[59]

Two other successful institutional development projects in Asia were the International Rice Research Institute (IRRI) at Baguio in the Philippines and the Indonesian Agriculture Institute at Bogor, Java. The Rockefeller and Ford foundations provided the first funding for these institutions, which thrive today and are directly responsible for many major breakthroughs in crop productivity technology and agricultural pest control.

Programs that decentralize planning and implementation from central bureaucracies to regional, provincial, and local levels have potential for later political impact. These programs have focused on rural infrastructure-oriented construction projects. They can have later political impact if the central governments permit provincial and local governments to establish their own tax regimes and collect revenues for maintaining and extending these types of projects.

In Indonesia, a deteriorating fiscal base in 1990 forced the central government to consider granting local governments the authority to collect taxes.[60] This situation increases the possibility of progress toward democratization. If the government eventually does relinquish its monopoly on the authority to raise revenues, U.S.-supported decentralization projects that began in the mid-1970s will have played a major role by helping local governments and organizations to develop the requisite planning, administrative, and fiscal skills.

U.S.-supported rural, decentralization/infrastructure projects also had a political impact in Thailand. During the late 1960s and early 1970s, A.I.D. and the Royal Thai government cooperated in the Accelerated Rural Development Project (ARD). One of this project's major accomplishments was the construction of a rural road network throughout northeast Thailand. At the time, the objective was to help combat rural communist insurgency. Yet, this same road network greatly facilitated political mobilization efforts by Thai university students in the months after the October 1973 student uprising.

That uprising brought an end to the military-led government and ushered in the process toward democratization that has continued ever since.[61] Many of the key student leaders had received university education in the United States. They used the rural road network to mobilize and bring farmers to Bangkok so that they could pressure the new parliament that followed the January 1974 elections. There is no question that political democracy in Thailand has benefited from the rural road network that A.I.D. helped finance during the 1960s.

Participant Training/Education

Participant training programs are a major part of most A.I.D. projects. Many of these training efforts are long-term and university-level, while others may last only several weeks or months. U.S.-supported training programs can significantly aid the political development process, even though A.I.D. has had difficulty supporting major education projects with implicit political purposes. Congress impeded such aid when it shifted A.I.D.'s mandate to basic human needs in the mid-1970s. During the Carter administration, A.I.D.'s leadership interpreted the new mandate as requiring a cut in many types of long-term education efforts. The primary objection of Senator Daniel K. Inouye (D-Hawaii) to A.I.D.'s involvement in higher education projects was that these programs tended to benefit the elite.

This objection, however, ignored the reality that most change has and will come from the elites, including their children. In the case of Indonesia, the Ford Foundation had supported U.S. training for the elites who replaced Sukarno. Collectively known as the "Berkeley Mafia," they developed a free market economy and promoted the private sector. Both of these are important U.S. political and development objectives, and both helped the people of Indonesia.[62] When Chinese students erected a goddess of liberty in Tiananman Square in June 1989 and called for democracy over communism, they proved the value of the transfer of technology and ideas.

The Thai student uprising in 1973 provided an earlier dramatic example of the political impact an education in the United States can have, whether provided through A.I.D. programs or other efforts. Thai history provides no precedent for this event. The Bangkok students, in their calls for democracy and a constitution, quoting from St. Augustine, Rousseau, Locke, and Abraham Lincoln, mobilized over 400,000 active participants, including students from up-country, and overthrew a government that the Communist Party of Thailand with seven years of active guerrilla, psychopolitical warfare in the countryside had never even come close to threatening.

In the end, the thoughts of Mao Tse-tung had less impact on Thai students and professors than those of Rousseau and Abraham Lincoln. "The Thanom-Praphass Government was destroyed not by a communist revolution, but by a democratic revolution led, in part, by the children of its leading bureaucrats."[63] The democratization process has continued in Thailand even though many in the Thai military have tried to turn the clock back. The last attempt began with a coup in February 1991. It was brought to an end in May 1992 when students, joined by many in the emerging middle class, brought down the government that was to be headed by the general who had led the earlier coup but had not stood for election in the 1992 parliamentary elections. One of the conditions for restoring order after more than forty people had been killed in the street demonstrations was a constitutional amendment requiring that all prime ministers be elected.[64]

The Central American Peace Scholarship program (CAPS) has been the most advanced A.I.D. effort to capitalize on participant training as a major diplomatic and development tool. This program resulted from the National Bipartisan Commission on Central America (NBCCA), which, under former Secretary of State Henry Kissinger's leadership, recommended expanding development aid programs in the education sector. In August 1985, Congress approved the Central American Initiative (CAI) as a five-year, $8.4 million A.I.D. program with a comprehensive strategy for achieving economic, social, and political stability and recovery in the region. The CAPS program is part of the CAI.

Though A.I.D. had invested heavily in participant training during the 1950s and 1960s, funding and the number of trainees declined drastically in the 1970s. U.S.-funded training declined 52 percent from 1972 to 1982. Soviet-funded training, however, increased 200 percent (700 percent in Central America alone between 1977 and 1982). In 1983, A.I.D. began two projects—the Caribbean Basin Scholarship Fund (500 trainees) and the Latin America and Caribbean (LAC) Regional Training Initiative I (670 trainees) —that reversed the decline in U.S. scholarship aid. The Caribbean and Latin America Scholarship Program (CLASP) reestablished U.S. scholarship programs in the LAC region.[65]

By June 30, 1988, a total of 9,476 CLASP trainees had begun training in the United States, including 7,184 who had completed training and returned home. An additional 5,000 trainees were to begin their programs during FY 1990. Subsequent A.I.D. studies have asked: To what extent do participants benefit from the program; what effect does the training have on the participants, their communities, and on LAC societies themselves; and what lessons can be learned for future CLASP design?[66]

Early case studies found that most trainees had advanced professionally due to the training and to increased job responsibility. One complaint was that the training had not been sufficiently adapted to local realities. The studies found that the U.S. training had favorably changed most trainees' views of the United States and its people. An interesting finding was that short-term participants were the most likely to introduce development changes in their communities because they returned after only a short time to established positions from which they could institute change. Longer-term participants, however, had to reestablish themselves and legitimize their training. Finally, the studies had difficulty measuring development impact directly related to the training.[67]

This program is still in its early stages. Most trainees have only recently returned to their countries and communities. Many more are in the training process. Nonetheless, they add to the larger mass of returned trainees who, if they can organize networks among themselves and receive support from their governments and other economic assistance programs, will have development and political impact. The development impact will come from the trainees' empowerment as they apply their skills to further their communities' social and political organization.

The political impact for U.S. objectives can occur as the trainees demonstrate the benefits they have received from the U.S. training experience. More important, as A.I.D., embassy, and other U.S. contractor personnel retain contact with the trainees, they can gain special insights into the countries' social, cultural, economic, and political events. This insight is prerequisite for the development and implementation of U.S. foreign policy toward Central and South America.

Thus far, post-training follow-up, including periodic, informal, and professional networking, has been among the weakest parts of most U.S. participant training programs. Final assessment of the political impact of the CAPS program depends on A.I.D. and U.S. embassy commitments to creating and maintaining the necessary follow-up efforts in the participating countries.

Finally, the dramatic improvements in U.S. relations with the emerging states of the former Soviet Union following the collapse of Marxism-Leninism have provided additional evidence of the potential value of participant training programs. These states have decided that the United States offers unparalleled training opportunities. Though the first official exchange program began in 1958, the number of participants was limited or even frozen. In 1985, 7,600 Soviet citizens came to the United States on exchange programs. The State Department estimated a flow of 100,000 Soviet visitors in 1990, most of them on exchange visas. The visitors include police chiefs, firefighters, cinematographers, cooks, puppeteers, computer programmers, scholars, and scientists. Georgi Shekochikin of the Soviet embassy in Washington noted the "basic feeling in the Soviet Union that we need these exchanges. We need the expertise and skills of others."[68]

The Chinese and Thai experiences suggest that U.S. training will significantly affect Russian thinking and social-political organizations. Quite likely, it will lead toward greater democratization than has occurred to date. Moreover, these exchange participants will undoubtedly broaden communication networks. Clearly, such networks are the base for advancing the most important political objective: peace.

The end of the Cold War and the collapse of Soviet communism have created other unprecedented opportunities for open, direct U.S. aid to emerging democracies throughout Eastern Europe and the former Soviet Union. By 1992, the United States, through A.I.D., was planning and even beginning to implement human rights–related activities in all these countries, including support for labor organizations; women's groups; constitutional, criminal, commercial, and administrative legal reform projects; political party development; electronic and print media development; and development of new electoral processes. It is far too early to know how successful these programs will be. But it can no longer be said that the United States is not directly involved in the promotion and extension of political freedom and human rights with its foreign aid resources.[69]

HUMANITARIANISM

The United States has provided more economic aid for humanitarian and disaster relief needs than any other nation. From 1964 through 1988, the United States spent over $4.2 billion to help meet serious, short-term humanitarian and disaster crises around the world.[70] By 1990, the United

States had helped the victims of 1,048 disasters in 140 countries in all regions of the world, including countries as diverse for U.S. interests as the Philippines, the Soviet Union, Ethiopia, Sudan, Bangladesh, and Jamaica. These disasters killed over 3 million people and another 1 billion were adversely affected. The PL 480 Food for Peace program is also an expression of U.S. humanitarianism. Since 1954, nearly 2 billion people in over 100 countries have received some 320 million metric tons of U.S. food.[71]

The people of the United States respond instinctively to the needs of those who suffer the consequences of natural or man-made disasters. The need to respond is so strong that their hearts often blind them to the possibility that humanitarian assistance can become counterproductive to the humanitarian cause they want to serve. During a trip through drought-stricken parts of Africa in 1984, U.S. Ambassador Millicent Fenwick reflected on Mozambique, where children were dying by the dozens in each village: "Whenever there is such a disaster—whether man-made or natural, whether war or cyclone—few Americans ask who is sitting in the palace, only if there is starvation in the streets. Provided there is honest distribution of the food, this is almost axiomatic. The Secretary of State stated it clearly, 'when people are hungry and dying America responds.'"[72]

Many argue that this was also the case in Ethiopia in the late 1980s, where U.S. food aid actually relieved the burden for a murderous regime. On the other hand, evidence suggests that had U.S. relief officials not been present in Ethiopia during the famine in 1987–1988, the slaughter of refugees by the Ethiopian government would have gone unnoticed. An A.I.D. official learned of the slaughter and revealed it to the press.[73] The resulting firestorm of criticism actually forced the Ethiopian government to change its policies toward the refugees and increased the international community's access to those victims.

Clearly, U.S. economic assistance, primarily food aid, has saved the lives of millions of people throughout the Third World. This aid will and should continue. Even in cases like Ethiopia, U.S. humanitarian aid has sent the valuable message that the U.S. public cares about the condition of people everywhere. The remaining, salient question is whether that aid contributes to long-run solutions to the problem of hunger. Or does it increase the survivors' long-term burdens because their political leaders remain unprepared for the changes in power balances that come with the development of the people they rule?

THE IMPACT OF PL 480 FOOD ASSISTANCE

The PL 480 program has four basic objectives: expanding exports of U.S. agricultural commodities, combating hunger and malnutrition, encouraging economic development in developing countries, and promoting U.S. foreign policy interests. The PL 480 program provides immediate benefits for two specific groups: U.S. farmers who sell their food to the U.S. government and the poor people who receive the food, usually through PVOs working among these poor with the approval of the host government.

The PL 480 program has been a mixed blessing. It subsidizes the U.S. farmer as well as the government of the country receiving the aid. In developing countries, such subsidies often allow governments to avoid the agricultural reforms necessary to encourage domestic food production. Because PL 480 food is provided free or sold at a nominal price, it can become a disincentive for agricultural production in the recipient country. While this food promotes short-term political stability because the people in cities do not have to pay the higher prices that domestic production might require, it often is counterproductive to development of a self-sustaining economy.

Abdoulaye Wade, leader of the opposition party in Senegal, believes that development should be based on agriculture. For this reason, he has criticized his country's governments for turning "to food aid which permits governments to transform their people into eternal dependents, always in need of a tutor."[74] Facing a similar problem in 1990, the Indonesian government asked the U.S. ambassador to stop shipment of over 70,000 tons of grain that would have put many Indonesian farmers out of business.[75]

A 1985 evaluation of the PL 480 Title I program's impact concluded that the four objectives often contradict each other and cannot be served simultaneously. Providing food aid as U.S. political support for friendly countries or in return for rights to military bases reduced the leverage of the program for development-oriented policies or programs. The evaluation noted that politically important countries were usually not those most in need of development aid. "In the long run, host country agricultural development may raise incomes and create an increased market for U.S. (and other) exports. However, . . . in the short run, promoting agricultural self-sufficiency runs counter to the objective of increasing the market for U.S. agricultural products."[76]

In the summer of 1990, the U.S. Congress finally began serious revisions in the Food for Peace program. Congress accepted A.I.D. officials' testimony that mismanagement and conflicting political interests had stymied the well-intentioned foreign aid effort to distribute surplus grain. While interagency turf battles slowed food delivery, using food for foreign policy political objectives meant denying it to the neediest countries in favor of the politically important countries. Tony P. Hall (D-Ohio), who heads the House Select Committee on Hunger, charged that the Food for Peace program "has so many bureaucratic and political players that it usually serves the political ends before it works to end hunger."[77]

Moreover, Owen Cylke, a retired former acting director of the Food for Peace program, described the program as a "slush fund of the State Department to meet political requirements around the world."[78] Proof lay in the fact that over a third of U.S. food aid goes to countries that do not have food shortages but that are important politically to the United States. For example, Morocco, with one of the highest per capita calorie rates in the world, received more than $70 million in food aid in 1989, while Angola, where malnutrition reigns, received less than $3 million.

Egypt receives the most U.S. food assistance, though A.I.D. has been at odds with the State Department for well over five years in an effort to cut the program. The State Department resists because the PL 480 assistance level ($182 million in FY 1988 and $171 million in FY 1989)[79] helps keep the overall aid level for Egypt at $1 billion per year. This retains the aid level parity with Israel and avoids the political difficulties that would arise if parity between the two countries were lost. At well over 2,000, Egypt also has one of the highest per capita calorie rates in the world. While the food aid serves its political purposes, many Egyptian farmers feed loaves of bread, made from U.S. staples, to their cattle.[80]

Despite these weaknesses as a development tool, the PL 480 program is an effective expression of U.S. humanitarianism. It has been an effective resource when countries could not know what their next year's crop surpluses would be, and therefore the PL 480 food provided a cushion. This program can also provide food that cannot be grown in certain countries; for example, wheat is not grown in Sri Lanka but is desired for its nutritional value. Thus, the PL 480 program remains one of the most effective tools for U.S. foreign political objectives. And, the U.S. farmer needs the export opportunities this program creates and sustains.

THE PEACE CORPS

The U.S. Peace Corps' contributions to U.S. political and development objectives are probably beyond measure, though when the Peace Corps was originally established, Sargent Shriver and his successors worked to distance it from those agencies most directly responsible for U.S. diplomacy, such as the State Department, A.I.D., and the Department of Defense.

Foreign Policymakers and Implementors

The Peace Corps experience is an unparalleled educational process. It directly contributes to the development of State Department and A.I.D. foreign service officers, members of Congress and their staffs, state and local political leaders, and teachers throughout the U.S. educational system. The Peace Corps enhances cross-cultural communication and empathy. It creates pools of people with foreign language capabilities not otherwise available, along with friendships and personal contacts that can help in future diplomatic relations with countries that have had Peace Corps volunteers. As former volunteers become members of Congress or congressional staffers, they improve foreign aid legislation. When former PCVs join A.I.D., private voluntary agencies, or contractors involved in the foreign assistance process, they improve the design, planning, and implementation of aid programs. When returned volunteers join the Foreign Service or serve in the White House and the Departments of Treasury, Commerce, and Defense, they can benefit U.S. foreign policy. Finally, as PCVs become teachers or otherwise participate in organizations concerned with foreign economic policies and programs, they broaden the education of the U.S. public about foreign affairs issues. In this regard, the Peace Corps has provided an essential cadre of new scholars and area specialists on countries such as Korea. Steinberg suggests, "This alone has justified the total Korean Peace Corps program."[81]

Diplomacy and Development

The Peace Corps helps transfer U.S. ideals and values abroad, as volunteers work in villages and cities in less developed countries. They can also help the development process in these countries, although their contribution may not be recognized by statistically-minded macroeconomists.

Peace Corps volunteers have become symbols of the U.S. interest in the welfare of the people of the recipient country. Evidence of this symbolism has been seen at the United Nations when U.S. foreign service officers with Peace Corps experience addressed development issues. Diplomats from developing countries tended to listen more carefully to these officers during negotiations on development-oriented resolutions in the General Assembly's Second Committee, because they respected the insights garnered from the Peace Corps experience. When the U.S. position could be presented in terms of serving development objectives, the Peace Corps experience added the necessary element of credibility to the U.S. policy. Moreover, many diplomats were often more willing to relax and exchange views when they were talking to a former Peace Corps volunteer. Such friendly conversations usually began with, "Do you know [so and so] who was a PCV in my country in [such and such years]?"

Nevertheless, the Peace Corps can be a double-edged sword for both U.S. diplomacy and foreign aid. The Peace Corps must do more than learn about other cultures and teach about Americans. A 1989–1990 GAO study of the Peace Corps recognized the historic success of the Peace Corps as an expression of U.S. goodwill toward the developing world. The study also found that to meet the challenges of the 1990s, the Peace Corps needed to adopt new mechanisms to attract and retain volunteers with critical skills. The GAO found that the Peace Corps was unable to fully meet countries' requests for volunteers with special skills in agriculture, education, industrial arts, and home economics. The agency had difficulty recruiting minorities, and thus showing the ethnic diversity of the people of the United States. In seven countries, the GAO found unevenness in volunteer assignments and some volunteers who had little to do while others lacked needed support from host government agencies. These weaknesses had "contributed to the fact that one of every three volunteers leaves the Peace Corps before the end of their 2-year assignments."[82]

CONCLUSION

Although driven by U.S. political objectives, U.S. economic aid has given developing countries the means to avoid the Soviet model for economic and social development and bought enough time to allow the weaknesses of communism to become undeniably obvious. In this sense, the aid may have helped create opportunities to develop the conditions for sustainable peace, instead of sustaining a balance-of-power status quo for states with no real interest in resolving the conditions of conflict, even with their own people. Nevertheless, far too many of these countries have used U.S. aid—including ESF and sometimes DA—to postpone the social, political, and economic changes that could have promoted development and political stability.

As the last decade of the twentieth century began, the world faced a new correlation of forces and new realities. The challenge for U.S. aid policy in the 1990s is to recognize and apply the lessons from this thirty-year experience and use assistance resources to advance social, political, and economic development objectives in the future as well as they have advanced U.S. political-security interests in the past.

NOTES

1. A.I.D., *Development and the National Interest*, p. 111.
2. Hamilton, "Foreign Assistance," p. 29.
3. A.I.D., *U.S. Overseas Loans and Grants*, pp. 13, 19, 20, 22, 25, 29, 30, 31, 121, 136.
4. Ibid., pp. 4, 35, 69, 89.
5. A.I.D. cable, "French Criticism of U.S. Economic Assistance," State 256425, September 9, 1983), p. 2.
6. George Lardner, Jr., "U.S. Officials Defend Prewar Support for Iraq," *Washington Post*, May 22, 1992.
7. Michael Wines, "U.S. Aid Helped Hussein's Climb; Now Critics Say, the Bill Is Due," *New York Times*, August 12, 1990.
8. Ibid.
9. Elaine Sciolino, "'89 Bush Order Says Ply Iraq with Aid," *New York Times*, May 29, 1992.
10. Wines, "U.S. Aid."
11. Lardner, "U.S. Officials."
12. Ibid.
13. Elaine Sciolino, "Slanting of Intelligence Becomes Issue for Nominee," *New York Times*, September 19, 1991.

14. Charles Babington, "Bush Botched Iraq Policy, Gore Charges," *Washington Post*, September 30, 1992.

15. Harrison J. Golden, "Hussein's Support: Deeper Than We Think?" *New York Times*, August 28, 1990.

16. R. Jeffrey Smith, "Bush Secretly Approves More Arms for Egypt," *Washington Post*, August 15, 1990. See also Edward Cody, "Anger at Saddam, Financial Need Seen Motivating Mubarak," *Washington Post*, November 6, 1990.

17. Moreover, when the Egyptians first arrived in Saudi Arabia, they came without their own equipment. All their logistic support was covered by the United States or the Saudis.

18. John Kifner, "Arab Role Unclear," *New York Times*, August 10, 1990.

19. Patrick E. Tyler, "Major Sale of U.S. Arms to Saudis Set," *Washington Post*, August 29, 1990.

20. John M. Goshko, "U.S., Saudis Agree to Delay Proposed Weapons Purchase," *Washington Post*, January 5, 1991.

21. A.I.D., *U.S. Overseas Loans And Grants*, p. 20.

22. Joseph B. Treaster, "Jordan Denounces U.S. for 'Explosive' Tactics," *New York Times*, August 13, 1990.

23. Philip Shenon, "West Is Rebuked by Jordanian King," *New York Times*, November 18, 1990.

24. Tyler, "Major Sale."

25. Tom Diaz, "Jordan Denies Arms Aid to Iraq Despite Evidence," *Washington Times*, March 1, 1991.

26. Reuters, "Joint U.S.-Jordan Military Exercise Postponed Over Sanctions Charges," *Washington Post*, June 9, 1992.

27. Ibid.

28. A.I.D., *FY 1990 CP*, Annex II: Asia and the Near East, p. 149.

29. It should be noted that by September 1992, King Hussein had begun changing his public stance toward Saddam Hussein. He expressed dismay that Saddam could so callously continue to cling to power at the expense of the Iraqi people.

30. Caryle Murphy, "Arab League Aide Urges Easing Iraq Sanctions," *Washington Post*, May 25, 1992.

31. Al Kamen, "Reagan-Era Zeal for Central America Fades," *Washington Post*, October 16, 1990.

32. Ibid.

33. Ibid.

34. Ibid.

35. The common pattern was Soviet and Cuban support for the insurgents, which impelled the United States to support the existing government despite its inadequacies, which very likely had generated the social unrest and "just cause" that in turn fed the insurgency.

36. John P. Mason, "A.I.D.'s Experience with Democratic Initiatives: A Review of Regional Programs in Legal Institution Building" (A.I.D. Program Evaluation Discussion Paper No. 29, Washington, D.C., February 1990), p.4.

37. Ibid., Appendix B: A.I.D.'s Civic Participation Division.

38. J. Bryan Hehir, "The United States and Human Rights: Policy for the 1990s in Light of the Past" (draft chapter, September 1990, for Kenneth A. Oye, Robert J. Lieber, and Donald Rothchild (eds.), *Eagle in a New World: American Grand Strategy in the Post–Cold War Era* [New York: Harper Collins, 1992]), pp. 9–10.

39. Mason, "A.I.D.'s Experience," Appendix C: Notes on the Human Rights Initiative.

40. Hehir, "The United States and Human Rights," pp. 35–36.

41. Mason, "A.I.D.'s Expereince," p.5.

42. When viewed against a total military and economic aid level in excess of $14 billion, $3 million seems a small commitment to human rights and probably reflected their priority within the hierarchy of U.S. political objectives.

43. Mason, "A.I.D.'s Experience," pp. 7–9.

44. Zimmerman, personal journal notes, December 1974.

45. Ibid., 1980

46. Mason, "A.I.D.'s Experience," pp. 3–4,

47. Ibid., pp. 14–18.

48. Ibid., pp. 22–23.

49. Ibid.

50. Ibid., p. 26.

51. A.I.D., *U.S. Overseas Loans and Grants*, p. 4.

52. A.I.D., *Development and the National Interest*. This was the first effort at a comprehensive study of the global impact of aid. But there have been many smaller evaluations of impact on people at the project level since 1979.

53. Ibid., p. 111.

54. Millicent Fenwick, "African Trip: Observations Re Foreign Aid" (Cable to Washington from Rome, *Rome* 03833, February 10, 1984), p. 1

55. A.I.D., *Development and the National Interest*, pp. 112–113.

56. Steinberg, interview with author. David I. Steinberg is a leading authority on the U.S.–South Korean aid relationship. He served in South Korea for many years in the early 1960s and has returned almost annually either for personal visits or official evaluation missions for A.I.D., the South Korean government, or the World Bank.

57. A.I.D., "Costs of Initiating Mechanisms for New Relationships with Advanced Developing Countries (ADCs)" (A report prepared for A.I.D.'s Asia-Near East Bureau by Robert F. Zimmerman, December 23, 1987), p. 1.

58. Ibid., p. 2.

59. Ibid., p. 5.

60. R. William Liddle, "Development or Democracy?" *Far Eastern Economic Review* (November 9, 1989), p. 22.

61. Robert F. Zimmerman, "Student Revolution in Thailand: The End of the Bureaucratic Polity?" *Asian Survey* (June 1974), pp. 509–529.

62. Ambassador Masters, interview with author. The problem today, however, is that the early success of these economists has not been reinforced with development in the political sector, and Indonesia's subsequent apparent political stability masks a situation not unlike that which led to the 1973 student uprising in Thailand—and again in 1992. For some observers, including myself, the prospects for peaceful political transition grow dimmer by the month.

63. Zimmerman, "Student Revolution in Thailand," p. 512.

64. William Branigan, "Thai Legislators Approve Steps Toward Reform," *Washington Post*, May 26, 1992.

65. Ray Chesterfield et al., *CAPS Case Studies, Phase II: Clasp II Design-Related Data Collection*, Final Report. (Prepared for A.I.D./LAC/DR/EST by the Academy for Educational Development and Juarez and Associates, August 1, 1989), p. i.

66. Ibid., p. ii.

67. Ibid.

68. "Soviet Exchanges with the U.S. Booming," *New York Times*, May 28, 1990, p. 7.

69. A.I.D. in 1992 provided grants for supporting these programs to the American Bar Association, the Free Trade Union Institute of the AFL-CIO, the International Republican Institute, the National Democratic Institute for International Affairs, the International Foundation for Electoral Systems, the National Endowment for Democracy, and Internews Network, a California-based media consulting firm.

70. A.I.D./Office of Foreign Disaster Assistance, *Disaster Relief Assistance and Related Data*, Summary Tables FY 1964–1988 (November 1989), Table 2, p. 9.

71. A.I.D., *Foreign Aid Facts* (Office of Public Inquiries, Bureau for External Affairs, A.I.D., August 1990), p. 4.

72. Fenwick, "African Trip."

73. This A.I.D. career officer, Dr. Ric Machmer, became A.I.D.'s representative in Somalia in 1993, directing the U.S. humanitarian relief effort.

74. Fenwick, "African Trip," p. 2.

75. "Revisions Sought in U.S. Food-Aid Program," *New York Times*, July 29, 1990.

76. Rogers and Wallerstein, *PL 480 Title I*, pp. 2–3.

77. *Newsday*, July 29, 1990.

78. Ibid.

79. A.I.D., *FY 1990 CP*, Annex II: Asia and the Near East, p. 81.

80. *Newsday*, July 29, 1990.

81. Steinberg, interview with author, August 19, 1992.

82. GAO, *Peace Corps*, p. 3.

9

Dollars, Diplomacy, and Independence

The United States and most of the Third World countries that received U.S. Economic Supporting Assistance resources over the past forty years lost innumerable opportunities to use that aid to stimulate effective political, social, and economic development. Moreover, the ESF program's sheer magnitude and its impact on the priorities for all U.S. aid also adversely affected many other efforts to promote development with non-ESF programs.

These lost opportunities may never be regained because the leaders of less developed countries will no longer be able to use political leverage to obtain high levels of aid from both East and West as they did for over forty years during the Cold War. The end of communism, the collapse of the Soviet ideological and military threat, and the sorry record of past foreign aid programs—for whatever reason—all work against the argument for foreign aid. Moreover, Japan has become a close second to the United States as the major foreign economic aid donor, and the newly industrializing countries (NICs) elswhere in Asia have created new sources of economic competition for the United States. All these factors affect the willingness of the U.S. public to support foreign aid programs.

The end of the Cold War also means changes in all the donor nations' aid and trade priorities. The United States currently appears to be placing a higher priority on Eastern Europe and the states of the former Soviet Union, with Latin America not far behind. Japan is expected to give more priority to China, while Western Europe's attention is shifting almost exclusively to the former East bloc states. Fewer resources will be available for the poorer countries, and for this reason alone, the United States and other aid donors will have to condition their provision of aid more directly on the willingness of developing countries to implement policies that will promote political change and stimulate internal economic development.

These considerations notwithstanding, the end of the Cold War has created unparalleled new opportunities to expand peace and human freedom and to use both ESF and DA foreign assistance *for* social-political change rather than *against* a foreign ideology. At the same time, there are new threats to the security of the people of the United States and their economic and social well-being that are probably more real than the probability of nuclear war with the Soviet Union ever was.

These "new" realities include increased civil strife within many countries that were once U.S. allies and within reemerging states of the former Soviet empire; mass migrations of people who are driven away by this civil strife and other increasingly unbearable social, economic, and political conditions; massive environmental degradation throughout the developing world and the former East bloc; the enormous debt crisis that is in part a consequence of the failure of ESF and other aid resources to stimulate economic *and* political development in the past; the probability that significant reductions in international drug trafficking will be impossible without alternative economic opportunity for those who produce opium and cocaine; the growing weariness of LDCs and donors with foreign aid that does not work; realization that the United States cannot overcome its own economic difficulties unless it restores its capacity to compete in the world market; and the no longer deniable evidence that sustainable economic and social development must be based on wealth created by skilled, educated, and politically empowered people in increasingly democratic political systems.

Given these political realities, the inadequacies of "economic growth" as a measure of development, and clearer understanding of the differences between modernization and development, it may now be possible to accept the idea that development should include processes that empower people, organizations, and institutions to articulate and control their own destinies. Measuring such development will require realistic indicators that relate economic growth statistics to broader social-political development. Clearer understanding of this relationship will help the United States and its aid recipients establish more effective guidance for ensuring that the aid, along with the additional efforts of developing countries, will attain development objectives. This understanding will also guide changes in the purposes of aid, program implementation criteria and processes, the numbers and skills of development and diplomatic personnel, and the funding required in recipient countries. While this study has focused on ESF assistance and most of the lessons relate primarily to that type of aid, for the remainder of this chapter the recommendations offered should be considered applicable to all types of U.S. foreign aid.

CHANGING U.S. FOREIGN AID PRIORITIES

The Agency for International Development is well into the process of delineating new priorities for all types of economic assistance. According to the 1990 A.I.D. Mission Statement, the agency's global objectives for the 1990s are (1) to assist developing countries to achieve their full national potential through the development of open and democratic societies and the dynamism of free markets and individual initiative, and (2) to improve the quality of human life and expand the range of individual opportunities by reducing poverty, ignorance, and malnutrition.[1] The six principles that will guide all aid programs toward these objectives are support for free markets and broad-based economic growth; concern for individuals and the development of their economic and social well-being; support for democracy; responsible environmental policies and prudent management of natural resources; support for lasting solutions to transnational problems; and humanitarian assistance to those who suffer from disasters of natural or human origin.[2]

One need not reflect for long on the A.I.D. Mission Statement to realize that virtually all of these objectives and principles to one degree or another have been part of U.S. economic aid policy guidance almost from the inception of U.S. assistance programs and their enabling legislation. The statements of Presidents Roosevelt and Kennedy, Ambassadors McGhee and Bowles, Representative Hamilton, and many others have reflected these goals. The problem has been less one of goals than of commitment to *implementing* aid programs that will achieve them. In light of the history of past purpose and actual practice, attaining A.I.D.'s objectives, with planning and implementation guided by the six principles in the Mission Statement, depends on the viability of the following assumptions:

- That the stated objectives and agreed principles for U.S. aid for development—both ESF and DA—reflect the highest U.S. national interests as determined by the White House, the executive agencies, and the Congress, and that the White House, agencies, and Congress support implementation of the aid programs in accordance with these objectives and principles
- That economic aid be used as a diplomatic tool only when the political objectives to be advanced are fully consistent with the development aid criteria
- That aid planning and implementation criteria fully reflect and directly advance the objectives and principles outlined in the A.I.D. Mission Statement
- That foreign aid resources be provided at adequate levels, have limited earmarked restrictions, and enjoy the flexibility necessary to respond rapidly and meaningfully to unexpected opportunities to support political changes consistent with democracy
- That U.S. foreign service officers be available in the numbers and with the necessary political, economic, cultural, and language skills to meaningfully collaborate with recipient country government officials and academic, business, and other political and social leaders
- That the PVOs and private contractors A.I.D. expects to rely on for field-level activities fully share the official U.S. objectives and priorities
- That potential partner countries themselves be committed to change, especially in the way political, social, and economic power is created and shared

An additional assumption might be that both the providers and the recipients of development-oriented foreign aid share some understanding of the differences between modernizing people and empowering people.

MODERNIZING AND EMPOWERING PEOPLE

People have long been *exploited* as labor in fields, factories, and mines. In this condition they are used much like the natural resources they themselves process for other use. People can be, and are, *modernized* through skill training and education to perform new tasks with increasingly sophisticated levels of technology in factories or high-tech glass towers. They can produce high-tech products with sanitary gloves or they can move money and stocks in crowded, frenzied stock exchanges. People who are *developing* already have or can acquire the capacity to empower themselves—politically, socially, and economically—as individuals or in groups to make their own choices in the life they want to live, and to be responsible for those choices.

A successful free market economic system, in turn, depends on the productivity, risk behavior, and imagination of individuals and corporations. The free market depends on people who are free—with access to whatever information they need to control their own lives and make their own investment decisions. These are the people who will produce the base of wealth in a society that can be responsibly taxed to generate revenue to support development of opportunities for others. From this perspective, it seems that an efficient free market system can best emerge and be sustained in democratic states, or where the political environment includes at least the following four characteristics: a free and independent judiciary and legal system; a free, broad-based education process and information base; free nongovernmental organizations in business, labor, and other fields; and respect for the freedom and responsibility of individuals to create their personal utopias.

This last point may require additional elaboration. First, democracy is a political process. It is not an ideology like socialism or communism that promises to create a social and economic utopia for the people. Were it to try to guarantee one utopia for all people, democracy would have to become something else—democratic socialism?—and develop a system of state control over most aspects of people's lives. Instead, a democratic political process constantly tries, often imperfectly, to balance changes in political, economic, and social power in a society. The democratic political process achieves its highest efficiency in direct proportion to the degree that individuals and families accept responsibility for defining and pursuing their own utopias. It is individuals that make democracy work, even when they are functioning through or with other individuals in families, organizations, and ad hoc groups. These individuals also tend to share moral and ethical principles, including a work ethic, responsibility for personal behavior, risk orientation, common respect for all individuals, and civility toward one another. Finally, democracy also requires a sense of the history and religious origins of democratic development.

IMPLICATIONS FOR THE FUTURE OF U.S. FOREIGN AID

One of the most important lessons of the forty-year history of foreign aid may be that a state whose social-political process does not encourage development of people, including some degree of empowerment, most likely will be unable to stimulate self-sustainable economic growth with the financial resources it often demands from donor nations. Ignoring this basic truth and pretending that a given country's poor economic and social condition is somehow caused primarily by outside forces—and therefore can only be overcome with foreign aid—serves only to perpetuate aid programs that become essentially state-to-state welfare programs.

Purposes

Foreign assistance programs need to encourage cooperative study of the linkages between political and economic development in country-specific terms and delineate how these may affect economic growth and the material well-being of people. Given this type of understanding, all aid donors can develop aid programs more compatible with different political and economic processes in less developed countries.

New foreign aid priorities in the 1990s depend on the answers to old questions. Should foreign aid attack underdevelopment by creating new self-sustaining capacities in the developing countries, regardless of whether or not these capacities enable them to compete with U.S. businesses? Should aid simply subsidize modernization and the *near-term* export of U.S. goods and services? Should the allocation of foreign aid in the post–Cold War world continue to be determined by the extent to which these resources serve short-term U.S. political objectives? Should foreign aid merely relieve LDC governments of the burden of change or should it stimulate change? The answers to these questions will determine whether U.S. foreign aid continues to act as state-to-state welfare or meaningfully attacks the root causes of underdevelopment.

The near-term answers are not encouraging. As the end of the Cold War removed the single most unifying rationale for foreign aid, members of Congress and other proponents of foreign aid have tried to find new rationales. Many believe that U.S. foreign aid should be used primarily to promote U.S. exports, as has been the case with Japan's foreign aid from its inception. These people, including many U.S. senators, back legislation that would "require the administration to increase the percentage of aid directed toward expensive infrastructure projects, such as airports and telecommunication networks." This type of aid would be provided "in the form of credits, which would have to be spent in the United States, rather than cash."[3]

This study has already shown how any aid, including ESF, DA, and other types, that supports such modernization projects, while it clearly benefits U.S. business, has little if any impact toward creating the conditions of peace on which U.S. national security depends. Indeed, one of the major criticisms of the Bush administration's aid policies and practices toward Iraq in the years prior to Saddam Hussein's 1990 invasion of Kuwait was that U.S. aid credits (in this case, agriculture loan credits) had been used to modernize the Iraqi war machine, including the development of a nuclear weapons program. The fact is that aid that primarily supports only modernization of infrastructure cannot help resolve the conditions of conflict within and between states. Worse, it can increase the capacity of a modernizing state, such as Iraq, to wage war on its neighbors.

No less discouraging is the major recommendation for clarifying the purposes and uses of ESF and DA funds in the Draft Action Plan of the President's Commission on the Management of A.I.D. Programs. The commission recommends: "The Administration and Congress should make a clear distinction between ESF and DA monies. ESF should be used only to achieve political foreign policy objectives and DA for legitimate economic development. If the situation in a given country or region designated for ESF requires "development" uses, those funds should be transferred to the DA account and managed as such."[4]

This recommendation appears to ignore the most obvious lesson from the forty years' experience in using any type of economic aid to advance U.S. political objectives: Even when ESF resources do help achieve political objectives, that gain cannot be sustained without continued infusions of aid unless real social and economic development objectives are achieved. These achievements would include an increasingly stable political situation in the recipient country based on legitimization of the governing power as a result of steady progress in the social, economic, and political empowerment of the people. Liberia, the Philippines, Zaire, Somalia, and Egypt all testify to this reality. The first four countries became economic and social disaster areas as the Cold War ended and the U.S. aid umbilical cord was cut. Egypt continues to serve U.S. interests because the United States maintains the political and military aid umbilical cord that enables both countries to mask Egypt's political, social, and economic frailties.

Equally unrealistic is the suggestion that ESF resources could be transferred to the DA account if the development situation in a given country warranted such a change. This type of transfer would not work in a country where the United States has the type of high-priority political objectives that would warrant use of the ESF account in the first place—*unless* the United States was prepared to sacrifice its short-term political objectives whenever a recipient country would not fully cooperate in the use of aid resources for truly developmental objectives. Since all development will create some instability, and given the previous history of using U.S. aid to ensure short-term stability whenever necessary to advance U.S. political objectives, this seems an unrealistic assumption.

A difficult truth is that long-term social, political, and economic stability depends on empowering change for people and their organizations throughout a society. If such stability is ultimately a prerequisite for sustaining the overriding U.S. political interest in a world free of military and political threats to U.S. national security, then all U.S. economic aid should be allocated only where recipient governments are committed to such development purposes. This would mean that foreign aid should be considered an investment, with profit defined in terms of how well aid-funded projects become self-sustaining.

Adhering to the condition that the United States would provide economic aid only to recipient governments that share a commitment to specific development purposes would require considerable empathy and patience. How clearly have LDCs *first* identified *their* purposes? How candidly have they studied and understood the policy and institutional obstacles that may need to be resolved before "investment" can be effective?

This study does not define specific political and economic purposes for different countries or regions. However, if economic aid is to successfully serve any political or economic development purposes, it seems imperative that we try to define a fundamental objective that can serve as a reference point for all country-specific purposes. Such an objective might be:

> To help expand self-sustaining governmental and private institutions with the capacity to determine and effectively respond to the people's basic economic, social, and political needs. These institutions and organizations must be able to design and implement programs that will help increase agricultural and industrial productivity, expand educational opportunities, improve basic health services and, finally, empower people to control their own lives and to participate in the political process.

At a time when assistance resources are increasingly scarce, it is useful to note that aid programs aimed at developing people and their political institutions are much less expensive than those that traditionally have supported large infrastructure modernization projects. The United States may spend $50 million on a power plant for Egypt and benefit the General Electric constituents of U.S. senators, but that same money would go much further and have greater impact—even for future U.S. export opportunities—if it could be spent in ways that empower people. However, such commitments require precise criteria for allocating aid and implementing the projects this aid supports.

New Criteria for Allocating ESF and DA Assistance

Criteria for allocating limited foreign economic aid might include at least the following:

- Commitment by a recipient country to delineate its role and responsibilities for ensuring conditions that will enable foreign aid to support the development of people, such as willingness to consider changes in domestic policies, people, and administrative procedures that obstruct the development process
- Consideration of the degree to which the United States and the recipient country share or can develop common political and economic development purposes and commitment
- Commitment to increasingly responsive government and free political process; for example, commitment to freedom of speech, organization, and basic human rights as defined in the UN Declaration of Human Rights
- Commitment to development-oriented policies and programs that will expand empowerment in at least the following four areas: an education system free of government-directed censorship of subject matter; opportunity for business and labor to participate in development of economic and social policies that affect productivity; freedom and opportunity for individuals to pursue their personal growth goals; and a legal system and process that ensure equal treatment and opportunity for all groups and individuals in society

For ESF, in addition to the above criteria, the following considerations should apply: political position and influence of the recipient country in the region involved, capacity and commitment of the country to reject military aggression by itself or on behalf of another power, geostrategic considerations, and historical relationship to the United States.

Besides these criteria for allocating aid to specific countries, it is also necessary to establish more precise criteria for measuring an aid recipient country's progress and commitment to empowering types of development. It should be possible to develop criteria that define the relationship between democracy and development and the status of conditions that are conducive to empowering a country's people.

Historically, a country's gross national product (GNP) has been the primary measure of economic growth in developing and industrialized countries, but it is an inadequate measure of a government's commitment to improving the people's quality of life. To overcome this weakness, development theorists established the Physical Quality of Life Index (PQLI) to measure the quality of life in terms of life expectancy at birth, infant mortality, maternal mortality, birth rates, death rates, and literacy. However, GNP and PQLI do not measure a country's capacity to develop and sustain the economic, social, and political policies that empower people to control their own lives, including the capacity to create wealth. The PQLI, for example, does not reveal the scope of the population's participation in political and economic development. It does not measure intangibles such as freedom, justice, opportunity, self-respect, and the human development process.

This deficiency has spurred efforts to find better measures. The United Nations Development Program in a recent report, *The Human Development Report 1990*, draws attention to the crudeness of the efforts of Western governments and international aid organizations to measure world economic and social development. The report suggests that this weakness has contributed to the ineffectiveness of development strategies. The report notes that economists have traditionally measured development in terms of how much wealth is produced per person. This measure, however, fails to show how the wealth is used for human advancement.[5]

The UNDP report includes a "human development index" that measures quality of life in terms of life expectancy, literacy, and ability to buy basic goods. The UNDP's human development index continues to focus on quality of life in nonpolitical terms. It measures those factors that are essentially welfare-oriented and that governments are expected to provide *for* people. In essence, the UNDP is measuring aspects of modernization, not development. The authors apparently intend to refine their index by including measurements for democratic freedoms.

In support of this effort, I suggest in this chapter a set of criteria that might help measure the extent to which the capacities of a country's population are employed in the development process. These criteria constitute a "political-social-economic quality of life index" (PSE/QLI). This index illustrates the breadth of *participation* in a country's political, social, and economic process. The PSE/QLI would measure performance that reflects the extent of individual empowerment emerging in the development process.[6]

Initially, applying this index will be difficult because most developing countries still do not have the required base of reliable statistics. Nevertheless, it may be possible to delineate the necessary criteria, or indicators, and then select a few countries for pilot measurement activities, including data collection processes. These criteria and measurement techniques could then be tried in many different countries or selected cities. A suggested set of criteria might include all or a selection of the following:

1. *Education and Employment*
   - teacher/classroom/student ratio
   - public/private educational institution ratio
   - percent of population with elementary, high school, and college education
   - percentage of college, high school, and elementary school graduates employed
   - percentage of each type of graduate employed in skill and wage categories relevant to their level of education

- percentage of these graduates involved in government or political organizations
- percentage of applicants accepted into universities
- percentage of foreign-educated employed in areas relevant to their foreign degree/training
- percentage of women in all of the above categories
- existence and censorship status of public and university libraries

2. *Health Services*
   - doctor/population ratio
   - doctor/nurse/patient ratio
3. *Labor and the Private Sector*
   - number of labor unions (independent/government) and percentage of labor so organized
   - percentage of productive enterprise controlled by private sector
   - percentage of population at different education levels employed by private sector
   - number of government and private sector cooperatives, by production activity
   - government/private bank ratio
   - savings rate
4. *Social/Political Organization*
   - existence and type of elected legislature
   - existence of a periodic election process for executive and/or legislature
   - existence of independent political parties
   - number and fiscal viability of private voluntary organizations
   - percentage of seats in national legislative body held by each political party
   - percentage of high school and college educated participating as political party members and representatives
   - percentage of graduates of each level participating in nongovernmental organizations, including PVOs
   - number and type of public interest groups
   - existence and number of independent business and labor organizations
   - number and independence of newspapers and electronic media outlets
5. *Justice and Legal Process*
   - existence of constitutional guarantees for basic human rights
   - existence and operational freedom of human rights organizations
   - degree of political independence of the court system
   - existence of independent lawyers and legal organizations capable of protecting individual human and property rights

Personnel

Given these types of purposes and criteria for U.S. foreign aid, the next measure of U.S. commitment to the development process will be the skills of the personnel who plan and deliver that aid and how that aid is programmed and evaluated.

The quality and commitment of the people who design and implement programs and projects are critical elements in any effective foreign assistance program. This principle, though a truism, has been routinely ignored in the assignments and career promotions of the majority of U.S. foreign service officers, despite the recommendations of many studies and task forces over the last two decades. Very few A.I.D. and State Department senior management and program officers are able to do their work in Third World languages or have the area expertise to understand the political and social cultures in which U.S. aid programs are supposed to work. Fewer still have both these capacities.

If the planning and implementation of U.S. foreign aid programs is to have *development* impact, application of at least the following practices seems essential: Language facility and area expertise should be required for career officers appointed to the senior levels of the Foreign Service. A.I.D. should place high priority on recruiting political scientists in order to redress the current overwhelming imbalance of economists and other technical personnel. Personnel responsible for project planning and implementation should be based in the relevant ministries of the recipient government, to the extent acceptable to that government, rather than at A.I.D. or other U.S. embassy offices. Officers should spend a minimum of two tours of duty, with a third automatic for those requesting it. And overseas assignments must begin only *after* the requisite language and area training has been completed, with mandatory ongoing language training at post.

Programming Criteria and Practice

Inattention to the administrative structure and processes of the recipient government has been one of the weakest links in the planning process. Current planning guidance requiring analysis of the political-administrative environment is either not followed or the analyses submitted are carefully crafted to avoid discussion of difficult realities. In future, all programming documentation should include careful analyses of political and administrative processes in terms of their eventual capacity to provide self-sustaining support for development projects and economic policy reforms. Such analyses would, for example, attempt to understand political power bases and relationships within and between ministries.

Given high-quality analyses in these areas, programming criteria should ensure that all projects directly create capacities for the recipient institution or organization to sustain projects and programs without continual infusions of external support. Initial project and program objectives should be achievable within the existing sociopolitical-economic environment, given that some difficult change may initially have to be incremental. Immediate success would not depend on fundamental, broad policy reforms but incremental changes would have to be measurable. Resources also should be provided according to the capacity of the recipient institution or organization to use the resources to create self-sustaining capacity with each increment.

Evaluation

Until the end of the 1980s, evaluation did not receive sustained, priority attention in the planning and implementation of U.S. foreign aid programs. The problem was less one of lack of techniques or knowledge than of lack of sustained commitment to excellence and integrity in the evaluation process at all levels. Over the past five years, A.I.D. has given higher priority to evaluation and has used evaluation findings in the programming process. Continued enhancement of these efforts will require separate evaluation officers in each country mission reporting directly to the mission director; project agreements that require the recipient government to be involved in all evaluations and to name an evaluation counterpart to cooperate with the U.S. evaluation officer; evaluation officers who are language and area experts; and project officers who receive periodic evaluation training and participate in mission evaluations of projects outside their responsibility. Finally, A.I.D. and the recipient government should undertake joint studies of social and political processes as they affect different aspects of development, including social-economic policies, people (training, experience), attitudes, political power balances and rivalries, and resource allocations in the recipient government's budget. A regular series of joint seminars on development issues aimed at increasing mutual understanding of development issues, obstacles, and alternative solutions would greatly enhance the cooperation between donors and recipients in all assistance relationships.

U.S. FOREIGN AID TO THE SUCCESSOR STATES OF THE SOVIET UNION

Since the late 1980s, the leaders of the Western democracies, the International Monetary Fund (IMF), the World Bank, and innumerable other public and private economic development organizations have been struggling with the most daunting development challenge since the end of World War II: the social, economic, and political dimensions of the human consequences of Soviet communism. These donors are pressing for major economic reforms designed essentially by the IMF, Harvard University's Jeffrey Sachs and Yegor T. Gaidar, President Boris Yeltsin's chief economic advisor and former acting prime minister.[7] The media headlines and the donors' priority focus stress the importance of macroeconomic reforms with high levels of aid totaling in the tens of billions of dollars. The major assumption behind these levels is that they will help "buy time" for the reform process. Another argument is that these levels strengthen President Yeltsin's position against the former communist leaders. Both the assumption and the political rationale reflect the continuing hold of traditional aid approaches.

It is increasingly apparent, however, that traditional economic reform approaches are inadequate to the development challenge. The emerging probability is that despite provision of billions of dollars in macroeconomic stabilization aid, the opposition to the reforms together with increasing chaos on both sides of the Ural Mountains will continue. Other forces must be found to drive the development process in the successor states of the former Soviet Union.

Perhaps more attention and priority should be given to the probability that the determinant variable in the successor states is the social-political-psychological condition of the people. This condition includes their capacity, defined in terms of technical skills, values, attitudes, and patterns of political and economic behavior, as well as their political will to commit themselves to the scope of change required for self-sustaining development, as distinct from modernization. Seventy years of Soviet communism destroyed the work ethic and, more important, precluded the development of imaginative, risk-oriented people with the education, skills, and attitudes required to take advantage of reforms suggested by the IMF, other donors, and Yeltsin's advisers—be they U.S. academics or Yeltsin aides, or even the opposition.[8]

Yet, Yeltsin's future, the effectiveness of the reforms he and others propose, and the possible impact of easier credit and trade provisions assume and demand people who are able and willing to take advantage of these new opportunities. Moreover, they assume that Russia's and other successor states' leaders will permit their people to attain the political power to create the desired economic environment and then enjoy the rewards of their risks. We do them and ourselves harm when we assume early and measurable benefits from reforms and imaginative leadership alone, without explicit recognition of the fact that developing the necessary human capital will take years, probably a generation. This is especially true if the government leadership is unwilling to provide the freedom and the educational opportunities that will empower the people and inspire them to want even more control over their own destinies.

Fortunately, there are some fledgling efforts underway, funded at levels in the single-digit millions, that are appropriate to the challenge. These efforts are targeted in sectors that must experience the earliest sustained change so that the billion-dollar programs can successfully buy time for macroeconomic change rather than just delay a future day of reckoning. However, these aid efforts will not succeed unless they receive the highest political priority and consequent planning and implementation support.

In 1992, A.I.D. began providing grants to support changes—read, "development"—that directly affect the political process in the successor states and the development of their people.[9] A.I.D. is providing grants to:

- The American Bar Association, to support activities in constitutional reform, criminal, business, and administrative law reform, and the training of lawyers, law school faculties, and judges;
- The International Republican Institute and The National Democratic Institute for International Affairs, to provide technical assistance in the development and organization of political parties and other civic organizations, training for party activists, and training for youth leaders and women's organizations;
- The International Foundation for Electoral Systems, to provide technical support for planning and implementing national elections in several successor states;
- The Free Trade Union Institute, to support development of new free trade unions; and
- Internews, a media consulting firm, to provide technical and commodity assistance for news broadcast systems that will offer reliable, current news and information to all regions of the former Soviet Union.

In addition to these A.I.D. grant programs, the U.S. Peace Corps is sending volunteers who will focus on small business development.[10]

Although these efforts are only beginning, each activity targets special areas essential to any democratic political process and free market economic system. These efforts are and will become increasingly people-to-people. Although funds can be provided only in small increments, they must be sustained, constantly monitored, and adjusted as new opportunities emerge for supportable, democratic political change.

The success of these new U.S. aid efforts depends on the sustained, high-priority political attention and patience of U.S. political leaders in both parties. Several other key conditions for success include:

1. That the political leadership in recipient states be fully committed to legal and political reforms based on democratic and free market models, values, and principles;
2. That current power struggles and possible coups or shifts in power and leadership personalities among political leaders not prevent lower-level technical cooperation on all U.S.-sponsored democratic initiatives projects;
3. That there be no significant political or legal obstacles to training programs in the media, legal, political, labor, and electoral sectors;
4. That potential participants in any long- or short-term training

programs, workshops, and seminars provided by A.I.D. grantees be readily available to receive the training and then able to return to positions where they can immediately apply their new skills and perspectives;

5. That the operating condition of recipients' transportation and communications equipment and infrastructure not impede timely and efficient provision of the logistical support required by the grantees' various training and technical assistance programs;
6. That long-term liaison personnel placed by the grantees in the recipient states be able to identify and establish collaborative working relationships with the key political leaders and the potential beneficiaries of their assistance efforts;
7. That A.I.D. and all grantees be able to recruit and support personnel with the requisite language and other communication skills, political and historical knowledge, empathy, patience, and humility for the people-to-people development challenge they face;
8. That the responsible State Department and A.I.D. officials receive, and in turn provide, high-priority political, conceptual, and personnel support to the Washington backstop offices that in their turn provide the planning and logistical support for these low-profile, long-term democratization efforts; and finally,
9. That Congress understand and provide intelligent, sustained support for the myriad democratization projects carried out by current and potential A.I.D. grantees.

It is crucial that Yeltsin, his supporters, and those who lead the other new states recognize and accept that accelerated economic and social development, and the equitable distribution of the benefits thereof, necessitate redistributing political power and expanding opportunities for their people to participate in the national development process.

CONCLUSION

This study has focused on the use of U.S. Economic Supporting Assistance to advance U.S. foreign policy objectives. It has described the policy process that establishes the political objectives, along with the ESF resources that are used to advance those objectives. The study demonstrates the consequences of using ESF or any other type of economic aid to pursue simultaneously both political and development objectives, because the political objectives receive such high priority that they are pursued in ways that undermine the achievement of development objectives. Although U.S. diplomacy that so used ESF resources to pursue U.S. political-security objectives was very much determined by the Cold War environment, this experience and its consequences provide many lessons of value now that U.S. foreign policy is no longer driven by Cold War concerns. There is a new agenda, driven by the failure of economic, political, and social development efforts in much of the Third World, along with new challenges to continued improvement in the quality of life.

This study has tried to focus on past experience to ascertain how foreign aid might best be used in future to advance economic, political, and social development objectives. Paraphrasing Norman Jacobs, a commitment to development might best be defined as a commitment to the kind of change that maximizes the power of people, as individuals or in organizations, in a given society, regardless of limits imposed by the existing social, economic, and political structure. Foreign aid that effectively helps countries to resolve the causes of violent conflict within their societies, eliminate environmental degradation, eliminate the causes of mass emigration, reduce or eliminate drug production and trade, and reduce their international and domestic debt burdens requires no less a commitment to change.

Is the United States prepared to use foreign aid more as an agent of change and less as a tool for achieving short-term U.S. political and commercial interests? Can foreign aid be applied in ways that will enable the majority of the world's nation-states to experience the United States as a creative force in their development process? It was never enough for the United States to be against the spread of Soviet power or any other perceived threat. Can we now define creative development purposes and positive goals? Can others identify with our purposes and we with theirs?

In a world free from significant military threats to U.S. security, the question becomes: Are the people of the United States prepared to accept the challenges likely to arise from the genuine development of currently weak countries as they claim control of their own destinies and alter existing international power balances? Does the Nebraskan farmer really want to be challenged by capable and productive Egyptian, Nigerian, and Ethiopian farmers? Though a rising tide of self-sustaining development may raise all countries, it also increases the level of competitive skill required by all players—be they nation-states or farmers, international bankers, or steelworkers.

Ultimately, only the developing countries can create the capacities they need to enter this competition. They cannot effectively use foreign aid until they and their people have begun to control their own destinies. The path to economic and political development lies in placing in the hands of the people the power to direct the course of their own lives. This is a function of the political process, particularly its capacity to provide the broadest possible opportunity for people to be what they want to be.

If development is the objective, it seems clear that foreign aid donors and recipients alike will have to begin with the arena they have so long and regrettably avoided—the political process. As uncomfortable as it will be for some, this may mean accepting that political democracy is, if not a prerequisite, at least the essential companion in any long-term effort to establish self-sustaining social and economic systems. And this means that foreign aid must be applied *with* increasingly empowered people rather than as an act of grace *for* them by others who control how those resources are applied.

Finally, it is worth remembering that foreign aid that helps enable recipient countries and their people to establish and control their own economic and social destinies also helps the United States. We are not diminished as a consequence of other peoples' development. Indeed, we are enhanced as a people whenever we employ our empathy to create effective aid programs for the growth of self-sustaining and just societies.

NOTES

1. A.I.D., *Mission Statement*, September 14, 1990.
2. Ibid.
3. Carroll J. Doherty (of the *Congressional Quarterly*), "Economic Woes Could Precipitate Cuts in Foreign Aid," *Washington Times*, May 27, 1992.
4. President's Commission on the Management of A.I.D. Programs, "Action Plan Working Draft," March 2, 1992, p. 28.
5. James Rupert, "GNP Disputed as Index," *Washington Post*, May 25, 1990.
6. Robert F. Zimmerman, "Democracy, Development, and Foreign Assistance." This paper, prepared in 1988 for consideration by A.I.D. and submitted, unsuccessfully, for publication in *World Development*, included the PSE/QLI discussed here.
7. Abraham Brumberg, "Russia's Demonized Politics: Zealots on Both Sides Threaten Yeltsin's Reforms," *Washington Post*, Outlook, November 22, 1992.
8. Ibid.
9. A.I.D., Project Memorandum, "New Independent States: Democratic Pluralism Initiatives" (110-0007), authorized April 10, 1992.
10. Reuters, "Russia, Reaching for Free Market, Welcomes Lift From Peace Corps," *New York Times*, November 22, 1992.

APPENDIX

Figure I.1 AID/W Organizational Structure as of May 1991

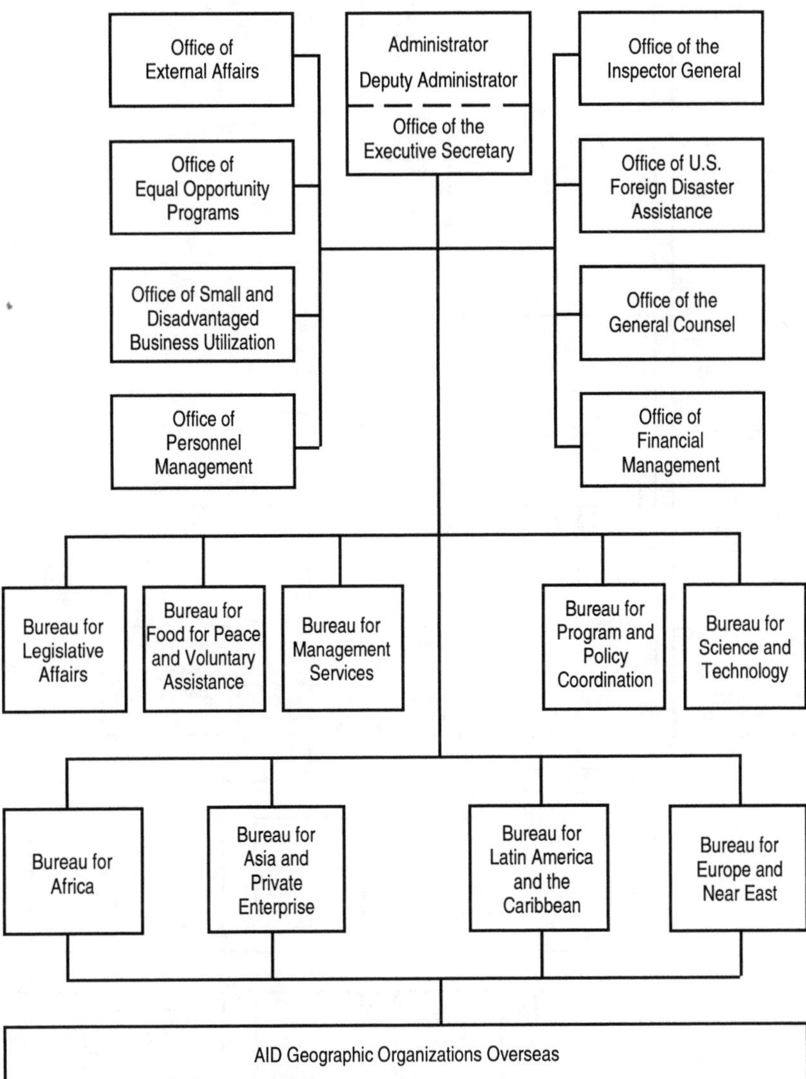

Source: GAO/NSIAD-92-148 Profile of AID

Figure I.2 AID/W Organizational Structure as of October 1991

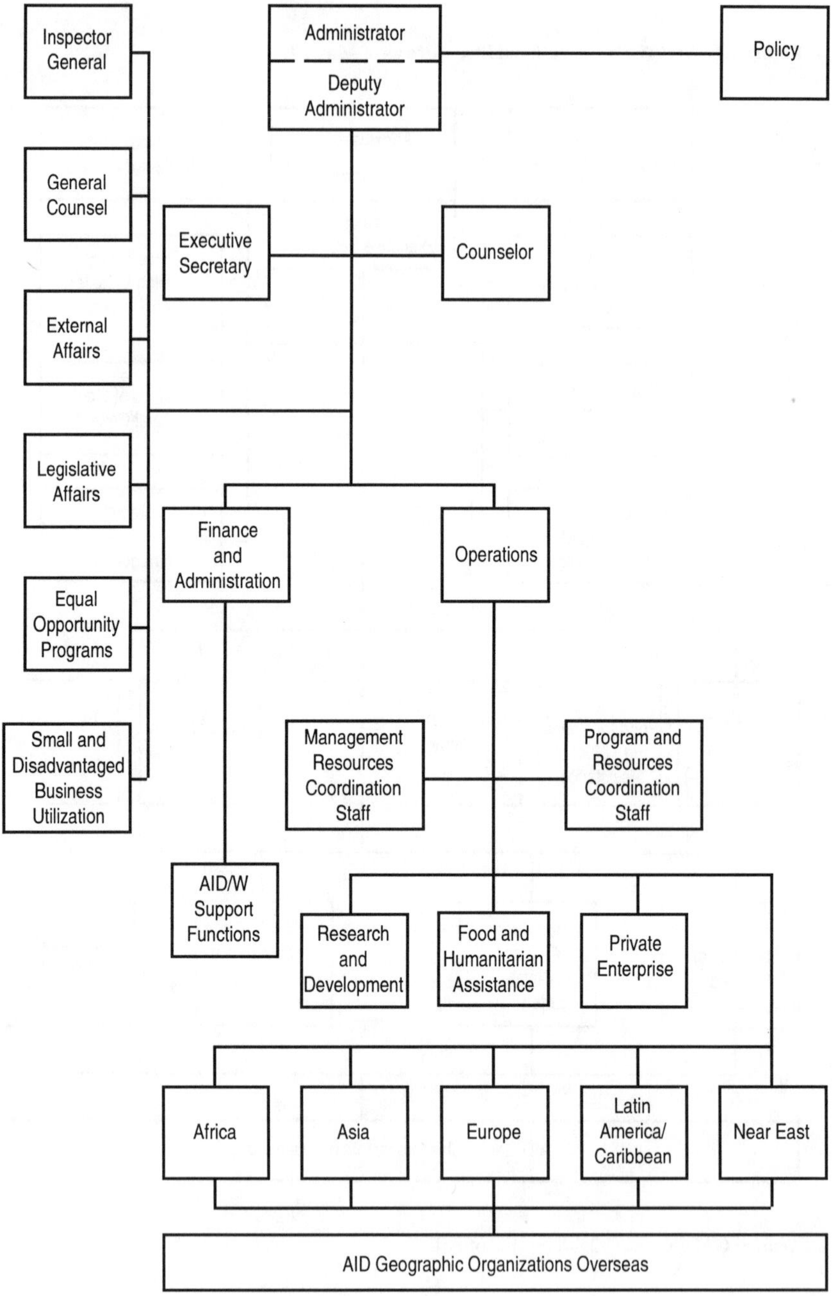

Source: GAO/NSIAD-92-148 Profile of AID

Figure I.3 Groups Concerned with AID's Mission

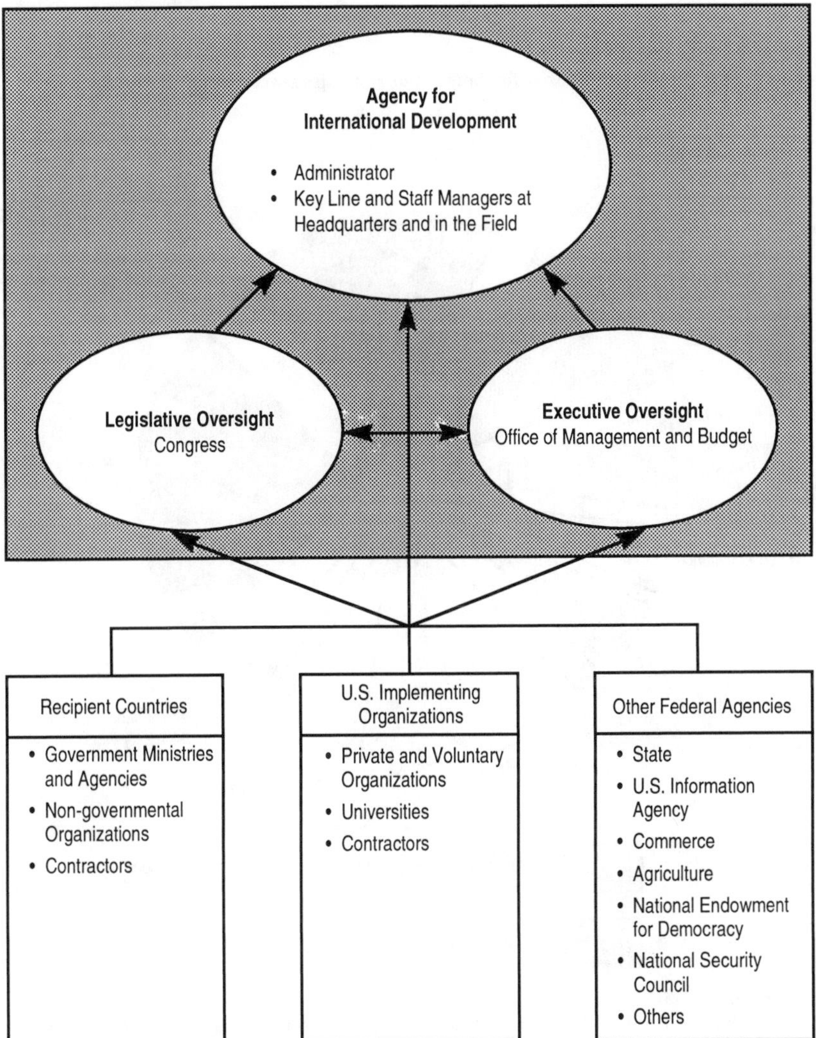

Source: GAO/NSIAD-92-148 AID Strategic Management
Note: Groups concerned with AID's mission are generally any individual, group, or organization that can place a claim on AID's attention, resources, or output, or is affected by AID's output. The Congress and AID's administrator and key managers are directly concerned with AID's mission and may also represent other concerned groups.

Figure II.1 Budget Authority for International Affairs Discretionary Programs, Fiscal Year 1990

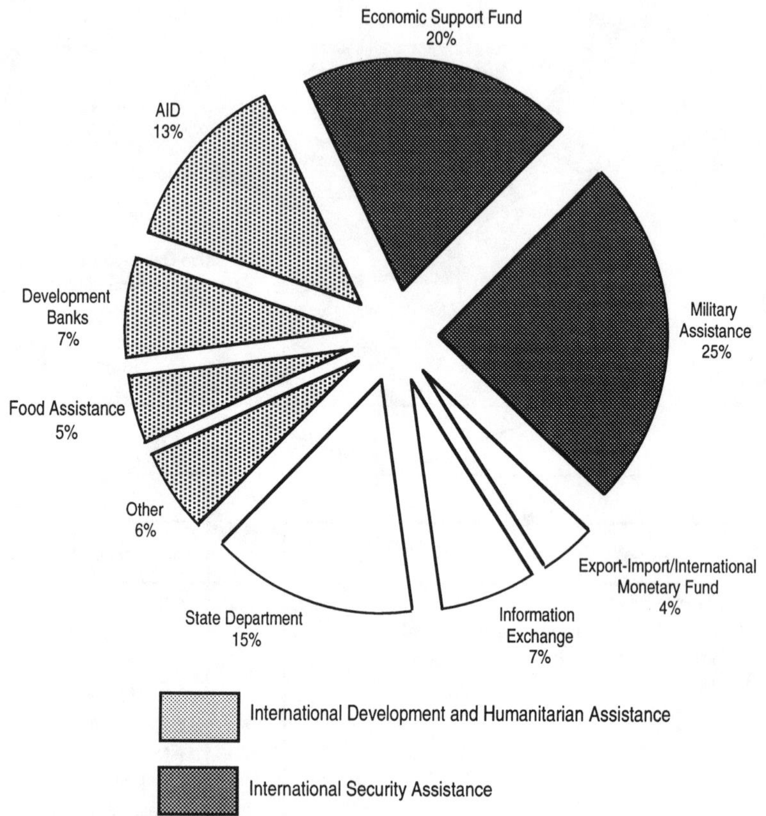

Source: GAO/NSIAD-92-148 Profile of AID
Notes: Budget authority for the programs totals $20 billion. State Department total includes U.S. annual payments assessed by the United Nations for its programs. Percentages do not equal 100 due to rounding.

Figure II.2 Functional and Geographic Develoment Assistance, Fiscal Year 1990 (dollars in millions)

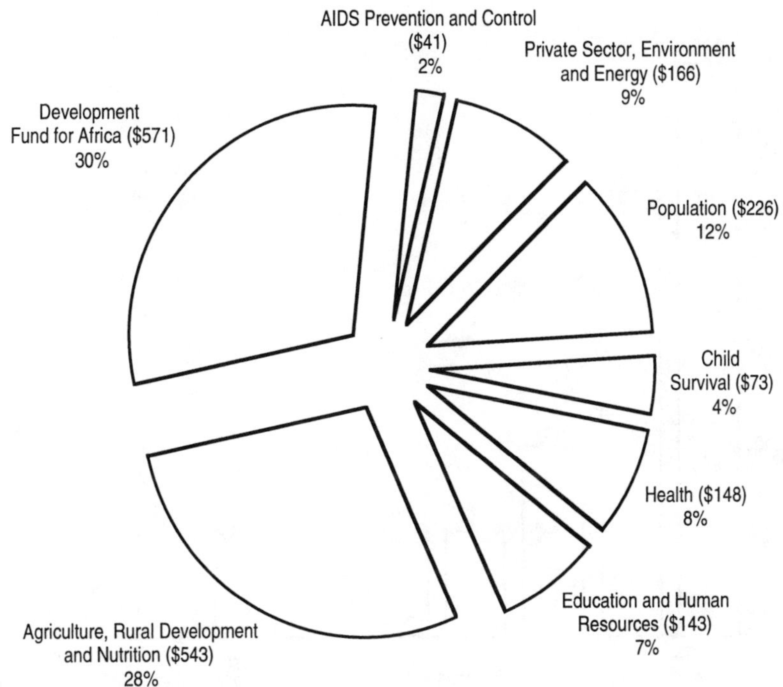

Source: GAO/NSIAD-92-148 Profile of AID
Notes: Figure represents actual obligations. Obligations for development assistance programs total $1.9 billion. Excluded from the analysis are (1) funds obligated for research activities of the Office of the Science Advisor and (2) the Sahel Development Program, which has been terminated.

Figure II.3 Major Recipients of Economic Support Funds, Fiscal Year 1990

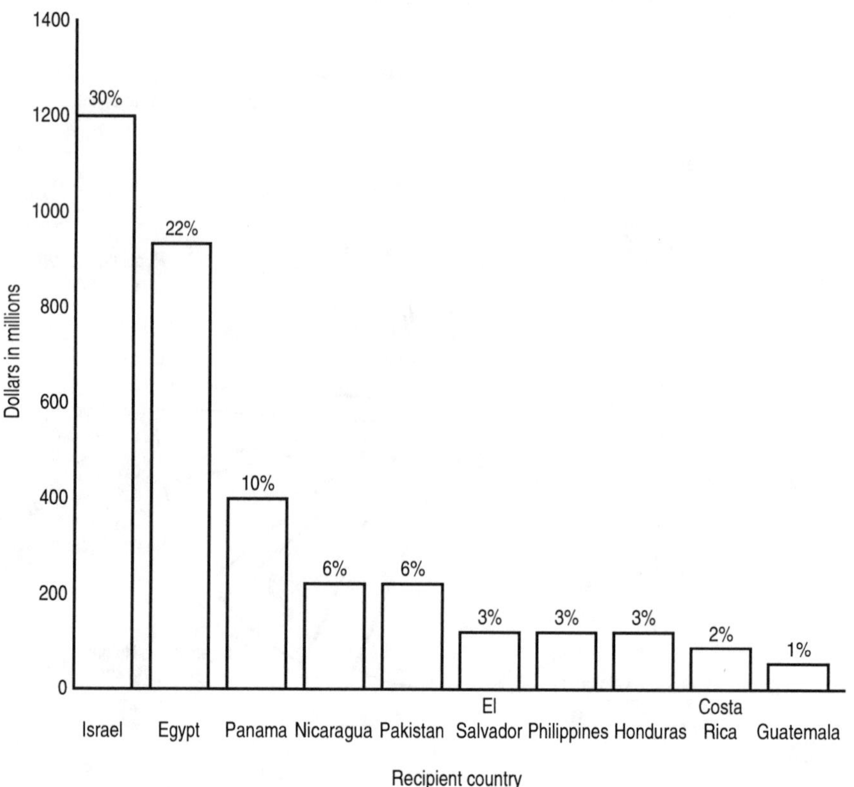

Source: GAO/NSIAD-92-148 Profile of AID
Notes: Figure represents actual obligations. Obligations total approximately $4 billion.

Figure II.4 Major Recipients of Development Assistance, Fiscal Year 1990

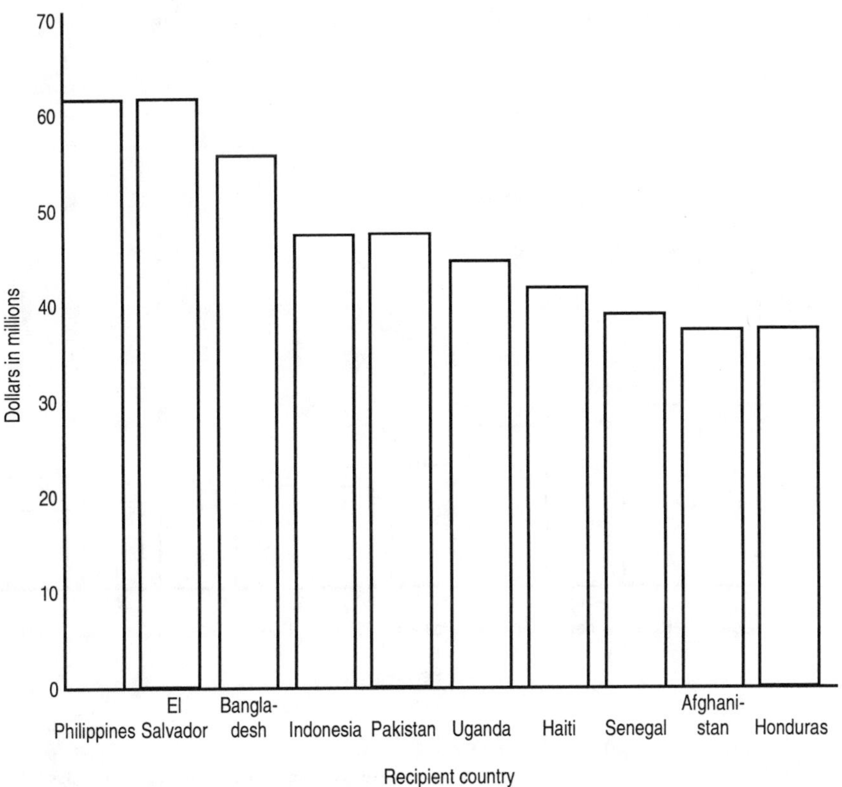

Source: GAO/NSIAD-92-148 Profile of AID
Notes: Figure represents actual obligations. Obligations total approximately $1.9 billion.

Figure II.5 Major Recipients of Food Assistance, Fiscal Year 1990

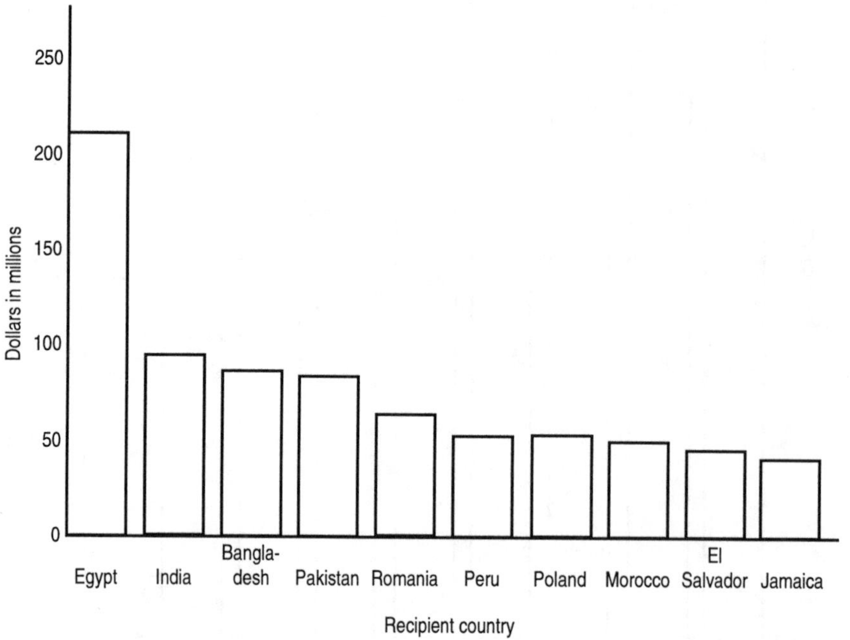

Source: GAO/NSIAD-92-148 Profile of AID
Notes: Figure represents actual obligations for assistance provided under Public Law 480, titles I, II, and III (net of receipts), and the value of surplus commodities provided under Section 416(b) of the Agriculture Act of 1949. Total is approximately $1.1 billion.

Figure III Overseas Work Years by Personnel Type, Fiscal Year 1990

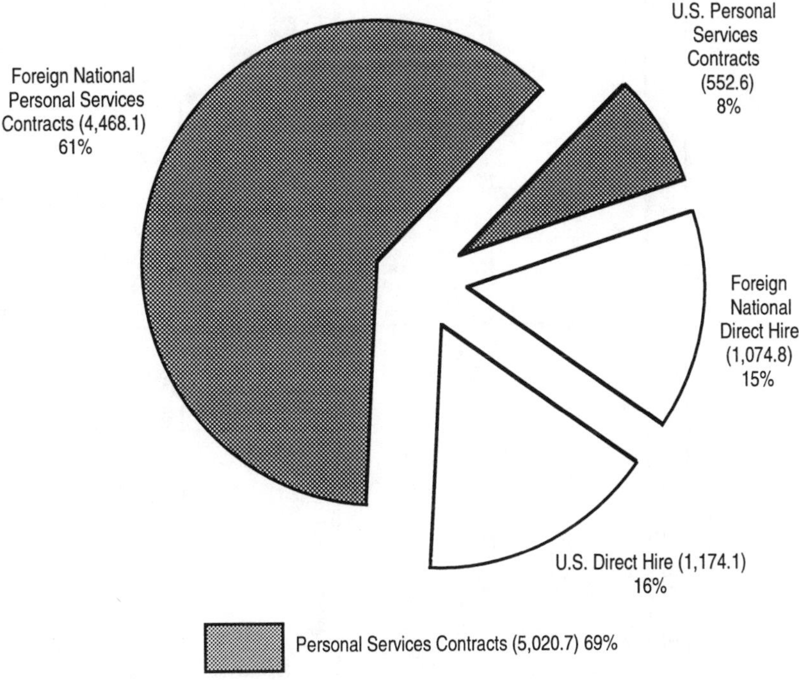

Source: GAO/NSIAD-92-148 Profile of AID

Figure IV Project Design Summary Logical Framework

Life of Project:
From FY ________ to FY ________
Total U.S. Funding ____________
Date Prepared: ____________

Project Title & Number: ____________________

NARRATIVE SUMMARY	OBJECTIVELY VERIFIABLE INDICATORS	MEANS OF VERIFICATION	IMPORTANT ASSUMPTIONS
Program or Sector Goal: The broader objective to which this project contributes: (A-1)	Measures of Goal Achievement: (A-2)	(A-3)	Assumptions for achieving goal targets: (A-4)
Project Purposes: (B-1)	Conditions that will indicate purpose has been achieved: End-of-Project status: (B-2)	(B-3)	Assumptions for achieving purpose: (B-4)
Project Outputs: (C-1)	Magnitude of Outputs: (C-2)	(C-3)	Assumptions for achieving outputs: (C-4)
Project Inputs: (D-1)	Implementation Target (Type and Quantity): (D-2)	(D-3)	Assumptions for providing inputs: (D-4)

Source: AID, Office of Development Program Review and Evaluation, *Project Evaluation Guidelines*, 3rd ed., August 1974.

Figure V Countries Receiving Economic Support Fund Assistance in Fiscal Year 1990

Countries		($Millions)
Near East and South Asia		
Cyprus		5.0
Egypt		898.4
Israel		1194.8
Jordan		3.8
Lebanon		3.7
Oman		12.5
Pakistan		229.0
Turkey		14.3
	Sub Total	2261.5
Latin America		
Bolivia		33.4
Costa Rica		64.9
Ecuador		.1
El Salvador		136.4
Guatemala		56.5
Guyana		1.7
Haiti		1.5
Honduras		130.1
Jamaica		13.7
Nicaragua		214.7
Panama		392.8
Peru		3.3
Uruguay		.1
Other West Indies/Eastern Caribbean		2.0
	Sub Total	1051.2
East Asia		
Laos		.9
Philippines		130.4
Thailand		2.5
Asia Regional		48.1
	Sub Total	181.9
Africa		
Botswana		.8
Chad		2.9
Djibouti		3.2
Ivory Coast		7.0
Morocco		19.9
Seychelles		3.0
South Africa, Republic of		10.0
Sudan		.3
Tunisia		12.7
	Sub Total	59.8
Europe		
Portugal		39.4
European Regional		44.2
	Sub Total	83.6
Oceania and other		10.0
	Grand Total	3648.0

Source: *U.S. Overseas Loans and Grants*: Obligations and Loan Authorizations (July 1, 1945–September 30, 1990). This document is prepared annually by the Agency for International Development/Bureau for Program and Policy Coordination. This table is prepared on the basis of data in this report.

ACRONYMS AND ABBREVIATIONS

A.I.D.	Agency for International Development
AIPAC	America-Israel Public Affairs Committee
ANC	African National Congress
BHN	basic human needs
CAI	Central American Initiative
CAPS	Central American Peace Scholarship program
CIP	Commodity Import Program
CP	Congressional Presentation
CDSS	Country Development Strategy Statement
CLASP	Caribbean and Latin America Scholarship Program
DA	Development Assistance
DFA	Development Fund for Africa
ESF	Economic Support Funds
FAA	Foreign Assistance Act
FAS	Foreign Agricultural Service
FMS	Foreign Military Sales
GAO	Government Accounting Office
GNP	gross national product
GOE	Government of Egypt
GOH	Government of Honduras
GOJ	Government of Jordan
GOL	Government of Liberia
GOZ	Government of Zaire
HIG	Housing Investment Guarantee Program

IFIs	international financial institutions
IMF	International Monetary Fund
ISC	Interagency Staff Committee
KIST	Korea Institute of Science and Technology
LAC	Latin America and Caribbean
LDC	less developed country
MSA	Mutual Security Administration
NDP	National Democratic Party (Egypt)
NIC	newly industrializing country
O&M	operations and maintenance
OMB	Office of Management and Budget
ORT	oral rehydration therapy
PSE/QLI	political-social-economic quality of life index
PT	participant training
PCV	Peace Corps volunteer
PID	project identification document
PQLI	Physical Quality of Life Index
PVO	private voluntary organization
SEAMEO	Southeast Asia Ministers of Education Organization
SSA	security supporting aid
TAF	The Asia Foundation
TDY	temporary duty
UNDP	United Nations Development Program
USDA	U.S. Department of Agriculture

INDEX

About the Book and the Author

Over the past half-century, the United States has spent more than $233 billion on foreign economic assistance. This book demonstrates that this assistance has largely failed to achieve its economic and social development goals primarily because it has been used first and foremost as a tool to promote U.S. political and security objectives.

Zimmerman focuses on A.I.D.'s Economic Support Funds (ESF), which account for more than half of all U.S. bilateral economic assistance. Emphasizing that politically driven aid too often promotes the trappings of modernization, but not necessarily development, he argues that lack of attention to such objectives as the empowerment of people ultimately undermines short-term political and security successes. He supports his case with evidence from Africa, Asia, the Middle East, and Latin America.

An underlying theme of the book is Zimmerman's belief that aid that does not address the causes of violent conflict within or between states cannot create the conditions for what must be one of development's ultimate goals: international peace and security.

ROBERT F. ZIMMERMAN has had more than twenty-three years of experience as a foreign service officer with the Peace Corps, A.I.D., and the U.S. State Department. He is currently a consultant with Management Systems International, assisting A.I.D. and private contractors working on democracy-building initiatives in Eastern Europe and the former Soviet Union.